Travels with 20/2(

i

Garden Route & Langkloof

Travels with 20/20 Vision

Bartle Logie

Published by:

Write-On Publishing
Tel: +27(0)614855491
frank@writeonpublishing.co.za
www.writeonpublishing.co.za

Edited By Saskia Boonzaaier
Book Design & Layout: Frank Nunan

ISBN: 978-1-920700-30-0

Other books by the same author:

Published by Blue Cliff

- 1999. *Governor's Travels. A journey along the Kouga/Tsitsikamma Coast.*
- 2001. *Traveller's Joy. A journey into the Eastern Karoo.*
- 2003. *Two for the Road. In the wagon-tracks of de Mist and Lichtenstein..*
- 2006. *Water in the Wilderness. A journey down the Great Fish River.*
- 2008. *Dusty Road to Long Ago.*
- 2011. *Sundays – Tales from a Winding River.*
- 2013. *Boots in the Baviaans.*

Published by Write-On Publishing

- 2016. *Tales from an Unmapped Country*
- 2017. *Toasted Marhmallows & Obies*

Together with Caryl Logie, and Published by Blue Cliff.

- 2010. *Gazetteer of the Humansdorp Division of the Cape Colony prior to 1910.*

Together with Margaret Harradine and Published by the Port Elizabeth Historical Society.

- 2014. *Gazetteer of the Port Elizabeth and Uitenhage Divisions of the old Cape Colony.*

Dedication

To the memory of
Brian and Ann Snaddon
With whom once we went a'wandering

Acknowledgements

The pandemic gave rise to changes that frequently complicated our lives. Under the circumstances I cannot stress too much how grateful I am to all those who assisted in any way with this book.

In particular I wish to thank Richard Cowling who read and commented on various sections. However, he is in no way to be held responsible for the views expressed.

As in the past Frank Nunan has worked tirelessly to correct my many mistakes and to produce a well laid-out and indeed handsome book. That he manages to cope politely with an elderly and tetchy author is to be commended.

Saskia Boonzaier, despite a busy life and a personal and family battle with the virus, supported and guided the writer from start to finish.

A special word of thanks to Caryl, my fellow traveller and helpmeet. Without her it would not have been possible.

Contents

ix

The City Hall and Vuyisile Mini Square as seen
from the Africana Section of the Public Library

1.

Port Elizabeth[1]

Before one sets out on a journey plans must be made. A good place to start, here in the Eastern Cape, was always the Africana Section of the Port Elizabeth Municipal Library (now the Africana Library, Nelson Mandela Bay Library Service).

---

1 Port Elizabeth's name change to Gqeberha occurred just about when this book was in the production phase.

There under the friendly guidance of the late Alf Porter or later the equally knowledgeable and well-loved and re-membered Margaret Harradine one was assured of a good start. Today (2020) Carol Victor has assumed their former responsibilities, but the library is closed for repairs and maintenance. Plans are made at home and we are forced to start from the adjacent Vuyisile Mini Square.

Making plans is all very well, but we were no sooner on our way than we were faced with the 2020 Covid-19 pandemic and associated lockdown. This resulted in enforced "virtual" travel while seated at home in a comfortable chair. Ultimately, in dribs and drabs, the journey was completed in reality, but unlike any other that we have undertaken.

The Library

Alfred Porter

Diagonally opposite the City Hall is one of my favourite Port Elizabeth buildings, the Public Library. The Library started life in October 1848 in a room of the Commercial Hall. There were 154 members.

Maragaret Harradine

The Library was highly regarded by the citizens of the town, so it is no wonder that in 1897 the family of local merchant Mr William Savage donated £8 000 towards the construction of a new library building in his memory, a sum that was matched by the Town Council. The Cape Government agreed to give £12 000 towards the cost. The new building was designed by Henry Cheers of Twickenham, England. Local architect Orlando Middleton supervised the actual building and placement of the imported and numbered terra-cotta tiles on the façade.

As ornate and attractive as is the exterior, the real treasures are to be found inside the building. When the library opened in 1902 it contained 38 000 books, but it was said that there was room for a further 60 000. The shelves are now full, but perhaps the first thing one notices are not so much the books but the wrought iron spiral staircases and balconies. Countless children have enjoyed this unusual jungle-gym. Playwright Athol Fugard did and he wrote how, peering over the iron railings he looked "down with disdain on the common folk grubbing around for cheap thrillers and love stories on the ground floor".

The more popular books, as Fugard noted, were stored on the ground floor, for the librarians soon discovered that many borrowers were unwilling to or incapable of climbing the steep staircases. The original public reading room had to give way to the extensive card-index, the first in the country to use the Dewey classification system. Then, in the 1980s the catalogues entered the computer age.

The books were the treasures, but faced with thousands, how did one make a choice? The librarians were ever helpful under the watchful eye of Mr Alf Porter, surrounded by books and with model ships everywhere. He was a founder member of the Port Elizabeth Historical Society and an editor and regular contributor to the Society's journal, *Looking Back*. He wrote items of what my family chose to call "useless information" under the *nom-de-plume* "Khitab". These happened to be right up my street and even today, long after Porter's death in 1998, I delight in going through old copies of the journal reading his columns.

The Porter family, Alfred, Edith and baby Isobel, arrived in Port Elizabeth from Lancashire in 1947 and at once set about establishing themselves as a part of the local community. Alf during his years at the library, apart from his everyday work and many other cultural contributions, became a font of local knowledge. So it was that when the *Eastern Province Herald* received a letter from Captain B Bell requesting information-

3

about the visit of a ship, the *Mount Stewart,* to Port Elizabeth, they immediately referred the inquiry to the Public Library.

Captain Bell wrote that in 1920 the *Mount Stewart* brought a cargo of wheat to Port Elizabeth from Buenos Aires. As a result of severe weather lighters were unable to reach the ship to off-load the wheat which was urgently needed by the SA Milling Company. Supplies were running short because of a fire. It was decided to bring the ship in alongside the Dom Pedro jetty.

"This was the first time a full-rigged ship had been placed alongside in such a difficult position," wrote Captain Bell, "and it aroused considerable interest among the local population while it lasted."

Such was this interest that when the *Mount Stewart* sailed some weeks later, the Harbour Master provided a large tug to provide Bayonians the opportunity to witness the ship sailing away. On board the *Mount Stewart* were two local young men, 20 year-old Mr G Whitmore as a cadet to start training as a master mariner, and 17 year-old Nicholas Bodo as a deck boy.

Alf Porter was, of course, able to find those issues of the *Eastern Province Herald* that recorded the visit of the *Mount Stewart.* He also noted how in the previous year the ship was thrown on her beam ends and was up to her hatches under water when her cargo of maize shifted during a severe gale 594 nautical miles off the coast of Ireland. Heavy seas swept the deck and the men were only able to reach the holds through the lazarette – a locker in the stern used to store ropes and other equipment, but originally used to store the bodies of important passengers or crew who had died during the voyage, lesser mortals being buried at sea. For 80 hours under the most difficult circumstances the crew fought to save their ship. Boats were smashed and while some men struggled to move the cargo and so right the ship, others pumped frantically. Finally, with the men at the point of complete collapse, the storm lessened.

In 1923 Captain Bell returned to Port Elizabeth, but this time as third mate on the steamer, *General Lukin.* The master, Captain Davis, had died during the voyage from Cape Town to Algoa Bay and is buried in Port Elizabeth. It was not recorded whether or not his body was stored in the lazarette.

Mr A P "Chatty" Knight of Amsterdamhoek, who we will meet again later, was able to finish the story of the *Mount Stewart.* In 1922 she was laid up for a year. Then she was ordered to Liverpool to load salt for Sydney. From there she sailed to the west coast of South America, was sold and went to the breakers.

Another former librarian with a huge treasure chest of Port Elizabeth stories was Margaret Harradine, formerly in charge of the Africana section of the Public Library. She too was a frequent contributor to the Historical Society's journal and even in her retirement was fielding the questions that once came the way of Alf Porter.

A story she told in *Looking Back* concerned the German-owned ship, *Hans Wagner*, and a brindle bulldog named Rex. The *Hans Wagner,* a 938 ton barque built in 1877 in Sunderland, England, was wrecked in Algoa Bay during the Great Gale of September 1902. It had arrived from Melbourne with a cargo of wheat, flour and butter. Rex, the bulldog, belonged to the master, Captain Müllman. No lives were lost when the ship went aground, and Rex managed to swim to safety. Captain Müllman was in no position to keep the dog and sold him to a local man, Thomas Blaine Dalziel.

A Relief Fund was set up for the stranded mariners and on the Saturday following the gale there was a street collection. Rex did his bit and as "The Sailors' Friend", collected £30 8s 7d, a considerable amount at the time.

Dalziel was a commercial traveller and appears to have left Port Elizabeth in 1909. Perhaps, notes Margaret, Rex went with him.

The *Hans Wagner* was repaired and refloated and sailed away.

Despite the harbour being a mere hop, step and jump away across the Market Square from the Library, the librarians were not solely concerned with matters maritime. Margaret Harradine, who enjoyed puzzles, had as part of her job a daily hunt for clues, delving into the past in order to find another piece in the jigsaw of the past. She did some wonderful detective work while tracking down the builder of Fort Frederick. She knew, having seen the plans for the fort in the Bayworld Museum that it was built under the supervision of a Lieutenant in the Engineers. She even knew that his first name was Septimus and that his surname was apparently of only four letters and ended *oas*. The date was too early for it to be found in the Cape Calendars nor could she trace any such name in other records.

One day she was examining a second-hand anthology of poetry. She noticed that the name of the compiler was Guy Boas. Suddenly the penny dropped. The name Boas, to rhyme with "doze", is of Cornish origin. It is a rare name, but according to the Boas site on the internet there is an entry in the British Naval Biographical Directory for 1849 for a veteran soldier named Septimus Boas. Bingo! There could be little doubt that she had found the man responsible for the building of Fort Frederick. There's no telling when a little useless information will come in handy.

A favourite spot of mine in the library is the window seat in the Africana section, housed in an octagonal corner tower of the building. From here one has a commanding view out over the Market Square (since 2010 the Vuyisile Mini Square) and City Hall. The Market Square, of course, was there long before the Town Hall, now the City Hall, or the Public Library were built. Actual trading probably took place on the site of the old Post Office, behind the present City Hall.

In January 1826 Captain Francis Evatt was called to the Market Square to deal with "circumstances of a most lawless and outrageous nature". Some men had acquired a cask of wine and were handing out tots to any passerby who showed interest. Evatt was requested to deal urgently with the situation. He contacted Port Elizabeth's only policeman and ordered that the cask be staved in. The constable took an axe and headed for the Market Square. Ignoring the protests of the bystanders, the constable carried out his orders.

The drinkers were outraged. They marched up and down chanting threats before disappearing briefly and returning with a cask of brandy. Then the British flag on the Square was hauled down and a notice pinned to it: "Pachter in distress". The flag was again hoisted, but upside down.

The men now retired to a neighbouring house, inviting all and sundry to join them. A number of bystanders, including some soldiers, accepted the invitation. When the constable tried to restrain the mob he was drenched with brandy. Captain Evatt, reckoning that it would not be long before they passed out, decided to leave the drinkers be. No arrests were made and no charges laid. According to Evatt no law had been broken. The remaining onlookers moved off and activities on the Square returned to normal.

Vuyisile Mini Square (formerly Market Square)

Over the years there have been many changes to what is now Vuyisile Mini Square.

Photographs, taken from the Public Library collection of course, tell the story of the Square. An 1853 photograph shows bare earth and a rocky outcrop. Five wagons together with their teams of wide-horned oxen stand on the Square. A man sits on the ground in front of one wagon. A small huddle of pedestrians stands in the middle of Main Street. There is no likelihood

of them being run down by traffic. No doubt the southwester whipped up dust storms at times and the spring rains turned both the Square and Main Street into a mud-bath.

A decade later the town hall is under construction and the Market Square is packed with wagons and a single horse-cart. The new building was to be a fine colonial edifice. When the English novelist and travel-writer, Anthony Trollope, visited Port Elizabeth in 1877 he was much taken with what he saw.

"The town is built on a steep hill rising up from the sea, and is very neat. The town hall is a large handsome building, putting its rival and elder sister Capetown to shame."

By 1882 ox-wagons are still to be seen, but also horse-drawn carriages and trams. The Obelisk, brought from Europe by merchant John Paterson and erected on the Square to commemorate the wedding of the Prince of Wales (later Edward VII) and Princess Alexandria, stands on the Square surrounded by four granite troughs: water for all those oxen and horses. Main Street is far busier and most pedestrians are on the pavements. The first streetlights are in place beside the Obelisk and on the corner of Main Street.

There is a dog, but neither an ox nor a horse in sight in the 1922 photo. The trams, still single-decker, are now electrically propelled. The Obelisk has gone, replaced by a large field gun; the Heavy Artillery Memorial. Electric trams, motor-busses and a few box-like cars are the only vehicles to be seen on the well-surfaced streets. The statue of Queen Victoria stands outside the Library. Is her expression one of disdain? Not all British visitors were as enthusiastic as Anthony Trollope. An earlier visitor in 1838, Sir Charles Bunbury, although excited by Cape plants, described Port Elizabeth as "an ugly, dirty, ill-scented, ill-built little hamlet resembling one of the worst fishing villages on the English coasts". Bayonians however, were proud of their city, its status having been raised to that of city in July 1913.

By the 1930s this pride was very evident. The old Market Square was now the Mayor's Garden. A photograph shows people wandering through the Garden, while some sit on the benches beside the lily pond soaking up the sun. All the men wear hats. In the centre of the lily-pond is a small statue, *The Water Catcher*. Because it was vandalised on Market Square this charming statue was later moved to outside the Pearson Conservatory in St George's Park. Sadly there too it caught the eye of vandals and no longer graces the city.

In 1972 the City Hall, looking out over the Mayor's Garden, was declared a National Monument, but five years later the building was destroyed by fire and shortly thereafter the Garden was demolished. An entirely new interior for the Hall was now built and bolted to the exterior walls of the original building, and in November 1981 it was officially re-opened. One hundred and twenty-three years separated the laying of the foundation stone of the Hall by Cape Governor Sir George Grey in 1858, and the re-opening by Cape Administrator, Eugene Louw.

Sir George arrived in a horse-drawn carriage and was taken to Wasley's Hotel for a "wash and brush-up". Louw and his wife arrived by plane and went to the VIP lounge at the airport.

On both occasions the men of Prince Alfred's Guard together with the regimental band provided a guard of honour. In 1981 the PAG band was joined by that of the Grey High School.

After laying the stone, Sir George was presented with a silver trowel. After opening a door, the Administrator was presented with a radio-cassette player.

Both men were in a hurry to leave, Sir George to board the paddle-steamer *Hermes* bound for Cape Town where he had an appointment. Eugene Louw needed to catch a plane for Pretoria where he too had an appointment. The Governor, however, stayed long enough to be vaccinated, while the Administrator and his wife left a finger-lunch early in order to catch their plane.

Political demonstrations on the Square or in its vicinity are not unknown and the first recorded strike in South African history took place in 1846 on the beach that adjoined the Square. At the time both cargo and passengers were carried

9

across the waters of the Bay by surf-boat. These were then unloaded by scantily clad black men. Women and children were carried through the surf by the same men. Cargo was taken from the beach to the Market Square, and passengers to their hotels or waiting family and friends.

At first Khoekhoen labourers undertook surf-boat duties, being paid about two shillings (the equivalent in 2020 of approximately R20) a day, but after the Sixth Frontier War (1834-1835), when Mfengu were settled in the colony, the Khoekhoe were replaced by Mfengu who were thought to be more sober and industrious.

The Seventh Frontier War (1846-1847) saw many of the Mfengu leave Port Elizabeth to obtain, they hoped, a share when the division of the neutral territory took place. This was at a time when there were far more boats than ever in the Bay waiting to off-load military supplies. In November 1846 a record 25 vessels were at anchor.

The beach labourers were well aware of the powerful position they held and thus it was that on Monday, November the 9th 1846, they went on strike for higher pay. Under the circumstances the authorities were forced to bow to their demands. After the cessation of hostilities, wages continued to rise until the building of a jetty and the influx of starving Xhosa after the cattle-killing of 1857 broke the power of the Mfengu beach labourers. High unemployment gives employers a wonderful upper hand!

A second strike in 1852 protested against a town regulation which required the beach labourers to work fully clothed. Lieutenant Governor Sir Henry Young, after a visit to Port Elizabeth, had written an indignant letter to the civil authorities about the beach labourers and the "state of NUDITY" in which they worked, describing it as "filthy, abominable and beastly".

The 19th century strikes were relatively peaceful, but the 20th century saw violence in the Market Square. There are few today who remember the 1920 Market Square Massacre, or the name Samuel Masabalala. Born in Uniondale in 1877, Masabalala was at the time an employee of Lennon's wholesale chemist and a leading light in the Industrial and Commercial Workers Union (ICU). This was a mixed union of coloured and black workers, the first in South Africa. During 1919 and 1920 there were strikes, riots and mass meetings of workers throughout South Africa. In Port Elizabeth a meeting, chaired by the Mayor, Councillor J S Young, was held on the 21st of January 1920 to hear representations from a black delegation to employers calling for an increase in wages.

Not having achieved their object the ICU called for a mass meeting to be addressed by Masabalala in Korsten on 23 October. The Port Elizabeth Council invited Dr Walter Rabusana, a founding member of the African National Congress (ANC) from East London to come to Port Elizabeth and use his influence on Masabalala. This was not a popular move amongst the workers. Rabusana was assaulted by a hostile crowd, the police moved in and Masabalala was arrested and taken to the Baakens Street Police Station, behind the City Hall. No charge was laid, but bail was refused. Indignant workers and supporters armed with *kieries* gathered on Market Square demanding the release of Masabalala. After several attempts to disperse the crowd failed, there was a general movement towards the Police Station. Stones were thrown and allegedly a shot was fired at the police. The police responded by firing on the crowd, killing 23 including three white bystanders and wounding 126 of whom 12 were white: a harbinger of subsequent events in South African history.

Much later an *ex gratia* payment of £2 857 1s 0d was made to the dependents of those killed or wounded. Of this amount £2327 11s 0d went to the whites, £377 7s 6d to the dependents of three coloured victims, and the balance of £152 2s 6d to the black victims.

The funeral of the dead workers was attended by a crowd of 30 000. Masabalala was later tried on a charge of "public violence", but was acquitted.

* * *

11

All of which brings us to Vuyisile Mini after whom the former Market Square is now named.

Mini was born in 1920, the son of a Port Elizabeth dockworker active in labour and community struggles. The son followed in his father's footsteps and became a founding member of the Port Elizabeth Stevedoring and Dockworkers Union. He was also known as a good dancer, a gifted poet and a singer. In the Port Elizabeth Male Voice Choir he was renowned for his deep bass voice.

From his union activities it was an easy step into politics and in 1951 he joined the ANC. Within five years he was Secretary of the Cape region.

He was first gaoled in 1952 together with Govan Mbeki, after whom Port Elizabeth's former Main Street is now named, and Raymond Mhlaba. They were charged with having participated in the Defiance Campaign. Mini had deliberately used a "Whites Only" entrance to an area of railway property reserved specifically for whites. Those whites, sympathetic to the black cause, who deliberately made use of areas reserved for blacks were not arrested, but simply warned and directed to those areas reserved for their "racial group".

In 1956 Mini was again arrested and became one of the 156 defendants in the Treason Trial. The majority of those arrested were held in communal cells in the Johannesburg Fort resulting in what Nelson Mandela described, in *Long Walk to Freedom,* as "the largest and longest unbanned meeting of the Congress Alliance in years".

The case against Mini and many others of those accused collapsed in 1959 through lack of evidence, and he was released. He was not out for long.

On the 21st of March 1961 a crowd of between five and seven thousand marched to the police station in Sharpeville, near Vereeniging, to protest peacefully against the pass laws. They offered themselves up for arrest as they were not carrying their passbooks. Later in the morning they were joined by thousands more. Police reinforcements were rushed to Sharpeville and Air Force Harvards and F-86 Sabre jets flew

12

low over the crowd in an effort to disperse them. When police attempted to arrest one of the protestors the crowd surged forward. Later it was claimed by the police that inexperienced officers lost their nerve and opened fire. This started a chain reaction. Within minutes 69 were killed. There were 29 children among the 289 casualties.

Nine days later, on the 30th of March, there was a nationwide crackdown. Vuyisile Mini was one of the many detained for 90 days without trial. It was in the same year that Mini was one of the first to enlist in *Umkhonto we Sizwe,* the Spear of the Nation, the ANC's armed wing founded, amongst others, by Nelson Mandela in answer to the Sharpeville Massacre. Mini became a member of the Eastern Cape high command.

Two years later, on the 10th of May, Mini was again arrested, together with Wilson Khayinga and Zinakile Mkaba. They were charged with 17 counts of sabotage and other political crimes. In March 1964 they were found guilty and sentenced to death and on the 6th of November were hanged in the Pretoria Central Prison. They went to their deaths singing freedom songs. Perhaps one of these was a song Vuyisile, the Port Elizabeth Male Voice Choir bass, had himself composed, *Pasopa nantsi 'ndondemnyama we Verwoerd* – Look out, Verwoerd, here are the black people!

* * *

We strolled across Vuyusile Mini Square and between dodging cars and car-guards pondered the changes that have taken place. Gardens require constant attention and are far more expensive to maintain than paving. The Council "saw the light" and the Market Square was paved. The design was inoffensive and if need be it could be used as a car-park. (We tend, particularly in cities, to go out of our way to accommodate the needs of cars and their owners.) It was now also much easier to hold mass meetings or demonstrations. We preferred the garden, but unkempt gardens are another matter.

We wondered how many on the Square that day knew anything of its history and of the man after whom it is named, and the supreme sacrifice that he made.

Mrs Hannah Cadle, seated and dressed in black and white, surrounded by her guests and "nieces and adopted daughters".

2.

Van Stadens to Gamtoos

Driving through the well-ordered lands that the Puttergill family farm today, it is difficult to imagine a time, little more than 200 years ago, when elephants roamed the banks of the Van Stadens and in the vicinity of Thornhill, while early travellers camped beneath a tree into which a gallows was carved. This resulted in the camp-site being known as *Galgenbos* – Gallow's Bush. Later the nearby SAR Road Motor Transport bus stop was given a derivative of the name: *Galbos*.

Cadles Hotel

From early in the 20th century it was possible to travel by train to Van Stadens seated in miniature coaches running on rails just two feet (60.96 cm) apart. The journey to Cadle's Hotel no longer took the better part of a day. At Witteklip Siding, just short of the Van Stadens gorge and only one hour and twenty-three minutes from Humewood Road Station in Port Elizabeth, trains were met by the horse-drawn carriage operated by Cadle's Hotel. In its hey-day the hotel was popular with honeymoon couples, to the extent that it became known as "Cuddles".

Henry William Carpenter Cadle, fifth child of settlers John and Sarah Cadle, married Hannah Shepherd and in 1862, aged 41, was granted a licence to run an accommodation house at Van Stadens Heights. He died two years later, and in the same year as his death, his daughter Elizabeth Ellen Cadle married Isaac Newton. The hotel was now run by Henry's widow Hannah with the help of her daughter and son-in-law.

Many photographs of the old hotel still exist. Perhaps some were taken by hotel guests, or by honeymoon couples; reminders of those first few happy days of marriage.

The earliest photo that I know of is so faded that one can barely make out the building. Someone has taken the trouble to pencil in the crest of the Witteklip Mountains in the background. In the foreground the water of a dam is visible, a dam that still exists.

Only one photo has in it an image of Hannah Cadle, known to some as Ouma Cadle. She has on a black dress, as befitted a widow, together with a white V-necked front and frilly-edged black apron. She is seated in front of the hotel and surrounded by a number of young women and bewhiskered, pipe-smoking men wearing an assortment of hats. Some of the hats look as though the men sat on them before putting them on. There are also men sitting on, or leaning over the railing of an upstairs balcony

Marianne North, a distinguished English botanical artist, stayed at Cadles in the 1880s and noted that her "kind" hostess was "almost immovable from dropsy". She was fortunate to have "half a dozen nieces or adopted daughters who did the work, looked after everything, and kept the place lively and in order. One felt more like a friend than a boarder."

Today, in a gallery specially constructed at Kew in London to hold her paintings, one can see the *Protea cynaroides* Marianne North painted while sitting on the upstairs balcony of the hotel. There is not a whisker, squashed hat or a pipe to be seen in the painting. There is however, a green winged, magenta lined touraco provided at the last moment by "the landlord", presumably Isaac Newton, Mrs Cadle's son-in-law. Also in the picture is a pine emperor moth, but no mention is made of how it came to play a part in the composition of the picture.

Very shortly after Marianne North's visit, Hannah Cadle died and was buried not far from the hotel. Her daughter and son-in-law, Elizabeth and Isaac Newton, took over the running of the hotel.

Isaac was the son of William Newton who was the builder and first keeper of the Bird Island light. In 1854 he pointed out that "the regular transmission of rations" was of vital importance to him, situated as he was at the time "on a barren rock". One hopes that the authorities took heed and that there was an immediate improvement in the situation.

After retiring from the lighthouse service William came ashore and settled at Van Stadens Heights, the farm on which the hotel was situated, his final resting place being a grave adjoining that of Hannah Cadle.

In September 1897 a distinguished visitor arrived at Cadles, none other than Sir (later Lord) Alfred Milner. As part of a journey to acquaint himself with the colony, Milner, the recently appointed Governor, took a trip in a horse-drawn spider from Uitenhage to Cape Town. He was met near the toll, just west of the hotel, by the local Field Cornet, Isaac Newton, "together with a number of other mounted burghers". They proceeded to the hotel, only about a kilometre away, and were served breakfast. This no doubt consisted of fried eggs, pork sausages and lashings of bacon with plates of hot, buttered toast and all washed down with gallons of tea.

The Governor then said goodbye to Mr George MacPherson, Mayor of Uitenhage, and other notables who had accompanied him on the first part of the journey. On the next leg he was to travel with Newton and his burghers.

In the early years of the 20th century, Newton sold the hotel to a Port Elizabeth businessman and photographer, Mr Charles Smart. Various additions and alterations were made, but the railway together with improved roads and the advent of the motorcar signalled the gradual downfall of the hotel. It had become so much easier for newly weds or those seeking a brief break in the country to travel, that Cadles was not as attractive a destination as was once the case. In 1910 Smart was insolvent and moved back to Port Elizabeth. It was stated at the time that the Avontuur Railway meant that there was no longer sufficient traffic making use of the hotel. Cadles struggled on for a while, but in 1916 closed its doors for good.

Charles Smart bounced back. Two years after his insolvency he was running the Central Hotel in Port Elizabeth. Always a keen musician - he was a teacher, violinist and founder of the Operatic Club – the move back to the city enabled him to give greater attention to his duties as choirmaster at St Augustine's.

Woodridge c1940

Woodridge

In 1924 the former Cadles property was bought by Dr George Porter Mathew as a weekend retreat and possible retirement home. His daughter, Mervynne, married to a fellow teacher, Leslie Carter, had other ideas. They envisaged a preparatory school. Eventually, and against his better judgment, Dr Mathew was persuaded. In January 1936 the new enterprise, Woodridge Preparatory School, opened the doors of the old Cadles Hotel to three pupils: two boys and a girl.

Times were often difficult. A shortage of cement and bricks during the Second World War left Leslie Carter scratching his head. How was he to build the new dormitories that were needed? General Motors and Ford factories in Port Elizabeth provided the answer. They were churning out military vehicles that arrived in Algoa Bay in a knocked-down state in wooden packing-cases. The upstairs dormitories went ahead with wooden walls.

The Carters with seeming boundless energy, self-sacrifice and faith forged ahead to overcome many difficulties. In 1967 they were on hand to witness with pride another new

18

development, the official opening of Woodridge College. Just in time, for in October the following year Leslie Carter died and was buried at Windygates, the Carter property on Woodridge, and within a short walking distance of the graves of Hannah Cadle and William Newton.

By the time the Prep celebrated its first 50 years in 1986, more than 1300 pupils had passed through the two schools.

Woodridge is no stranger to fires. Situated as it is at the eastern end of the fynbos biome, the Cape Floral Kingdom, in which fire plays a vital role, this is not surprising. In 1958 the preppies were evacuated to Gilson's Tearoom, near the present-day Flower Reserve, when a veld-fire threatened the old Cadles Hotel building. The fire was brought under control, but the Divisional Council firefighters stayed through the night to ensure that there were no flare-ups.

It was at a time when boarders wrote weekly letters home to their parents. One of the young boys in his letter home described the excitement: "It was a huge mix-up. We had supper for lunch and lunch for supper and firemen for breakfast."

By the 1960s it was not only indigenous plants that surrounded the school, but also large areas of exotic gums, pines and wattles, all fire-prone and capable of producing blazes of far greater intensity than the native blombos, besembos and ericas of the fynbos.

In the 1980s it seemed that Matopos, a house on top of the hill over-looking the schools, was in danger. The financial manager of the school at the time was housed there, but was nowhere to be found. Then someone remembered that he might be having a music lesson. A boy was sent at once to fetch him.

The door of Ida Cumming's music-room at the Prep burst open and a breathless boy gasped, "sorry Miss Cumming, but sir, there's a fire at Matopos. Come quickly!"

The financial manager remarked calmly, "Right, my boy, I'll be there as soon as I can, but I have paid for this music lesson, so you'll have to wait for me." Accountants it seems, march to the beat of a different drum.

Everyone's priorities at Woodridge were fairly focused during the fire of June 2017.

On Tuesday the 6th of June there was a foretaste of the disaster. The onset of a cold front along the Cape southern coast-line brought with it gale force winds. In Knysna wind-speeds of up to 100 km/h were recorded. The cold front together with the extreme winds moved rapidly eastwards.

During the morning of Thursday the school received reports of a fire in the Longmore Forest above Thornhill, just west of the Van Stadens River. As a necessary precaution all staff and pupils were instructed as to what they should do and where they should gather if Woodridge was threatened.

By Friday evening fires were visible on the Witteklip range north of the school and soon after 0600 on Saturday morning the school received a phone-call from the team monitoring the fire. All children and staff were to evacuate the school as soon as possible. Before 0700 the fire alarm sounded. Pupils grabbed what valuables they could and moved towards the assembly points.

Mrs Sue Carter roused the junior boys and thought to provide them with some breakfast, in the form of cupcakes she had baked for a birthday-party later in the weekend. Having delivered the children she began to collect elderly residents and members of the domestic staff and ferry them to safety. Her brother-in-law, Mr Roger Carter, son of the founders of Woodridge, was at first reluctant to leave his house. He eventually drove his car to the assembly point and locked it. Later in the day firefighters had to break into the car to move it.

Several buses arrived at the school early to take rugby-players to Despatch. The buses were immediately commandeered to help with the evacuation.

Grade 12 pupil Bevin Potgieter described how thick smoke blanketed the school while they waited to take their seats. Another matric pupil, Sean Darnborough, commented how there had been no chaos, but rather a mixture of "excitement and panic". There was really no time to think about the situation, everything happened so quickly. His sister Holly, in

Grade 10, had rescued only her shoes. By the time they drove out it seemed that flames were "jumping over the bus".

Those evacuated were driven to the Baywest Mall where they were cared for until the arrival of their parents.

At the Woodridge Equestrian Centre, adjoining the school, volunteers moved the horses to safety.

Firemen now blocked the entrance to the school to prevent the entry of sightseers and others.

Academic staff began to make arrangements for the Grade 12s, who were in the midst of writing their mock-matric exams, to write at other centres during the following week.

Throughout the course of the afternoon fires swept through the Van Stadens gorge and across the N2, resulting in the closing of that road together with the R102. At Woodridge the first buildings were engulfed by flames and later the hydrants ran dry. A helicopter, filling its bucket at the swimming-pool, bombed the fires, but as wind speeds picked up, this became increasingly difficult. Meanwhile empty hoses lay like spilled spaghetti across the campus. Municipal spokesperson Mthubanzi Mniki stated that an appeal for water-tankers had been well supported and local farmers with tanks on their *bakkies* did all that they could to provide water to fight the fires.

Meanwhile across the valley at Thornhill, the fire claimed the life of 72 year-old Mrs Myrna van der Riet. Her 73 year-old husband, Walter, was taken to hospital, but later died of his injuries.

In Port Elizabeth Woodridge domestic and grounds staff-members were accommodated in the St George's Prep School Hall. Numerous offers of support were received and food and clothing began to arrive. St George's school staff did what they could to provide for the families that had suddenly arrived in their midst.

Woodridge driver and handyman, Fabian Fortuin, was one of those who spent the night at St George's. Interviewed by the press he said that his greatest fear was losing the job he had had for the past ten years. Woodridge Prep headmaster, Trevor von Berg commented that no one would lose their jobs. "There is a lot of loyalty, and we will look after them."

On Sunday 11 June, the Woodridge Trust met in the morning to assess the damage. This appeared to have been mainly to staff accommodation with 13 houses and flats destroyed. The College also lost six classrooms, offices, the kitchen and dining-hall, workshops and the old Woodridgeans' clubhouse known as the Woodpecker. The administration building housing the headmaster's office, the school library, finance department and school records was also completely destroyed.

At the Prep three classrooms and the accommodation for 29 girl-boarders went up in flames. The sanatorium was also seriously damaged. Miraculously a nearby building, the historic former Cadle's Hotel, was untouched.

Plans were made to source mobile and temporary classrooms, and to set up a dining-hall and re-install IT systems. Fortunately damage was fully covered by insurance. Donations and offers of assistance began pouring in, not only from old Woodridgeans and family members of pupils, but also from the general public.

Three weeks after the evacuation, fires were still starting up as logs continued to smoulder, but clearing up operations were well in hand.

As promised, the school reopened on the 4th of July and Derek Bradley, headmaster of the College, commented, "We see the situation . . . as an opportunity to rebuild an even greater school."

A year later the R110 000 000 restoration and re-building project was complete. The builders moved out and the staff and pupils, after nearly a year in temporary accommodation, moved into their new facilities.

Walking along the school drive is a man showing some signs of a middle-aged spread. He is wearing a green cap, and has on a T-shirt with the inscription "2015 Finished", a pair of dark blue overall pants and blue Chinese *takkies*. He moves quickly with a characteristic lope.

It is almost a quarter of a century since we last met, but there is no mistaking Richard "Greenback" Kulu, once a gardener and still on the maintenance staff at Woodridge. He advances with a broad, but somewhat shy smile. We greet and ask after one another's families.

With these formalities over I say, pointing to the former Cadles Hotel and without due consideration, "It's wonderful that you were able to save the old building."

"But this is my home," he answers, gently putting me in my place.

Nicholas and the three wise men

The three-man deputation was led by Bok and supported by Piet and Harry. Normally at this hour of an evening they were to be found in the bar of the Thornhill Hotel, and it was there that they first met Nicholas.

Today boarding schools do not receive a very good press. It was different in the 1950s and 60s. There were no lurid headlines in the weekend newspapers, and no stories of psychologists warning of the dangers of institutional life. For farm children there was often no alternative, they had to become boarders. Most settled down and enjoyed the experience, but there were always exceptions. Nicholas was one.

One day Nicholas decided that he was home-sick and tired of boarding school. He had a small suitcase, and into this he packed a pair of pyjamas and a clean shirt. Being a conscientious small boy and having reading to do for the next day, he also packed his reader. Shortly before supper when neither boys nor adults were about outside, he set out on the long journey home.

His presence was soon missed and search parties went out to look for him. One of these drove through the Van Stadens Pass. Nicholas was expecting this. Hearing a vehicle approaching slowly, he had time enough to find a hiding place. He knew that before long the car would return, which it did, but once again he was not spotted.

By the time he had walked through the pass the light was beginning to fade and he was feeling the first pangs of hunger. He knew that he would soon have to find a place to spend the night and also something to eat and drink. The road was lined with bluegums which in the failing light took on fantastic and rather frightening shapes. There were unexplained rustles in the bush beside the road and the strange calls of night creatures. He tramped on hoping before long to see a light. Eventually, in the distance, he noticed a faint glimmer and headed towards it.

In the bar of the Thornhill Hotel, Bok, Piet and Harry had already downed a couple, but when Nicholas walked in, blinking against the bright lights, they knew immediately from where he had come.

It was Piet who went across and introduced himself. Would Nicholas like anything to eat or drink? Within moments Nicholas found himself perched on a bar-stool, surrounded by three strange men. The elderly barman looked doubtful, the new arrival was definitely under-age, but he took Bok's money and placed on the counter in front of the boy a cool-drink and a packet of chips. The other men at the bar looked at Nicholas with quizzical but not unfriendly expressions.

The chips and liquid refreshment worked wonders and gradually Nicholas began to relax. Bok ordered another round of drinks and some more chips for Nicholas. The three men asked questions in a friendly manner and Nicholas found himself telling them exactly what had happened.

When Piet asked about the suitcase, Nicholas showed him the contents and told Piet why the reader was included. Piet offered to hear him read and when Nicholas started hesitantly the men in the bar stopped talking to listen.

With the reading done conversation resumed, but Nicholas, Bok, Piet and Harry sat in silence. Then Bok said, "Your mum and dad will be worried. You don't want that to happen, do you? Mr Carter at Woodridge will be worried too."

"Mr Carter will be very cross," said Nicholas. "He'll punish me."

"Oh, I don't think so," said Harry. "We'll make sure that he knows all about what has happened."

"And," said Piet, "we'll see that he knows about your reading book and that you did your reading homework."

The three men looked at one another, but after his long walk Nicholas was becoming sleepy. Eventually he agreed to return to Woodridge with the three who promised him that there was nothing to fear.

Mr Carter was much relieved to see Nicholas again, and surprised by his three companions. Bok insisted on talking to Mr Carter alone before allowing Nicholas out of the car. What was said was never disclosed, but eventually Bok came back and opened the car door.

"It's okay Nicholas," said Bok, "Mr Carter says Miss Lush will look after you in the San tonight. Look, here she comes now. It's all going to be okay."

And that is why in the bar of the Thornhill Hotel, Bok, Piet and Harry were sometimes referred to as the three wise men.

Nicholas is now a grown man. Does he still remember the three wise men that helped him in his time of need? He never really knew their names. Does he think of them in terms of Melchior, Gaspar and Balthazar? Probably not, but I do hope that when the opportunity arises he remembers them and cares as they did for young people who, for whatever reason are lost and lonely: that he is, so to speak, a modern-day St Nicholas.

Thornhill

There was practically no room for luggage in the boot of the 1967 Morris Mini-Minor, so almost all went on the back seat. This was no real problem. Caryl's luggage was a hold-all of clothes and toiletries plus a kitbag of tackies and odds and ends. Mine was much the same, the kitbag being replaced by a Pick 'n Pay plastic carrier-bag.

Over the years one accumulates a good deal of excess baggage. We now need an Isuzu double-cab *bakkie* to carry it all. Both the canopied *bak* and the back seat are filled not only with clothes, shoes, towels and toiletries, but *padkos*, a portable refrigerator, cameras, notebooks, maps, plant-presses, a spade and trowel, camping chairs, walking-sticks, a tow-rope, jump-leads, electric pump, spanners, pliers and screwdrivers, torch and a travelling library of botanical books, geological tomes, travel guides and historical works, and if the expedition warrants it, camping equipment.

Of course in my case at least there are also invisible impedimenta: sins of both omission and commission, unquestioned acceptance of the privileges of a white skin, ingratitude and acts of chauvinistic behaviour, all to add to various anxieties, fears and phobias. In the age of psychoanalysis, anti-depressants and social media we travel more heavily laden than ever.

In my paternal grandmother's day it was, or so I was told, easy enough to rid oneself of these latter problems. It was the job of the church, she maintained, to deal with such unnecessary baggage, which was the reason why weekly attendance was so important.

* * *

The Thornhill Church, perched on a hill overlooking the hamlet, was opened with a flourish on St Thomas' Day, 21 December 1884. It was built on ground given for the purpose by the Field Cornet for the area, Isaac Newton of Cadles Hotel. His wife, Elizabeth, née Cadle, had died the previous year. A plaque in the church records her death. Isaac Newton was himself later laid to rest in the church grounds.

Recently the church has had a wing added, an unusual event for a country church at the present time. Perhaps this is an indication that the people of Thornhill are acting as my grandmother suggested and attending church regularly. Are they as a result, more stress-free than the rest of us?

In 1969 our daughter Catherine was born. This led to a baptism in the Thornhill Church and my discovery of a cousin.

Mrs Sylvia McLaggan, the bursar at Woodridge, told me that a former Thornhill postmistress was coincidentally also named Catherine Logie. A little research resulted in my discovery that the postmistress was the daughter of Douglas, the youngest of my father's brothers, who once farmed on Sunnyside beside the narrow-gauge railway; Catherine the postmistress being a cousin I had never met.

A more unusual link involves the Puttergill family. For many years at least three generations of Puttergills have farmed in the Thornhill area, but originally the family was from the former Transkei.

Charles Edward Puttergill, from Nottingham, suffered from a respiratory problem. Like so many others in Victorian times he was sent, a mere teenager at the time, to the Cape in the hopes that the sun, together with a dry climate, would ease if not cure the problem. In due course he landed up in Queenstown where he worked for the wholesalers, Hodges & Co. There he met and married Mary Ellen Flowers.

The young couple was sent to St Marks in the Transkei to run a Hodges & Co trading-store. In time Puttergill was able to buy the store and there they lived for many years. While at St Marks they ensured the survival of the Puttergill name in South Africa by raising 13 children. More importantly they were well-respected members of the community. Charles was regarded as an honest and fair-minded businessman, while Mary was always ready to help those in need.

Wherever you go in South Africa today you are likely to come across the descendants of Charles and Mary Puttergill. You may also come across Xhosa speaking members of the Patekile family. They too are from St Marks in the former Transkei. Their surname, Patekile, is a derivative of Puttergill. It was adopted by local tribes-people as a tribute to a family that was much esteemed a century and more ago.

These familial links amongst groups such as English-, Afrikaans- or even Xhosa-speakers are not that uncommon. Similar links may be found world-wide.

It has been claimed that the majority of those living in England today, including the most humble members of society, and despite what the aristocracy may think of the matter, have royal blood in their veins Likewise the Logies and Mc-Laggans stem from a common Scots ancestor named after his place of residence, Luguen, the "valley of the yew tree".

"Don't ever trust anyone who claims to be related," said my father, "they'll probably want to borrow money, and you'll never see it again."

So far so good: to date all likely and some unlikely possible relations have refrained from asking for loans.

Gamtoos

It was in 1967 that Caryl and I first travelled through Thornhill on the R102, the old national road. An early European visitor described the countryside it passes through as English parkland, but it has been largely transformed by farming activities and the planting of blue-gums and other exotics. Today there are traces of the fire that came so close to destroying Woodridge and the old Cadles Hotel building.

A white-walled homestead on Nocton Farm to the left of the road before one passes under the modern N2 highway catches the eye. Shortly thereafter the road winds down through the aloes and euphorbias of the Albany Thicket to the valley of the Gamtoos.

The Gamtoos was a major obstacle to early travellers. The first recorded crossing of the river was in 1752 by an expedition led by Ensign August Frederik Beutler. He negotiated the river at a place still marked on the maps as Wagendrift, a few kilometres south of present-day Hankey. This remained a major crossing point for a century. At some unknown date a "punt" was introduced for the conveyance of passengers, but wagons and carts together with horses, cattle and other livestock continued to ford the river.

Then in September 1844 the 15 members of the Beresford family arrived in Algoa Bay from England aboard the *Warrior.* They brought with them a number of servants, farming implements, pedigreed livestock and four wooden "American" prefabricated houses, the latter for use on a future farm. Two of these later found their way to beside the Gamtoos.

The Beresfords had great plans for their new homeland. Their introduction of "the newest English farming methods" to the Eastern Cape proved to be a dismal failure. Far more successful was the building of a pontoon for use on the Gamtoos. For the first time it would be possible to carry not only passengers but also stock and vehicles across the river near the mouth, avoiding the long detour inland to Wagendrift.

The pontoon was put into operation in 1847 at the site of the present Gamtoos Ferry Hotel. It was operated by 20 year-old George Beresford, third son of the family. In the same year he married Maria Helena Kemp, daughter of a local farmer. The ceremony was conducted by the Rev Francis McCleland with the permission of both sets of parents, both bride and groom being under-age. Two of the American houses were erected and linked to form a home for the newly-weds.

Two years later George Beresford, ferryman and shop-keeper at the Gamtoos died, leaving Maria and two young daughters. It was said by some that he had taken his own life. There was speculation at the time as to what might have driven him to this.

The prefabricated Beresford home was later dismantled and moved to Nocton Farm where it now forms a part of the white-walled house we saw on the way down. It has been re-roofed, re-floored with local yellowwood, and the wooden walls plastered, but it is otherwise the same building that arrived in Algoa Bay in 1844. Some years ago, while repairs were being made, the name of the ship that brought the Beresfords to Algoa Bay, *Warrior*, was found on one of the interior walls.

For close to fifty years the Beresford ferry remained in operation. Farmers were at times critical of the service. On more than one occasion floods carried the ferry downstream towards the mouth. Farmers with wagon-loads of agricultural produce or driving stock on the way to market were forced to wait until such time as the ferry was dragged back upstream. Complaints were lodged and the Divisional Council was very aware of the farmers' views.

When at last the ferry was replaced the old pontoon was sold to the Williams family of the nearby farm Bergrivier (alternatively known as Jagersfontein). After half a century in the waters of the Gamtoos the timber from the old pontoon was in good enough condition to be used in the building of a barn that is still to be seen on the farm.

The bridge was officially opened in 1895 by Mrs Garcia, wife of the Civil Commissioner of Uitenhage, accompanied by Mrs Andrews, wife of the Humansdorp magistrate. The Humansdorp newspaper, *The Re-echo* of the 14th of December 1895, noted that transport-riders would no longer have to wait overnight to cross the river but could now cross whenever they pleased no matter the time of day or state of the weather.

Of course, not everyone was happy. Like most projects of this nature the final cost was 20% more than the original estimate. Likewise there were those who objected to paying a toll to cross, but as *The Re-echo* pointed out, a charge had to be made to ensure regular maintenance. (When in 2019 I mentioned this to a local farmer he remarked that there had been no maintenance done during the last quarter of a century, but that the bridge was still in use.)

The bridge serves as a monument to an interesting man: Joseph Newey, an English civil engineer who came to the Cape in 1873. On his arrival he set to work at King Williams Town erecting an iron latticework girder bridge across the Buffalo River. He then moved together with his wife and son, to Committees Drift on the Great Fish River.

By December 1874 work on the Committees Drift Bridge was well underway. Then on the 5th of that month the river came down in flood, washing away the wooden scaffolding and the second span. When on the 7th the waters began to recede, Newey set about repairing the damage. He took it upon himself to raise the level of the bridge by two meters. After communications were re-established, his superiors concurred with Newey's decision.

At this stage Newey was asked to check on any damage to other bridges along the river. He reported that the bridges at Fort Brown and over the Koonap had simply disappeared. The ironwork of the Carlisle Bridge lay mangled in the river, while that at Cookhouse had toppled from its piers. From the head office in Cape Town he was instructed to take control and repair the bridges as quickly as possible. He was not yet 30 years of age.

Newey worked with a will and not only made the repairs in record time, but completed work on the bridge at Committees Drift, rebuilt the Victoria Bridge at Fort Beaufort with enlarged outer spans and erected a new iron bridge of his own design over the Great Fish at Fort Brown. His prompt and appropriate action restored road links and brought him to the attention of those in head office. For Newey the flood was a blessing in disguise. He decided to stay on at the Cape.

In the years to come he bridged the entire Eastern Cape. In 1882 he was appointed District Inspector not only of bridges, but of all public buildings, and in 1893 became the Chief Inspector of Public Works in the Cape Colony. But it was a case of one and all laying loads on a willing horse. Ill-health brought on by exhaustion brought his retirement from public service. Two years later, in 1907, he died on his farm at Kei Road.

With the coming of motor vehicles the more than 70 single-lane bridges for which he was responsible were soon outdated and were gradually replaced. His name was all but forgotten, yet his contribution to the transport network of the Cape was on a par with that of the pass builder, Thomas Bain.

* * *

At the Gamtoos River Bridge we stopped to check its condition. At a quick glance it seemed that not only had Joseph Newey been forgotten, but also, as mentioned by the farmer to whom I spoke, his bridge, which is in dire need of a coat of paint if nothing else.

Walking across the bridge came a man in Johnson overalls and wearing a tattered, faded, floppy hat and white Wellington boots: Titus Ncama, dairyman.

"I use the bridge twice a day, like my father before me, and *utat'omkhulu* before him."

"And the new bridge?" I ask pointing in the direction of the N2.

"Sir, it is too far and too dangerous. Too many cars. But look at this bridge. See where *iloli* hit it? It is falling apart. One day it fall down. And then? Then where do we cross the river?"

Further upstream, near Gamtoos Station, is a railway bridge. The station at Gamtoos was, in the days when trains were still running, a busy junction. It was from here that a line ran up beside the river to Hankey and on to the terminus at Patensie. Shortly after leaving the junction, the main line crosses the Gamtoos on its way to Humansdorp and eventually Avontuur.

We walked across the bridge which, despite no longer being in use, is in better condition than the road bridge. Stopping above the muddy water of the river, we watched two small boys throwing stones at a swimming snake. Fortunately for the snake the stones seem to have little effect.

* * *

The first narrow gauge railway bridge, a wooden trestle, did fall down, or rather a 30 metre section was washed away. This happened in 1904 before the line was officially opened. The bridge was repaired in time for the first trains in 1905, but later in the year another massive flood, rising to 10 feet (3.048 m) above the rails, again swept away the bridge. The replacement lasted for seven years.

Finally, in 1912 the present bridge was built. It is made up of a large, arched span produced by Braithwaite & Kirk of West Bromwich and designed specifically for the Gamtoos crossing. The other three spans are a hodgepodge collection of bridges that happened to be on hand. From the north (the station) side there is an iron lattice work road bridge of typical Newey design made by Westwood Baillie and Co of London in 1884 and obtained by the South African Railways from the Cape Public Works Department. On the southern side of the arch are two spans, one by Westwood Baillie and believed to have come from the Free State, and a third undated Westwood Baillie span of unknown origin.

It was customary at the time for bridge mechanics, or civil engineers as we would call them today, such as Joseph Newey, to design a bridge and erect the necessary approaches and pillars, but to send to Britain for the required metalwork. One of the most prominent of these British engineering works was Westwood Baillie & Co., established in 1856. They produced iron and steel work not only for bridges, but also ships, boilers and milling machinery. The company was wound up in 1893 and Baillie declared insolvent two years later. Joseph Westwood, son of the Joseph Westwood of Westwood Baillie & Co, established his own constructional engineering firm, Joseph Westwood, in 1883. The company took over much of the business of the earlier firm and was still active in the 1960s. The iron lattice work on the road bridge was produced by Joseph Westwood.

The central arched span of the railway bridge, the only span designed for use over this particular crossing of the Gamtoos, was produced by Braithwaite & Kirk, a firm established in 1884. Initially it was involved exclusively in the manufacture of steel bridges, but in 1913 an Indian subsidiary, Braithwaite & Co, Structural Ltd, was established. The company is now owned by the Indian government.

How travel has changed! Yet we seldom nowadays give a thought to the surveyors, road-builders (including the convicts that often provided the necessary muscle), civil engineers and maintenance crews that made travelling in this country as easy as it is. One thing at least has not changed - we still complain about having to pay tolls!

The wooden railway bridge over the Gamtoos River

Humansdorp Cultural Centre 2020 - roof
in need of repair

3.

Kouga Coast

Symbolism in Humansdorp

An image appears on the television screen: a group of irate, white, Afrikaans-speaking farmers. In the background is an old South African flag.

It sometimes surprises us how certain symbols unite, or in this case divide a nation. In 1928 when the Union of South Africa adopted the flag, the grandparents of the irate farmers may well have been among those that protested against the

35

flag's use, for there in its centre, together with an old Trans-vaal *Vierkleur* and the Orange Free State flag, is a Union Jack, symbol of the hated Brits, the *rooinekke*. Today some of their descendants, unaware of their ancestors' protest, claim the flag as their own.

During the latter part of the 19th century, after the depar-ture of the Trekkers and before the onset of the Anglo-Boer War, there were relatively few in the Cape Colony with vio-lently negative feelings concerning the Union Jack. The war brought changes.

W S J Sellick, pro-British editor of the *Uitenhage Times* and founder of the Humansdorp newspaper, *The Echo,* and then of its successor, *The Re-echo,* was one of the admirers of the Humansdorp Park, designed by a Mr W A Muskett.

In 1904 Sellick wrote of the Park:

> *The walks are arranged in the form of the Union Jack, and radiate from a common centre, where an orna-mental fountain stands. Four broad carriage drives meet here, and four paths lead from hence to the cor-ners of the enclosure. Both drives and paths are well kept, and are 25 feet (7.6 m) and 16 feet (4.9 m) wide respectively.*

He went on to praise the flower beds, "bright and pretty" and made much of trees such as the "Caroub, which is said to bear finer fruit, or at all events as fine as that grown in Asia Minor, the natural habitat of the tree". What he called the *Pi-nus Insignis* (*P. radiata* or Monterey Pine) "never reaches the age of twenty years in South Africa, but in Humansdorp park are trees double that age, over eighty feet high and bearing fertile seeds which produce self-sown trees by the thousand". (Enough to make any modern-day botanist blanch at the thought of all those invasive aliens.) The most plentiful spe-cies in the park were Eucalypts and Blackwoods (yet more invasive aliens, and with no mention of a single indigenous tree).

"For shady walks and noble trees Humansdorp has not many equals in the Cape Colony."

While Sellick remarks on the "capital tennis courts and croquet lawns", there is no mention of the swimming pool. At the height of the British Empire its young men in the colonies, bearers of the white man's burden, were expected to be involved in the manly sports. In the absence of pig-sticking or fox-hunting, swimming was a lesser but acceptable sport. The pool at the southern end of the park was well screened by trees, thus safe-guarding young ladies from sights likely to cause maidenly blushes. (A later pool was built at the top of the town, and at long last provision was made for women swimmers, but not at the same time as men.)

The former "Union Jack" park is easy enough to find: it is located at the bottom end of Main Street. A large brick gateway advertises the fact that it later became, and was until quite recently, a municipal caravan park. As such it was popular for a number of years, but today it resembles a miniature Hiroshima after the Bomb. Roofs have disappeared, as have doors and windows. At least one of the buildings was apparently destroyed by fire. The bricks from a boundary wall lie scattered on the pavement. The swimming pool – the third in the line of municipal pools - lies empty other than for mud, loose bricks, rubbish and a puddle of water. The former "shady walks" are strewn with litter. An inquiry of a municipal official elicited the information that the present state was due to a lack of use caused at least in part by the fact that "it was too colonial". Perhaps Mr Muskett should have chosen a different design for the carriage drives and paths?

Main Street, like many other streets in town, was at one time lined with trees. Originally these were all indigenous, being easily obtained from the nearby Tsitsikamma forests, but as time went by some of these were uprooted and replaced with flowering gums and other exotics. Those in Main Street were removed in the 1940s in order to widen the road. At the same time the *leiwater* furrows were filled in: features that might today have attracted tourists were removed in the name of progress.

At the top of Main Street is a modern building loaded with symbolism. In June 2000 the local press announced that the

Humansdorp Transitional Local Council (TLC), headed by Mr Booi Koerat, was proposing to build a Cultural Centre at the top of Main Street. The Local Economic Development Fund, established by Central Government, was to award the Humansdorp TLC R1.5-million to help towards covering the costs. The building was to be designed by a former Humansdorp architect now living in Australia, Mr Ardea Oosthuizen, who would be assisted by archeologist Dr Johan Binneman. Mr Bokka du Toit was to act as "facilitator and cultural adviser on the Khoisan and Traditional Africa".

A later press release informed the public that organic materials were to be used in the construction of the Centre. The walls were to be of rammed earth, and elsewhere thatch, clay, mud, limestone and red and yellow ochre were to be used. The dome would be sheathed in copper, "one of the earliest metals mined in Africa". The design would be based on a typical anthill where the interior maintains a constant temperature, which would do away with the need for any "artificial" air-conditioning.

Du Toit stated that the project could act as a blueprint for future housing development, having low environmental impact together with natural aesthetic values. Apart from any other attractions that might be housed in the building, the structure itself would have enormous attraction value. There would be parking for coaches and cars and a separate area for taxis. The building was to be surrounded by an indigenous garden and on the northern side there would be an amphitheatre. Also to the north of the building would be a siding where passengers travelling on the Apple Express could alight before entering the building.

In the Centre there would be not only a display of cultural artefacts, but live cultural performances, traditional African art and crafts, and a labour exchange. A food market and stalls stocking traditional herbal remedies would cater for those making use of the adjoining taxi-rank.

Altogether it was to be a "must-see" experience and was bound to attract a majority of the 2.1 million foreign tourists that annually by-passed Humansdorp.

In general all the citizens of Humansdorp, no matter what their skin-colour or language group, looked forward to seeing this wonder completed. It was true that archeologist Johan Binneman had raised some tricky questions regarding the display and storage of artefacts and the movement of people through the Centre, but most people felt that these were minor problems that could easily be overcome.

On the 21st of December 2002 the R9-million Kouga Cultural Centre was opened at a ceremony attended by 500 VIPs. The building was blessed by traditional healers, there were African dances, a performance by a band, the *Melktertkommissie* and almost, but not quite, an interlude of *volkspele.* (The programme went on for longer than expected and the dancers had to leave.)

Mrs N Botha, Deputy Minister of Provincial and Local Government, said in her opening message that the gathering together of different cultures meeting and enjoying themselves would eventually become the real picture of the whole of South Africa.

It was planned to link the Centre to the Baviaanskloof and its caves, and to the burial site in Hankey of Sarah Baartman, who, exhibited as a freak in Europe during the early years of the 19th century, found a final resting place in the Kouga district. There would be visits to the Centre by schoolchildren who would come to discover the symbolism of the building and to learn about their ancestors and cultural beginnings.

Today (2020) the indigenous gardens are neglected, rubbish-filled and surrounded by a security fence erected to keep hitch-hikers, work-seekers and drinkers from sitting on the steps of the ceremonial front entrance. Thatch has fallen from the roof and copper-cladding from the massive dome is disappearing. There can be very few Humansdorpers who know anything of the symbolism of the building or who have learnt anything there about their ancestors, the ancestors of other people or anyone's cultural beginnings.

The lights are off and the doors are locked. It seems that, through lack of interest, the ancestors of the indigenous people of the district are about to follow the colonists into oblivion.

Colonialism

In 1897, as Britain celebrated the 60th anniversary of Queen Victoria's ascension to the throne, the nation could claim to have the greatest empire in history. Almost a quarter of the earth's inhabitants were the subjects of the Widow of Windsor. Wherever one went the Union Jack flapped. Why, the design of the flag even inspired the layout of public parks!

During the century from 1815, Britain, without any serious international rival, established the *Pax Brittania* and ruled the earth. The British were the winners of the ultimate World Cup. No wonder they became arrogant. No wonder they tended to look down their long noses, or the barrel of a gun, at the people of other nations, or the "savage" inhabitants of Africa, Asia and Australia.

They made derogatory remarks about their new subjects, but then they even referred to their fellow Europeans by such pejoratives as Frogs, Huns and Dagoes. The citizens of France, Germany and Italy were well aware of this British practice, but could do no more about it than the inhabitants of the Cape Colony, Bangalore or those living on the banks of the Murrimbidgee.

Whether or not the colonies ever produced for the mother country the power and income hoped for is doubtful, but there is no question that the vast splashes of red on the map of the world were enough to impress those gathered to celebrate the triumphs of the Queen's reign. Hers was "an empire on which the sun never set".

Britain was the commercial and industrial capital of the world. At sea the Royal Navy ruled the waves. The fighting spirit of its soldiers far outstripped that of any other nation. In the colonies British missionaries showed local inhabitants the error of their theology and of their ways, both morally and in the manner of their dress, which conveniently also boosted the sales of cotton goods from Manchester.

The young men of Britain, wholehearted colonialists, set forth to suppress savagery and to reclaim the wilderness: this then was "the white man's burden". The burden did not rest too heavily on the young men's shoulders, for in the process they found in the colonies a place to misbehave and an outlet for self-importance and cruelty not tolerated in their home country.

This left some outsiders in a quandary: did one admire and support the World Cup winners, or condemn their violent and inhumane ways? Even prior to 1945 it was perfectly clear that Britain's dreams of world hegemony were not a passing affliction restricted to a single nation, but a dangerous disease to which almost all are prone. As Nigerian academic Ropo Sekoni pointed out, "Colonialism has nothing to do with the colour of the coloniser and the colonised. Any group of people that uses advantage of power – military or material – to oppress, exploit, and inferiorise another group of people can be justifiably described as a colonising group." The battle against colonialism, in whatever form it takes, continues.

Not many countries, although there have been some marked exceptions, happily accept outsiders. Europe is at present faced with an influx from Africa and also the Middle East, Australia with people from South-East Asia, and the United States with refugees from South America. How are they to be housed and fed? Where are the children to go to school? They cause all sorts of problems. Even the most tractable and law-abiding newcomers are likely to wear unfamiliar dress, eat outlandish food and practise strange customs.

The majority of South Africans are immigrants or the descendants of immigrants. The earliest evidence of Iron-Age Bantu-speakers in southern Africa goes back only 2 000 years. The Dutch arrived just 368 years ago and the majority of the English a mere two centuries ago. Most but not all of the Dutch and British were, like their Iron-Age predecessors, settlers planning to make a new home for themselves in a strange land.

Not all immigrants are pimps, con-artists and drug-dealers. They often bring benefits with them. They are usually young, healthy, hard-working and ambitious. Yet it is these very attributes that often result in their unpopularity.

41

Jews who came to South Africa fleeing the pogroms of Europe between the World Wars arrived penniless, yet within a generation many established thriving businesses in their new home. There were stories at the time, stories that were enthusiastically spread by some politicians, of Jewish shopkeepers who supposedly fleeced their unsophisticated, *platteland* Boer customers. Prevalent as these stories were at the time, they were countered by the likes of Afrikaans author P H Nortje. He told of how Jewish shopkeeper Julius Musikanth of Willowmore helped him financially through school, enabling him eventually to go onto Stellenbosch University. Nortje was not the only one to thank a Jewish general dealer.

The children of these immigrants became doctors, lawyers, businessmen and academics. Of South Africa's eleven Nobel Prize-winners, four were born in South Africa of Lithuanian Jewish parents, one of Swiss parents, and one, Albert Luthuli, in the then Rhodesia.

None of my immediate ancestors, be they 1820 British settlers or their descendants, were as spectacularly successful as the former Lithuanians. Besides being colonists the majority were, I am sure, enthusiastic supporters of colonialism. They were, after all, people of their time.

Yet my father in 1910, at the time of Union, believed that all "educated" men should be able to vote - women as yet did not have the franchise. "Educated", so far as he was concerned at the time, meant that one could read and write and, because the Cape was a British colony, could understand basic English. He estimated that this would mean that at least 20% of whites would *lose* the vote, while roughly the same number or more of black and brown citizens would be enfranchised. Whatever one might think today of his distinction regarding "educated voters", at the time his views were regarded as radical.

Despite their beliefs and their comparative lack of financial, academic or even cultural success, my ancestors made a positive contribution to their new homeland.

They became farmers, watchmakers, printers, teachers, nurses, small businessmen and minor government officials, and of course, successful mothers and housewives. And some, being uneducated, would have lost the vote had my father had his way. Still, as citizens they paid their taxes and undertook what they regarded as their duties to the State and to their fellows, which in my father's case at least included the Xhosa amongst whom he had grown up. My father died aged 96. In his extreme old age he moved back to the Eastern Cape, There in what had become the Nelson Mandela Metro, he could see in front of the Public Library the statue of Victoria, the Queen in whose reign he was born. Around him he heard the lilt and clicks of the language of his childhood and youth. He had returned to the land of his ancestors.

Did any of my forebears hanker after the "green and pleasant land" of their European origin? Of those I met none ever spoke of "Home" as being anywhere other than in South Africa. Nor did they in my hearing express a wish to return to the misty shores of Albion, not even my English-born mother, though she did welcome what she called "grey days" with overcast skies and the promise of rain. But then so does many a South African farmer whatever his or her skin colour or home language.

Were they aware of their privileged position? Probably not, but even if they did, they accepted it as their "right": they were, after all, British, British South Africans.

Jeffreys Bay

Leading a column of vehicles up the hill from the Swartrivier is an elderly Nissan 1400 *bakkie* trailing a veil of light blue smoke. The cream bodywork is dusty and covered with chocolate brown splodges of rust-remover. From under the canopy a surf-board sticks out. No prizes for correctly guessing the *bakkie's* destination.

It is ten minutes to eight on a Monday morning and there is an equally long column of cars and busses coming in the opposite direction. Half of the population of Jeffreys Bay, or so it seems, is on the way to Humansdorp, while half of Humansdorp is going to Jeffreys Bay, or J-Bay as the surfers and most others these days would have it.

Finally a gap appears in the traffic and we hurry past the Nissan. We give the tangle-haired young man driving it a wave as we pass. He acknowledges this with an enthusiastic thumbs-up out of the window. There is no way of knowing how following drivers interpret this signal. We hope that they simply shake their heads while remembering that they too were once young. Perhaps they wish that they, like the driver of the Nissan, were on their way to catch a wave at Supertubes, Kitchen Windows or perhaps even the Boneyard.

South Africa has a claim to surfing fame of which very few are aware. In 1897 on a Durban beach a visiting mariner, Capt TW Sheffield, staggered down to the waves carrying a 75 kg, two metre long board, and took to the water to become the country's first recorded surfer. This was ten years before the sport was introduced to California. Australians only started surfing in 1915. Presumably Sheffield had witnessed the Hawaiian islanders surfing and shaped his own board before arriving in Durban.

Despite the early start, no one seemed to do much surfing along the South African coast before the late 1960s. Then suddenly one saw VW Beetles and Kombis with surfboards strapped to roof racks driving along coastal roads. To paraphrase *The Beach Boys,* everybody'd gone surfin', surfin' RSA!

The sudden popularity of surfing had a great deal to do with a film, *The Endless Summer,* in which Bruce Brown, the director, producer, writer, narrator, cameraman and editor, together with two surfers, Mike Hynson and Robert August, took a trip around the world in search of the "perfect" wave. (They found it off Cape St Francis!)

Brown, a surfer and an entirely self-taught filmmaker, first took still photos and eight millimeter ciné shots to show his mother what surfing was all about. Later he began using a 16 mm camera and produced surfing films for fellow enthusiasts in California. Finally, after raising $50 000, he was ready to produce a full-length film.

The Endless Summer, released worldwide in 1966, was an entirely new, relaxed approach to the making of documentary films. It appealed not only to surfers and prospective surfers, but also to the general public. Despite initial rejection by film distributors, it went on to gross more than $20 million (the equivalent of $159 680 000 in 2020). In the year 2002 it was selected for preservation by the United States Library of Congress, being considered "culturally, historically and aesthetically significant".

While in J-Bay we took the opportunity to question surfers and found that not everyone took to surfing because of the film. Ross Turner told us that he was too young to have seen Bruce Brown's masterpiece. He only became a surfer in 1982. At the time he was in Standard 5 and lived not far from the beach. Earlier he was, as a "nipper", a young member of a local Lifesaving Club. "In those days lifesavers scorned surfers. Today it is the surfers that maintain the lifesaving clubs."

Richard Cowling said that he became a surfer in 1968, but only watched *The Endless Summer* much later. "They didn't show films like that up in the Transvaal where we lived." It was the "counter-culture" of surfing that appealed to Richard. "And it was far more fascinating than fishing," he added. "Nobody had much money. We made do with whatever we had, but nowadays it's different, and surfers drive the most up-to-date four-by-fours."

Well, not all the surfers, we thought, remembering the smoky Nissan.

In Cape Town *The Endless Summer* was shown at the Labia. The first night audience was mainly under the age of 40 and casually dressed. A few of the men even wore sandals without socks. There was not a tie to be seen. A girl named Josephine, wearing only a floral blouse and black pantihose with no shoes attracted some interest, but was not barred from entry. "Rugger buggers" were noticeable by their absence. There were also no safari-suits, nor combs tucked into long stockings.

I did not realise it at the time, but as Richard remembered it I was witnessing the birth of a counter-culture. When next I visited J-Bay the pavements were full of young people with surfboards. Cheron Kraak was sewing baggies and on her way to creating a surf-related clothing empire. Every other young man, or so it seemed, was making sandals when not surfing. It was rumoured that some were even smoking dagga.

If you are at all interested in the early history of surfing in South Africa, call in at Trawlers (formerly Coetzee's), the fish and chips shop opposite the Savoy Hotel in Da Gama Road, Jeffreys Bay.

Behind the counter we found a tall, photogenic woman, Dora Ackerman. We placed our order and asked about the surfers' Guest Book. She ducked under the counter and began scratching around. "It's here somewhere," she said before emerging with a large, battered ledger.

Out on the stoep we had hardly sat down and opened to the first page when a fresh-faced, smiling, young man carrying a motorcycle safety helmet walked in from the street.

"Don't tell me you're Brian Murphy," he said to my mystification. Without pausing to explain his remark he introduced himself as Paul Richmond, son of Dennis Richmond who bought the fish and chip business from the Coetzees 26 years ago. We only just had enough time to introduce ourselves and explain our business.

"Please excuse me," he said, "but I am supposed to be at work." He hurried indoors.

Opening the ledger we came across a greeting: "The Coetzees Wish You All A Perfect Wave," and thereafter words of counsel:

Let this be the Surfer's Motto:

I will always endeavour to let my words, my deeds, my actions be as Clean as my body after a day's surfing.

Nothing wrong with that, but did the Coetzees find some of the young surfers a bit wild?

There followed some useful information: "We can supply repair kits @ R1 each". No doubt the price will have escalated in the past half-century.

The first entry by a surfer is dated 31 December 1967 and explained Paul Richmond's remark. South Australian surfer Brian Murphy from Nilpecia Avenue, Parkholme, commented on how the surfing was "too much" and the Coetzees, "beaut fish and chip people".

Paul must have realised as soon as we spoke that we were not from South Australia.

In 1989 Brian Murphy was back with his 11 year-old son, Jedd.

Then in 2005 Brian, now aged 60, was back yet again: "Surf very small, but still enjoyed memories of paradise . . . May all who come here still get gas waves and enjoy." This is followed by a comment by Liam Murphy, "youngest of the generation aged 15".

Looking through the Guest Book we found hundreds of others commenting on the surf and singing J-Bay's praises with barely a dissenting voice and definitely no "unclean words"!

Dark-haired Dora in her eye-catching red dress delivered our take-away order of grilled hake and chips to the outside table where we, sitting beside the vinegar and salt, were going through the book.

We put our heads in the door, returned the book, said goodbye to a busy Paul Richmond and walked across the road to the Isuzu.

Tell the teacher we're surfin'
Surfin' RSA.

Fishing and conservation

Before the 1850s, when Port Elizabeth surveyor Robert Pinchin laid out plots for sale on the farm Klein Zeekoei Rivier, there were Khoekhoen fishermen living beside the Bay of St Francis. They lived on the fish they caught and on *patats* – sweet-potatoes - which they obtained from local farmers in exchange for fish. This combination of *vis en patat* is today referred to locally as a Tsitsikamma-burger.

The plots sold by landowner M G Human (of Humansdorp) and others came to be named Jeffreys Bay, after an early trader and plot-holder, Joseph Avent Jeffery. The difference in spelling between the name of the trader, and that of the town, was probably due to an oversight by a careless clerk.

In 1860 Yorkshireman George Pell also bought land in the area, including a portion of the farm Klein Zeekoei Rivier, and established a general dealer's business and canteen. Most of the Khoekhoen fishermen, particularly after 1925 when Jeffreys Bay was officially proclaimed a village, lived in the vicinity of the Pells' shop. At this time the Pell business was run by George's son, William Pell. Various members of the Pell family were buried in the nearby graveyard and today the area has become the suburb of Pellsrus.

Pell and Jeffery were only two of the new white landowners. Both men realised the business opportunities offered by the local fishing industry. Others too were impressed by the catches of the Khoekhoen fishermen. Some of the newcomers invested in boats in order to exploit this bounty. These boats, built by Thesens of Knysna, were clinker-built rowing boats of a standard, double-ended design. For light on board the paraffin-fed flicker of a storm-lantern sufficed, and sandbags were used for ballast. On shore a driftwood fire might be lit to guide the boat in. Boats put to sea with a crew of nine: eight oarsmen and a skipper. After breasting the breakers a sail was set to carry them to the fishing grounds.

Thesen's boats were used by various fishing communities situated along the south and south-east coast of the Cape Colony. Returning with their catch, each member of the crew was allowed a number of *"eetvis"*. Then roughly 20% of the remainder was apportioned to the owner. Fishermen were free to sell what remained for what they fetched. Often this turned out to be to the boat-owner at ridiculously low prices.

With their primitive equipment; hand lines with scrap iron for sinkers and hooks fashioned from *bloudraad* – eight-gauge wire - they caught Kabeljou, Dageraad, Red Roman, Steenbras, Geelbek and Geelstert. Chokka (calamari) was used only for bait. In good times a fisherman might earn as much as £1-10-0 – say R3 - a day, but times were seldom that good.

A fishery officer was first appointed in 1900 to keep an eye not only on the fishing, but the boats themselves, for they were not often well maintained. Eventually from 1919 boat owners were obliged to license their boats and to keep them in decent order. It was at this time that dragnets were introduced and the old hand lines gradually disappeared.

By 1926 the fishery officer could report that 153 190 lbs (69 486 kg) of fish were caught during the year. Without refrigeration available, little fresh fish was sold, most was either dried or salted. Fences provided convenient drying lines and after a good catch the main economic activity of the village was very evident. Fish was sold not only to local farmers, but to Humansdorp merchants and the Thornhill Hotel. Fish was even sent to Port Elizabeth, travelling either by ox wagon or occasionally by boat.

Few if any of the crew were able to swim. Swimmers were unwelcome, for if the boat was in difficulties a swimmer might well strike out for the shore, leaving his companions in their hour of need. No one ever took cooked fish to sea, for this surely was tempting fate. Nor did anyone dare whistle: wind was their enemy and whistling – who knows? – might bring on a south-westerly gale. The boats never went to sea on a Sunday. Yet despite all precautions tragedies did occur. Families were left fatherless and without a breadwinner, and without pensions or child grants to support them, widows struggled.

Today most of the descendants of the oarsmen of the old clinker-built boats, the Hammonds, Tituses, Mentoors and Perils go to sea in refrigerated boats and like their great-grandfathers they use hand lines, but to catch chokka. Chokka, regarded by their ancestors as only useful as bait, is now "white gold", a multi-million rand export industry. No longer are the boats launched from the beach, but from Port St Francis, a harbour to the west of Jeffreys Bay.

Unlike their ancestors, today's chokka fishermen go to sea for three weeks at a time, not just for a day. The paraffin storm-lantern has given way to half-a-dozen or more giant halogen lamps that at night shine on the water to attract the different fish species on which the chokka feed. Gathered together, lamps ablaze, the fishing-boats resemble a small Venice that, having made a unilateral declaration of independence, is gently drifting southwards.

For three weeks the fishermen live and work in very cramped quarters, sleeping in the bows, head to head. "One can hardly imagine a situation better suited to the spread of a variety of diseases," remarked Jean, a local doctor. But for three weeks they live rent free and with food provided; not so the families they leave on land.

Each fisherman's catch, for which he has to have a permit, is weighed after a night's fishing. At the end of three weeks the fisherman is paid according to the weight of chokka he has caught. On occasion he may earn thousands of rand, but it can also be only a few hundred.

After three days ashore he is back again on the boat. At home his wife and children make do with whatever is left of his earnings. Then during the off-season, with the boats confined to harbour for three months, there is no income at all unless he can find a part-time job. Today's fishermen may in some respects be better off than their great-grandfathers, but it is nevertheless a hard life.

Chokka catches have diminished over the years. Over-fishing may be the reason, or global warming or a combination of factors: a worry to both the company owning the boat and the individual fisherman and his family. Research is on-going, for more and more people have come to realise that we, as so called "Lords of Creation" have a daunting responsibility. How do we establish a balance between our needs and a functional environment? To change just one interlocking piece in the jigsaw puzzle may have unexpected results.

* * *

In the 1960s the South African Government was worried about feeding a burgeoning population. A decision was made to grow wheat in large areas both to the east and west of Port Elizabeth. To do so the veld was stripped of its indigenous vegetation.

Botanists such as Timm Hoffman sounded a warning. The big constraint on growing wheat in the western part of the Eastern Cape is the lack of predictability in our seasonal rainfall. Mid-winter can be the driest time of the year. If the autumn (March-April) rains fail, then the crop fails. What is surprising is that government agrometerologists must have known this.

Timm was not the only one that was concerned. A Humansdorp traditional healer, selling his remedies in Main Street, Humansdorp was also reported to have doubts: "I worry what will happen to all the (indigenous) plants." Predictably his worries were ignored, yet as early as 1957 Prof John Taylor of Leeds University had written:

It is the gravest possible mistake for Europeans to suppose, because of the incredible technological success of modern Western civilisation, that other cultures can offer no way of looking at the world; Africa has another way. The white man must at least respect the African's right to be different, even if he is too slow to realise how much the world needs the African vision. (Cultural Imperialism.)

Paying no attention to any warnings, the plan went ahead. Feeding the population was regarded as more important than preserving *renosterbos* and *vetplante*. It was acknowledged

51

that at certain times of the year *blommetjies* produced a stunning flower-show, but one could not feed people flowers. Hoffman's prediction that they would be creating a dustbowl went unheeded. Not only was land cleared, but vast grain silos were built at railway stations in the area.

No sooner was wheat planted in the Humansdorp district than farmers noticed the arrival of Blue Cranes. This large elegant bird had only recently been proclaimed South Africa's National Bird. As the farmers soon discovered one pair of birds, following a line of germinating seeds, pecking out each plant in turn, could easily destroy an entire wheat field. Humansdorp farmers applied for permission to shoot Blue Cranes feeding on their lands. The National Bird had become, so they said, "a pest and a menace".

Mr R Liversidge, acting Director of the Port Elizabeth Museum noted that cranes were usually to be found in the grain-farming areas of the Orange Free State, where they were regarded as a pest. They had been nominated for national bird status by the South African branch of the International Committee for Bird Protection in 1961. Found only in South Africa, their beauty, dignified appearance and size were considered important factors. The Bokmakierie, the only other bird to be considered, lacked these features.

This was all very well, but what were the farmers to do about the problem? Liversidge was able to reassure the Humansdorp farmers: "Despite its status, the Blue Crane has been removed from the protected game list. You may shoot birds feeding on your lands."

Today (2020) the Blue Crane is classified as critically endangered. The population suddenly declined from the 1980s on, and at present only between 10 000 and 20 000 birds remain. In the last two decades the bird has almost completely disappeared from the Eastern Cape, and also Lesotho and Eswatini.

Not many years after the first Kouga wheatlands were ploughed, it was found that Timm Hoffman had been correct. The area from which indigenous vegetation was cleared was not suitable for the growing of wheat. The entire exercise was a complete waste of money and so far as biodiversity was concerned a disaster. Very little wheat is now grown in the district. The enormous silos at the Humansdorp railway station stand empty. They now serve as among the tallest, and surely the most expensive radio signal masts in the country.

If we are to continue enjoying stir-fried calamari or even Tsitsikamma-burgers we cannot allow similar mistakes to be made concerning our marine resources.

Perhaps at the same time we should look into ways and means of improving the lot of the fishermen.

Wildlife

It is the middle of the night and there is a bang outside the bedroom window. We stir, but snuggle back under the blankets. There is nothing to worry about. It is simply the porcupine calling in on his nightly ramble. Sometimes just one porcupine comes calling, while at other times the whole family arrives: granny, mum, dad and junior. Soft grunts indicate that they are enjoying the evening meal, or sometimes an early breakfast. They eat roots, bulbs, tubers, the bark of certain trees, fallen fruits and in fact most vegetable matter. An old bone lying under a bush is often gnawed to sharpen their teeth, and possibly to obtain minerals otherwise lacking in their diet.

It was in a desperate attempt to keep at least a part of our garden that we eventually, reluctantly started feeding the family. Every night a metal dish is put out containing avocado pear pips from the local pizzeria, plus any other delicacies that may be available. The porcupines appreciate this and, on the whole, leave the garden alone.

They are now almost members of the family and are far less skittish than was originally the case. They remain cautious, but they are obviously intelligent animals and have come to realise that we offer no immediate threat. Switching on a light or a torch in order to keep a check on their activities no longer sends them scampering off into the bush, unless a newborn happens to be there with its mother. We have become really quite fond of them, the largest of the African rodents.

We do not have to feed the bats that hang like heavy, brown, ripe fruit from the *koeboe bessie* tree beside the lawn. Apart from anything else that they may find to their taste in the neighbourhood, there is a Cape fig at the other end of the lawn. It produces a goodly crop of fruit in late summer that is obviously enjoyed by the bats.

Originally there was only a single bat, or so we thought. We identified it as a Wahlberg's epauletted fruit bat and were fairly sure that it was a female. This was confirmed one morning when we noticed an ear appearing from under her wing. A little later there was a small, dog-like face peering out from under the protective wing. We had thought that the bat looked a trifle fat, but not being familiar with these creatures had thought nothing more of it. According to the description of these bats a single pup is usually born, although a litter of two is not unknown. We were therefore delighted a day or so later to observe another small face looking out from its mother's wing.

Since then numbers in the tree have varied from one to five when another mother joined the group together with her pup. Apparently roosts may consist of as many as 100 individuals, but we are quite happy with our small select group. We have enough trouble trying to identify the ones that we have and enjoying their company while we can, for apparently they quite often change their roosts.

Birds tend to come and go rather more frequently than mammals. Some are always around. The *wit oogies* can be counted upon to visit the birdbath every day at about noon, or shortly thereafter and again in the late afternoon. Animated balls of fluff, they dash in and out of the water apparently oblivious of our presence barely two metres away.

Others, such as the Narina trogon in our driveway, or the Buff-spotted Flufftail in the back garden, make a single appearance and are never seen again. One other such bird was the Jackass Penguin we found in the bower next to the lawn. It must have waddled a good two to three hundred metres from the beach to the sheltered spot beneath the *taaibos*. We wondered what on earth possessed it.

Sitting alone in the house one day with the front door open I became aware that something or someone was at the door looking in at me. I slowly lowered my book, and we looked at one another. Looking against the light as I was it was at first difficult to make out the appearance of the visitor, but almost immediately I noted that it was not one, but two creatures; one on either side of the door. As my eyes became accustomed to the light I realised that my visitors were large grey mongooses.

These densely hairy animals are roughly twice the size of the Cape grey mongoose, are largely diurnal and in South Africa are found all along the south-east coast, near rivers, swamps or dams. These mongooses are at times seen hunting in shallow water and they swim well. They are also found throughout Africa and are known also in the Middle-East and Europe. In ancient Egypt they were kept as pets to catch snakes and rodents, and were regarded as sacred animals, often being embalmed together with their masters.

The two animals looked at me quizzically, and though obviously wary when I slowly stood up, they did not immediately turn and flee. After a last look at me they turned and trotted off down the stoep with heads held low and one animal closely behind the other. The last I saw of them was a flick of their black-tipped tails as they passed the coral tree and headed off down the driveway.

Ratels, or honey-badgers are quite common in the area and may often be seen when driving home at night. Their silver-grey saddles and white crowns on an otherwise jet-black body are unmistakable. They are described in some guides as solitary animals, but we almost always see them in pairs.

While plant-collecting along the top of what once was a dune situated in an area that is now a part of the St Francis

Links, we heard a huffing and puffing coming from the dune-slack. Looking down we noticed bush being shaken vigorously and the sound of breaking twigs. Into view burst a pair of ratels apparently in the midst of a wild game of catch-as-catch-can. They appeared to be quite unaware of our presence and the game continued for some minutes before they padded off to continue the business of finding something to eat.

Ratels will kill and eat virtually anything that can be over-powered, and they have a fearful reputation as opponents. However, as the late Charles Astley Maberly, British-born naturalist, wildlife artist and author observed, they are by nature shy and retiring animals, peacefully disposed to all that come their way. They normally show no inclination to interfere with innocent passersby, and we were delighted to have had the opportunity to watch them at play.

We were sceptical when first we heard the news: a school-boy playing near the top of the ridge claimed that he had seen a leopard in the forest fringe, less than two kilometres from an urban area. The other great cat and problem animal, the Cape lion, succumbed in the wild a century or more ago, but leopards being opportunistic hunters with nocturnal and secretive habits, have for at least two centuries successfully resisted the best efforts of farmers to eradicate them. So leopards still put in an appearance in the most unlikely places, but nevertheless there seems little doubt that their numbers are dwindling. Was this perhaps one of the lucky survivors?

The local farmers were willing to believe in the presence of the leopard. Although to date none had suffered any stock losses they feared the worst. Nor were their fears allayed when a local taxidermist stated that while he had no doubt that on occasion leopards attacked small stock, in his own experience he had found that the stomach contents of those brought to him usually consisted of dassies, young buck, guinea-fowl, partridges, jackals, domestic dogs and even rats and mice.

Farmers are realists and over the years they have increasingly come to accept that ridding their farms of leopards does not solve all their problems. In the absence of leopards, jackals or lynx make the most of having the field to themselves. And the absence of leopards often results in a population explosion of dassies. In some areas the number of dassies increases to such an extent that they move down from the kranses and on to the lands where the sheep graze, adding to the farmer's problems.

To protect their stock some farmers resort to the old method of *kraaling* their sheep at night, but new ways of controlling losses are also tried. Leopards normally make a kill by seizing the throat of their prey, so some farmers fit heavy gauge wire collars to their animals. The use of large Anatolian dogs to protect the flocks also seems to help. These dogs bond with the sheep and spend their lives with the herd and are quite capable of seeing off a leopard.

Despite those farmers who practice eco-friendly means to protect their animals, and the leopard being declared an endangered species by the Convention on the International Trade in Endangered Species (CITES), scientists believe that there are now fewer leopards in the Eastern Cape than there were 20 or more years ago. One reason for this is that the hunting of leopards has become a profitable business. An animal may be classified as "damage-causing" in which case a permit, specifically targeting a particular individual, is issued. Only South African citizens may use the permit, but a farmer is at liberty to allow another person to do the hunting, cashing in on this by charging hunters R120 000 and more for the opportunity to shoot a leopard!

Is this last great cat going to go the same way as the lion? The more we know of these animals the more likely we are to be able to protect them, so it is good to know that at various reserves and game farms in the Eastern Cape leopard research programmes are in place and operating. There is still hope for these magnificent creatures.

Some weeks went by and there was no news of the spotted stalker. Then when Caryl and I were walking in the veld one day we came across what remained of a porcupine lying in a sandy hollow surrounded by bush. Body parts lay scattered over a large area as if the animal had been hit by a ten ton truck. Some of the blood was still sticky indicating that it was not that long dead. We found quills up to 15 meters from the body and by following them and noting the disturbed ground and vegetation it was possible to make out whereabouts the initial encounter had taken place. We hoped that the porcupine was not one of "ours".

Porcupines, with their prickly armour, are treated with circumspection by leopards, but are still considered fair game; the leopard, gingerly, rolling them over to attack them from beneath. To judge by the evidence this particular porcupine had put up a spirited defence. It is not unknown for leopards to come off second best in one of these meetings, and there have even been instances of leopards dying when the wounds inflicted by the quills turned septic.

We have neither heard nor seen any more of the leopard since then and hope that it has gone on to enjoy rather more conventional meals of dassie and guinea-fowl – and for everyone's sake, no sheep or goats, or porcupines so far as we are concerned!

Jack, Mollie and the lighthouse

The old man is warmly clad. Despite the clear blue sunny sky there is a howling south-wester blowing. His daughter, Peggy, has his arm firmly gripped: she has to be careful in the wind and on this rough ground, to see that her father, in his nineties, stays on his feet.

The photographer braces himself and fiddles with the aperture on the camera, in order to ensure that both the human figures and the great bulk of the lighthouse in the background are in focus. He waits for the wind to drop for a moment before taking the photograph.

"Right, I think we've got it," he calls. "Let's get out of this wind before we're blown to pieces."

It is warm when sheltered from the wind by the wall of the lighthouse. The old man unbuttons his coat. He and Peggy head towards the camp-chairs. We sit in the sun like dassies.

Caryl produces hot drinks and some yoghurt-topped biscuits. When everyone has recovered their composure, the old man, Dr Jack Skead, nature-lover and historian, onomastician – one who studies the origin and meaning of place names - and former curator of the Kaffrarian Museum, now the Amathole Museum, begins his story.

Francis Skead was my paternal grandfather and har-bour-master in Port Elizabeth. There'd been a number of shipwrecks along the southern Cape coast and in 1871 the Governor, Sir Henry Barkly, appointed a commission to find the best way of lighting the coast. Francis Skead was a member of this body.

In November 1871, he and two others, Captain George Perry RN and Lieutenant Kibby Taylor, a navigating officer in the Royal Navy, set out to find a suitable spot for a lighthouse near Cape St Francis. They went off in a horse-drawn van, and with their camping gear in an ox-wagon.

They stopped at Van Stadens, at Cadle's Hotel, for the night, but the wagon took so long to arrive that next day they hired a cart to take some of the gear from the wagon.

Humansdorp was reached on the evening of the 23rd. They were met there by the magistrate, J J le Seur and spent the night. There were further hold-ups caused by the wagon and they were only able to leave for Mo-stert's Hoek at 10:30 am the next day.

The journey to the coast was extremely rough: thick bush, a mere track rather than a road, and finally scattered rocks and deep sand.

Mostert's farmhouse was small and of the poorest kind. It was situated about 2½ miles (4 km) north-west of Seal Point and just north of the wreck of HMS Osprey, which had gone aground there a few years earlier. There they waited anxiously for the arrival of their camping gear. It arrived at sunset and they hur-riedly set up camp.

59

The next day they set off on foot for Cape Seal (Seal Point) visiting all prominent points, and established a new camp near some fresh water between Cape Seal and Cape St Francis. Taylor took theodolite observations on possible points on both capes. During the day they decided on an eminence north 20° west from the pitch of Cape Seal, an isolated rock, about 20 feet high on which they carved an arrow.

There appeared to be plenty of rock suitable for building, and huge quantities of sea-shells together with driftwood for burning the lime. Another member of the commission, the Chief Inspector of Public Works, Murrell Robinson was due to visit the site later, and would be able to comment on building materials.

They left Cape St Francis the next day and arrived in Port Elizabeth on the 28ᵗʰ, having been away a week.

Soon after this Murrell Robinson visited Seal Point. He agreed with Skead regarding the shells and driftwood for making lime, and reported that the stone was suitable for building, but in addition a few loads of granite would be required. This could be taken to Seal Point from Port Elizabeth. However, the "road" from Humansdorp was in such an execrable condition that transport would have to be by sea.

The Governor accepted the Commission's report and hurried a grant through parliament. In July Robinson sent the plans to Joseph Flack who was still busy with the lighthouse on Bird Island. Flack asked a Mr B Godfrey of Long Street, Cape Town, to tender for the job, and towards the end of September his tender was accepted. On the 1ˢᵗ of October Godfrey, together with 12 men, left for Humansdorp.

J J W "Mollie" Moolman, a retired schoolmaster, takes up the story:

My great-grandfathers Moolman and Mostert were contracted to transport materials and workers from Humansdorp, or even Port Elizabeth to the site. Most of the building materials came from Port Elizabeth by sea. Moolman and Mostert carried mainly food sup-

plies and other necessities from Humansdorp. They also conveyed the labourers.

Mr Godfrey was the builder and sometimes he was very agitated. There were at times as many as 33 workers on site and some had brought their wives. This demanded outstanding management skills. There were also problems with drunkenness. At times Godfrey must have felt like tearing his hair out.

On one occasion Mostert had on his wagon some men returning to Humansdorp. A fight started on the wagon and at the Kromme drift, one man was thrown from the wagon.

"Klim op die wa!" shouted Mostert, but the man shouted back, "B---r the wagon!" and walked the six miles back to Seal Point.

Then there was the fight that took place on the site. During the fight one of the two men, both already bruised and bloody, lost his shirt, torn from his back. The next thing he was practically poedelnaak – naked. "Wait!" he shouted. "Friends?" he asked, putting out his hand. There was a pause. Then the other took the outstretched hand. "Friends," he said. Half-an-hour later the two men were sitting on a rock together fishing, as if nothing had happened.

My Scottish grandfather, John James Watson was the chief carpenter. When he was just 18 months old, his family was on the way to this country when the ship sank and the family returned to England. His father said, "Never again", but he died soon afterwards. The widow Watson set out once more with her three sons and a daughter, and this time they reached Port Elizabeth safely. There my grandfather trained as a joiner, and in due course got the job at Seal Point. You can still see his woodwork: doors, windows, gates, steps. When we move from here, have a look. After more than a century it still looks in good condition.

For 80 years the Moolmans and Mosterts delivered the post and supplies from Humansdorp to the light.

The carpenter's daughter, Charlotte Elizabeth Victoria Watson, married my father. They went to live on the Moolman family farm, Welgelegen, near Oesterbaai – Oyster Bay. That's where I grew up, but it was because of my Scottish grandfather that I was named John James Watson Moolman, but everyone calls me "Mollie".

Joseph Flack finished the Bird Island light and returned to Cape Town before leaving on the RMS Teuton for Port Elizabeth at the beginning of February 1876. By March he was on site and laid out the foundations for the new light, but soon after that he took ill. Mr Godfrey took him to Humansdorp. There the District Surgeon, a Dr Ward, laid him off for three months. However, Flack was obliged to apply for extra leave on half pay. He only returned to work towards the end of September.

He was still not a healthy man, and frequently had to leave the work to Godfrey. On the 14th of November, aged just 53, he died. Typhoid was given as the cause of death.

Today in a quiet corner of the Humansdorp cemetery you will find his gravestone. Apparently it was paid for by those with whom he worked at Seal Point. They also paid for the grave to be maintained in good condition. They must have held him in high esteem.

Some years ago I received a phone-call from a man whose name I did not recognise and with whose voice I was not familiar.

"Is there the grave of a Joseph Flack in Humansdorp?"

I could assure him that there was, but was intrigued as to why he wanted to know.

"I never met him," he replied, "but he was my great-grandfather."

The tower was completed in July 1878, and the lamp was first lit, a paraffin lamp in those days, on the 4th of that month.

That Godfrey was able, despite all the difficulties he encountered, to complete the work within two years, is to this day regarded as an outstanding achievement. Before ever starting on the tower he built temporary accommodation for his workforce and limekilns for the production of cement. Then he set about producing accommodation for the lighthouse staff, and only then began work on the tower.

The tower has proved to be an excellent lightning conductor. At one time a record of lightning strikes was kept, but the total has long since been lost. However, on one occasion at least 120 panes of glass were shattered by a strike, which kept the staff busy for some days repairing the damage.

For many years the light was considered to be the most remote on the South African coast. Long after Capt Skead's 1871 visit to Seal Point, animal-drawn vehicles, especially ox-wagons, remained the only means of carrying machinery, paraffin for the light, and later diesel fuel for the generators. Several photos exist of the rubber-tyred wagon that Mostert used to carry goods over the dunes and along the beach to the light. It was only in 1957 that a Jeep was provided for transporting staff, but even then heavy goods continued to be carried by wagon. Then, in the 1960s when Leighton Hulett and John Booysen developed the coastal resorts beside the Bay and at the Point respectively, a decent road was at long last built.

When Booysen was developing the Cape St Francis Lighthouse Township an unusual problem arose. It was discovered that the lighthouse was actually situated outside the 20 morgen set aside for its construction. It was always assumed that the whole Seal Point peninsula was Crown land, but the survey document attached to Governor Sir Henry Bartle Frere's 1878 proclamation regarding the lighthouse was confined to straight lines that did not include the actual coast.

Booysen, as owner of that portion of the farm Ongegunde Vryheid, now claimed the area between the straight lines and the coast. It was here that Skead had placed and Godfrey had built the lighthouse. Eventually a compromise was reached. The western boundary was adjusted to compensate for the

63

property in dispute, and as a result the lighthouse was safely situated on official property.

* * *

We finish our biscuits and pack away the coffee mugs. Jackets are zipped, or buttoned up, and Peggy once again takes her father's arm. We scurry across to the cars with the wind behind us. Jack and Peggy take a last look at the tower before we drive away.

Fossil find on St Francis Links

News travels fast. "There's a skeleton up at the big dam on St Francis Links. They"ve found a skeleton while digging a trench."

"Human?"

It appears not.

By the time we get there a small crowd is gathered beside a hole in the ground. Not much to see other than mud. Only later, after the archeologist, Dr Peter Nilssen, has arrived and had a look, do some answers emerge. It is probably a bovid of some kind, and a fossil. It died a long time ago, perhaps thousands of years ago. Gradually the crowd disperses.

When eventually there were definite answers to our questions, most people had forgotten all about the skeleton, or rather small portion of a skeleton. It turned out to be not of bovine origin, but a fossilised section of the spine and ribcage of a rhinoceros, and the age was given as 175 000 years ago.

What was more interesting was that a number of stone-age tools were found in the vicinity. It was conjectured that the rhino had become stuck in the mud beside the ancient wet-land. There it was discovered by a band of hunter-gatherers who proceeded to butcher the animal using stone tools, some of which were left on site. We felt privileged to have had this small glimpse into the lives of the earlier inhabitants of this land, which we tend to think of as ours.

Nowadays the trench, beside the tee-box on the 15th fairway at the St Francis Links, has been filled in to preserve the bones, but the site is marked by an information board. A photograph on the board shows the bones as they were when first found. Understandably the majority of golfers pay little attention to it.

* * *

It was barely 245 ago that the first European travellers visited the Tsitsikamma: Anders Sparrman in 1775, Hendrik Swellengrebel in the following year, and before the end of the century, John Barrow. They made mention of elephant and buffalo, hartebeest and eland, rhino and leopard. Of those the Knysna elephant and the leopard are now on the brink of local extinction, and the others are gone.

Those early travellers would not have seen possibly the most spectacular large mammal of them all, the formidable long-horned buffalo. This giant animal, with a horn spread of up to two metres, had an estimated mass of about 1 800 kg. It first made its appearance as much as 2.5 million years ago, and finally bowed out about 12 000 years ago.

What happened to the giant buffalo and for that matter all the other mega-fauna that once were found around the world? The answer lies beside the 15th fairway at St Francis Links. They were killed by *Homo sapiens.*

Extinction is a natural process which has always taken place, but the appearance of man has accelerated the natural rate of extinction. A great extinction event began more than 100 000 years ago in Africa. The magnitude and scale of the killing surpassed any other recorded. Climate changes, with associated sea-level changes, ice-ages or droughts, meteorite bombardments and volcanic eruptions have all played their part, but this extinction is greater than any other natural calamity.

It all began when *Homo erectus* acquired the ability to make and use tools. This led to a change in behaviour. From being a scavenger, man became a predator. The ability to make and use stone-tools meant that his lack of formidable teeth and strong claws was no longer a hindrance. Man was able to kill, and when once he had learnt how to attach a sharpened stone to a stick, to be able to kill from a distance.

In Africa the mega-fauna lived and developed alongside man. Animals became aware of the danger that man posed and instinctively avoided him. This explains why it was that by comparison with other continents; only about 13% of African mega-fauna was lost initially. The invention of the rifle tipped the balance in favour of humankind.

By the time the Dutch arrived at the Cape in the middle of the 17th century, the Bloubok was already endangered. Previously found over a wide area, it was, when first encountered by Europeans, restricted to the grasslands of the south-western Cape. Today all that remains of the Bloubok are four mounted specimens, all in European museums, in Stockholm, Leiden, Paris and Vienna. It was Dutch firearms that finished it off in its natural habitat.

Elsewhere in the world it was a different story. With no experience of *Homo erectus* and later *H. sapiens,* the mega-fauna were unafraid and perhaps even inquisitive about this curious new creature.

Charles Darwin described how the marine lizards of the Galapagos Islands were so unafraid of him that he could walk up to one, pick it up and throw it into the sea. It would swim rapidly back to shore and go to rest on the same rock from which he had picked it up. This, he reasoned, was not because it was stupid, but because it was instinctively aware of the dangers associated with the sea, where there were sharks that preyed upon the lizards. Unaware of any potential threat posed by the bearded scientist, the lizard returned to its supposedly safe resting-place.

Humans left Africa and a wave of extinctions swept across the earth in the wake of their advance. In the so-called "old world" this started early. In some places, extinction, timed to coincide with man's arrival, was comparatively recent: in Madagascar only 2 000 and in New Zealand a mere 1 000 years ago.

Everywhere large animals were particularly vulnerable. This was because of their lengthy gestation periods, and because they usually produced only one young at a time.

In the course of time a further change took place. It was the development of agriculture, also associated with the evolution of tools, but in addition with bush-clearing, forest-burning and the erection of fences that resulted in the destruction not only of animals, but also of natural habitats. The loss of biodiversity affected creatures both great and small.

The problem intensified with the expansion of population and the spread of industrialisation. So today we are faced with a possible sixth extinction event, and the dreadful possibility that humankind might be one of the species facing extinction.

The answer may lie in the marked excavation beside the 15th. The number of stone tools found, indicate that several individuals were involved. Butchering a 1.5 ton rhino is not a one man job. Co-operation was essential.

The change from scavenger to predator sparked another alteration in the behaviour of humankind. Hunting was more successful if two or more hunters were involved. Possibly for the first time, co-operative behaviour became essential. Not only was it a case of many hands making light work, as in the case of the rhino, but ideas were shared and it was noticed that frequently two heads were better than one. Speech developed, enabling the transfer of information not only from one hunter to another, but from generation to generation. For the first time we were able to build on the experience of the past.

It was through co-operative behaviour that mankind managed to overcome the many problems that arose during past millennia. Co-operative behaviour may yet enable us as a species to avoid extinction.

Perhaps the golfers at the St Francis Links should pause for a moment to consider the implications of the fossil find beside the 15th tee-box.

From the top, clockwise: Thornhill Station and Hotel a century ago (Ch 2); Dora Ackerman and the surfers' guest book at Trawlers, Jeffreys Bay (Ch 3). Bakkieshoek strawberry pickers (Ch 4); Church at Kruisfontein (Ch 4)

Assegaaibosch Hotel (Ch 5)

The memorial to T
homas Bain in the
Prince Alfred's Pass (Ch 8)

Haarlem church interior
(Ch 7)

Nico Hesterman at the
Attaquas memorial (Ch 8)

Spoorbek-se-erf

4.

Humansdorp District

Spoorbek-se-erf

Heinrich Schorbeck arrived in the Humansdorp District sometime early in the 19th century. According to him he had been born in the city of Dortmund, Westphalia, and had trained as a stonemason. Later he became a sailor, but tiring of a life at sea abandoned ship at the Cape. Settling in the Humansdorp district, he in 1816 applied for and was granted land beside the Kromme River about 25 km west of Humansdorp. Here, on what became known as Spoorbek-se-erf, he built a two-roomed house and set up a small water-powered Norwegian mill.

No one seems to know why these small mills were known at the Cape as Norwegian mills. Nor is it known who was responsible for introducing them to the southern Cape. They were common throughout Europe, not only in Norway, and were often referred to as Greek mills. They were not normally used commercially, but simply to grind the wheat produced on a farm. It seems, however, that Schorbeck ground both wheat and possibly maize in his mill, and operated as a miller for local farmers.

Norwegian mills were housed in an out-building approximately three metres high. A channel or race directed a strong flow of water through the building. Beneath the mill and in the channel was the horizontal waterwheel. It was made from an old wagon-wheel with wooden blades approximately 100 mm wide in place of 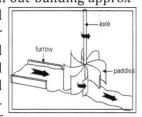 spokes. A vertical axle connected the wheel to the millstone. When water was allowed to flow through the channel, the wheel, and the mill-stone above it turned. The mill and its mechanism, other than for the grinding stones, was made of wood and Spanseriet (*Arundo donax*), making it easy to set up and, in case of need, to repair.

When not milling, it seems that Schorbeck had itchy feet and he was often away from home doing odd jobs, treating the sick or helping those in need. His assistance frequently involved the casting of spells, and as Hendrik Spoorbek he became possibly South Africa's best known *towenaar* – sorcerer or magician.

Spoorbek had a way with fires. When a farmer named Schoeman was having trouble with a fire in a manure heap, Spoorbek was asked to help. He arrived with his usual unkempt hair and beard, and considered the situation. "Have you a *skimmel?*" he asked. Schoeman fetched a roan horse from the stable. "Saddle the horse," said Spoorbek, "and ride around the heap with this," giving the farmer a piece of paper on which something was written. "When you have ridden around the heap, ride off into the veld and throw the paper away." Schoeman did so and when he returned the fire was out.

Frequently Spoorbek was called in to fire-proof thatched roofs. The Meiring family of Jagersbosch, to the west of Humansdorp called on him to treat their roof. Having done so, Spoorbek left the farm. A woman in the family found that he had left his tobacco pouch behind, and made some disparaging remarks about the old man and his possessions. Soon afterwards Spoorbek returned to Jagersboch to collect the pouch. Looking the woman sternly in the eye he repeated word for word what she had said. She was suitably abashed. "While there is no running water between us, I always know what people are saying about me," he claimed.

It was said that his fire-proofing was highly effective. Years later when thatch was removed from a roof fire-proofed by Spoorbek, it was still impossible to burn the thatch.

Just such a story is told of the original church in the district on the farm Kerkplaats west of Humansdorp. The walls of the old church are still standing and on a visit to it I hunted around to try and find some of the original thatch. I was hoping to test how inflammable or otherwise it might be. I could find none, but later was told by an elderly Humansdorp resident that the thatch, because it had been fire-proofed by Spoorbek, had been removed carefully for re-use.

Many people regarded Spoorbek as a sorcerer. His wild appearance and strange ways no doubt went a long way to convince them of his occult powers. If he were a wizard, his magic was strictly of the white variety. So greatly did he impress local people that his fame spread throughout South Africa and anecdotes have been handed down from generation to generation.

He was also known for his prophecies. He is reputed to have foretold of the South African War of 1899-1901, and of the invention of aeroplanes. One prophecy failed to come true: "When I die my body will never be found." He died on the 13th of June 1845 and was buried not that far from his humble farmhouse.

There are two different versions of another of his prophecies. "When I am gone the waters of the Kromme will flow upstream and cover this farm," being the one version. The alternative being, "When the waters of the Kromme flow upstream, this will signal the end of British rule at the Cape."

In 1943, with the completion of the wall of the Churchill (now Kromme) Dam on the Kromme River, the waters of the river rose and, "flowing upstream" covered the farm Spoorbek-se-erf.

Regarding the second prophesy any remaining form of British rule at the Cape may be said to have ended in 1910 when the former British colony became a part of the Union of South Africa. But in 1948, just five years after the waters of the Kromme flowed upstream, the National Party was voted into power. The NP victory in turn led to South Africa being declared a republic and leaving the British Commonwealth on the 31st of May 1961. There are those who maintain that it was the declaration of a republic to which Spoorbek was referring.

After Spoorbek's death in 1845 his estate was wound up. He was five years in arrears with the quitrent for his farm, and there was also an outstanding debt of £80. Despite his strange powers the former Westphalian stonemason, seaman and miller was not a wealthy man. His sole assets were listed as some tools, a saddle, a few articles of furniture, five shirts and two pairs of trousers.

For almost a century after his death there were others, Strydoms and Kritzingers, that farmed Spoorbek-se-erf. The old two-roomed house disappeared and new outbuildings were erected. Perhaps Spoorbek's mill was incorporated in these, but there is no way of knowing for certain. Then with the decision of the Port Elizabeth Municipality to build the Churchill Dam, the property was expropriated. In due course

Spoorbek-se-erf disappeared under the waters of the dam, but every so often in times of drought, it reappears. According to one informant, 1970 was when he first saw the *opstal* emerge from the waters. Then in 1989 when the dam was only 11% full the buildings were again visible. In 2018 the waters receded as the capacity of the dam dropped to below 15% and it was again possible to see the old buildings.

In the 2018 drought we went to see what we could find, but there was little to see. The house that replaced that of Spoorbek was constructed of sun-baked bricks. The foundations, front *stoep* and steps are all that remain. A long stone wall may have been part of a *kraal*. Some piles of stone and crumbling bricks marked the remains of out-buildings, one of which may have been the mill. Three upright stone slabs resembled gravestones, but probably served some other purpose for they are very close to one another. We could find no traces of a mill-race. Elsewhere on the farm there were stone walls that once bordered lands.

More than a century and a half after the death of Spoorbek, or Heinrich Schorbeck, there is still a good deal of interest in the old prophet and magician. Mention his name in the Humansdorp area and you are bound to hear about some of his feats. This may help account for not only our own interest in the farm Spoorbek-se-erf, but also for the stainless steel plate that we found. On it was scratched:

2010/03/28
Johan, Ilse en Juandre, Piet,
Rika van Heerden
Freddie, Tru(illegible), Werner en
Mariska (Els) Olivier
Morné, Pallo, Jason, Megan
Grobler
God is met ons vir ewig

Erik Roux, who works at the dam, was able to explain its presence. In the 2010 drought the old buildings were again exposed. Members of the Van Heerden, Olivier and Grobler families selected the site to pray for rain. They left the plate as a memento of their visit. They obviously believed that the site held some special significance. Was it perhaps the connection with Spoorbek?

Rondebosch Farm

In December 1819, just months before the arrival of the British settlers, two soldiers of German origin completed their period of service with the British Army on the Eastern Frontier. Normally they would be shipped back to Europe when a ship was available, but Christiaan Wagner and his friend, George Hippert elected to stay at the Cape. They set out on foot, probably from Grahamstown (now Makhanda) walking westwards, and before the end of the month arrived at Rondebosch, the farm of Johannes Scheepers, just north of present-day Humansdorp.

No one knows exactly why they decided to stay on at Rondebosch. Perhaps Scheepers was particularly welcoming, or it might have been the plentiful supply of water on the farm that suited the industry they intended to establish: a tannery together with the making of saddles and harnesses. For more than a century the holes that they dug beside the Rondebosch River in 1819 remained visible; one for black and one for red/brown hides.

Their business thrived and in April 1823 Wagner and Hippert bought an area of 3000 morgen (2570 ha) from Scheepers for 9000 guilders. Four years later Wagner married local girl, Agatha Vermaak.

Scheepers either stayed on at the farm, or kept a small portion for himself. Years later Wagner related to his family how Scheepers wished to be buried on a stony ridge overlooking Rondebosch. From there he would "be able to look out over the farm and see his red Africander cattle grazing". When the time came to bury the first owner of Rondebosch, Wagner found many good vantage points, but had great difficulty finding a place where a grave could be dug.

On the 16th of March 1839 Wagner was granted citizen-ship by Governor Sir George Napier and three days later he bought out his partner. The break-up of the partnership re-mains a mystery, although one descendant believes that Wag-ner and Hippert's wives could not see eye-to-eye.

In the 1850 register of farms, Wagner was recorded as be-ing the owner of both Rondebosch and the adjoining farm, Swartenbosch.

Rondebosch, today just seven kilometres north of Hu-mansdorp on the road to Hankey, remained a Wagner family property for the best part of two centuries. This is really no wonder for the farm is blessed with water. Not only is there a river, the Klein Zeekoei or Rondebosch, which in its lower reaches is also known as the Swart, but there are also a num-ber of springs on both Rondebosch and Swartenbosch. That nearest the old main house bubbles out in a wood and pro-vides 7500 litres per hour. It is now dammed. There are also several smaller springs, one, in the south-western corner of Swartenbosch, being the source of the Moeras River.

Adjoining the property is the farm Rheboksfontein, which in Wagner's day was farmed by Matthys Gerhardus Human. Human came to an agreement with Wagner that he, Human, could use the water of one of the Swartenbosch springs in re-turn for allowing Wagner to cut wood in Boschkloof, situated on Rheboksfontein.

In 1849 Human decided to donate 561 morgen (481 ha) of his farm to the Church Council of the Parochie Alexander, as it was known then, for the establishment of a church and new village. There was no specific mention of water, but it now flowed onto church land, and Wagner continued to cut wood on Boschkloof.

Nine years later this changed. The Church Council denied Wagner the right to cut wood on their land in Boschkloof. Wagner responded by cutting off water to the village. Ulti-mately the matter was settled when the Council bought the water rights from Wagner for £100.

Today if you enter the former village of Humansdorp from the N2, look to your right as the road winds down the hill towards the town. Crossing the narrow gauge railway tracks the large domed roof of the Cultural Centre lies ahead, and just north of it, to the right, a small white building. This was once the Humansdorp Mill. The millstones were driven by the water acquired by the Church from Rondebosch, *leiwater* - water led by conduit - to the plots in the village. The *leiwater* days are long gone, but in some of the quieter suburban streets of the town you may still see the channels that once carried Rondebosch water through the village.

1869 Disaster

Fires are an ever present possibility in the fynbos of the Cape Floral Kingdom. The most destructive fire to hit the Humansdorp district occurred in February 1869, two years after the death of Christiaan Wagner, the former soldier, leather-worker and farmer. To this day the 1869 fire is referred to as the Great Fire. It came very close to destroying the village. At one time, standing near the magistrate's court, flames or smoke were visible at every point of the compass. The flames that were seen to the north of the village were on Rondebosch.

Thanks to exceptional rains in the previous year, grass cover was good at the start of 1869, but drought conditions set in during the early summer and by February the veld was tinder dry. Hot berg winds began during the day of February the 8th and continued to blow the following morning. Smoke was in the air, and the captain of the *Knysna Belle,* sailing some eight kilometers out to sea, noted in the log that flames could be seen along 40 miles (64 km) of the southern Cape coast. Ash and soot were raining on the ship, with birds and insects on the decks and clinging to halyards.

On Rondebosch Freek Wagner, son of the former German soldier, together with Freek's brother-in-law, Dail Vosloo, began to take precautions. The shepherd, *outa* Kerneels with the help of Freek's eight year-old son, Christiaan, moved the sheep to a previously burnt area, where the two stayed to look after the flock.

Furniture and other precious possessions were carried from the house to the forest beside the spring: the indigenous trees were less likely to burn than the grass. The oxen and wagon were moved to a safe spot, but by the time that this was done, the fire was upon them.

Family and staff watched helplessly as their homes and all the outbuildings with the exception of the stables went up in smoke. Among the sheep *outa* Kerneels held tightly onto young Christiaan as the flames enveloped the Wagner's home.

Dail Vosloo's house, furniture and possessions were incinerated together with those of the farm labourers and of the Smith, Terblanche, Schreiber and Fortuin families, all resident on Rondebosch.

To the north, on the Metlerkamps' farm Zuurbron, eight lives were lost together with property, stock and the harvest of oats and corn, while on Misgund, situated not far from Zuurbron to the east, the entire property was burnt to the ground, but no lives were lost.

The Humansdorp magistrate reported that by two in the afternoon the temperature was 113° Fahrenheit (45° C), but shortly thereafter the wind swung to the south-west and the temperature dropped steadily, particularly during the night when it began to rain.

The weary, blackened, and now wet and shivering families on Rondebosch sought shelter in the one remaining building; the stables. Next morning, the 10th of February, Freek Wagner went out to select a site on which to build a new house. He chose a spot just a hundred metres north-west of the smoking ruins of the house his father had built.

In Humansdorp the magistrate began recording the losses. In addition to the loss of life on Zuurbron, other reported deaths included two women walking to Hankey, 14 Mfengu children in the Tsitsikamma, and two children and servants west of the town. On the road near Klipdrift, the wagon and oxen belonging to a Mr Kemp of Uitvlugt were overcome by the flames. The entire span and the wagon were destroyed, together with Kemp, his son and the *touleier* of the oxen.

The fire continued to burn for a further five days in the direction of the Van Stadens River, Uitenhage and Somerset East, but it was the Humansdorp district that was hardest hit. Before it had burnt itself out, the Humansdorp magistrate reckoned the financial loss to amount to at least £25 000, the equivalent in 2020 of about £3 million, (R60 million).

Apart from the loss of life, six farms had been completely destroyed.

A fund, the Humansdorp Relief Fund, was started by the *Eastern Province Herald* to help those in need. In December 1869 the newspaper reported that an amount of £1 418 (R3 400 000 today) had been disbursed.

There was no way in which those who had lost family members could be compensated, but the money did not go very far in covering farmers' losses. I was unable to discover whether or not any of the Mfengu or Coloured survivors received any form of monetary compensation after the worst disaster ever to have struck the Humansdorp District.

Sifting through the the ruins: Zuurbron, Misgund and Osbosch

The farm Zuurbron lies approximately ten kilometres north-north-east of Rondebosch on the road from Humansdorp to Hankey. At the time of the Great Fire in 1869, Zuurbron was farmed by Rutger Metelerkamp and his wife, Sarah, née Rawstone. The farm Klipfontein adjoined Zuurbron to the north-west, and was farmed by Willem Metelerkamp and his wife, Augusta, née Pullen.

Was it just a coincidence that the two Metelerkamps on adjacent farms were married to women with English surnames? Theirs are the only two English surnames to appear in the entire Zuurbron ward, of which Willem Metelerkamp was the Field-cornet, at the time. In fact Willem's wife Augus-

Misgund - Kabeljous River

ta, born in 1804, was the daughter of English settler Thomas Pullen, who arrived in 1820 aboard the *Nautilus*.

Zuurbron and Klipfontein may have been regarded as one farm when Willem Metelerkamp reported losses in his ward to the Humansdorp magistrate. At least nine different (white) families are given as living on Zuurbron, with no mention of any on Klipfontein, which seems strange.

On Zuurbron there was, you may remember, not only the loss of stock and property, but also the loss of eight lives: Mrs Frans Gertenbach together with her maidservant were consumed by the blaze, and six Mfengu children who were originally recorded as missing were later found to have died in the flames. All the buildings, including the "finest home in the district" were destroyed, but the owner's son managed to save the books from his father's library. (Whilst regretting the loss of life, I applauded his saving the books!) Apart from the buildings and furniture, 20 horses, 190 sheep and 14 oxen died, as well as an unknown number of other animals. Six carts and two wagons were reduced to ashes, together with a harvest of 120 muids of corn and 30 muids of oats. (A muid was a Dutch measure the equivalent of 91 kg.)

Nothing remains today on either Zuurbron or Klipfontein farm as a reminder of the Great Fire. There is one old building on Zuurbron which may at one time have been a house, but which was either re-built after the fire or more probably was erected post-1869.

Today Jacques and Liesje Steenkamp of Zuurbron[2] are involved with various mountain-biking (MTB) activities. There are MTB routes in the area that are popular with local riders. One such route follows the old gravel road to Jeffreys Bay, which is no longer maintained and has several gates to be opened and closed. Were it not for an old road sign or two, one might never guess that this was once a public thoroughfare. Along the way it passes through the farm Misgund and what remains of its *opstal*, all burnt to the ground in 1869.

After travelling through farm lands for some distance, the road from Zuurbron drops quite suddenly down towards the valley of the Kabeljous until one finally reaches the remains of Misgund, situated beside the river. It would appear that what one sees is what was left after the 1869 fire. Actually a far more recent fire caused the present damage, and prior to that there was also a fire in 1969. Nevertheless, the remains of Misgund today must resemble that which the survivors saw in 1869, for no lives were lost on this farm.

Close to the water's edge are the blackened ruins of what once was the Misgund mill. In 1869 Cornelis du Plessis and his sister Hester, lay in the water while the flames swirled overhead. Even the reeds that grew within their reach on the edge of the river burnt. The nearby farm buildings were gutted, but the water saved their lives. What must it have felt like to emerge sodden from amongst the blackened reeds to find the smouldering remains of one's home?

Life must go on, and the ruined buildings were either rebuilt or the bricks and stone used for replacements. The mill was restored and at one time it was possible to see the wood-

---

2 While this information was correct at the of writing, the farm Zuurbron has since been sold, and biking activities appear to heve been discontinued.

en steps inside, worn alternately left and right, as sacks of grain were carried up to be ground into flour.

By strange coincidence another fire started on Misgund almost a century to the day after the Great Fire. A candle was knocked over, a curtain caught alight and within next to no time a building made from the old mud-bricks salvaged from the earlier fire was ablaze. Unfortunately two people died in this fire, although far less damage was done, but those susceptible to such thoughts wondered whether or not there was some curse on the old farm.

Little of the farm buildings still remain: some stone walls but not the millstones, for these were transferred years ago to the small mill at the entrance to Humansdorp.

I picked up a shard of Victorian blue-and-white pottery before we left for the long climb up the hot, dry, stony slope leading out of the valley.

The farm, to which we were heading at the mouth of the Kromme, was originally named Krommerivier, after the river. When it was bought by a former British Army officer, John Henry Hartley Boys, it became St Francis Bay. In 1848 his mother died and was buried on the farm. Her gravestone, which incorporates a memorial to her late husband, may still be seen.

S A C R E D
To the Memory of
John Paramor Boys Esqr.
Formerly Deputy Paymaster General
to the Forces in the Peninsula.
He died at Bloise in France (Oct. 11 – 1821)
and was buried in the Protestant Cemetery
there aged 55 years.
Also to the memory of
Jane Hartley Boys
wife of the above
John Paramor Boys Esqr.
Who died at Saint Francis Bay,
Cape of Good Hope
April 27th. 1848
Aged 75 years.
P. Bodily, Sculp. Port Elizabeth.

82

This is an interesting link with the Napoleonic Wars, the culmination of which was at least in part responsible for the arrival of the British settlers at the Cape.

Today the farm, now known as Osbosch, is farmed by the Du Toit family. It has other historical connections. Not far from the grave of Jane Hartley Boys, on the banks of a small stream, are the ruins, mere foundations, of what once was the home of Great Trek hero, Piet Uys. It was from here that he and his family set out on the Great Trek, an historical event that at one time bedeviled many a school-child's life when faced with History exams. The Trekkers made their way at the pace of an ox-wagon to what was then Natal. Then, at the Battle of Italeni, father Piet Uys and his young son Dirkie lost their lives and joined the pantheon of Afrikaner heroes.

Perhaps one day, when we have sorted out our differences, the Great Trek will come to be regarded in a different light to that of today, and South Africans of all racial groups will treat it as a source of adventure stories appearing in comic-books and TV thrillers.

At some stage Hermanus Bernadus Swart and his family moved into the old Uys home on the farm. In a nearby graveyard lie the mortal remains of four generations of Swarts. There you will find the antecedents of the last Governor-General of the Union of South Africa, who was also the first State-President of the Republic of South Africa, Charles Robberts "Blackie" Swart. Somewhat surprisingly, Swart spent a brief period of his early life in Hollywood. This was still in the days of silent films and his South African accent made little or no difference to his portrayal of cowboys in the American Wild West.

But what has happened to the original house? After the Swarts had moved on, the farm was acquired by the Du Toit family. Today it is farmed by Mikey, the great-grandson of the first Du Toit on the farm.

After the 1938 centenary celebrations of the Great Trek, there was much interest in those places and artefacts with Voortrekker connections. There was a proposal that the old home on Osbosch, then in a poor state of repair, should be restored and declared a national monument. The site was visited by members of the Monuments Commission. One of the members, while admiring old Mr Du Toit's bushbuck, remarked how on his next visit to the farm he would like to shoot one. This enraged Mr Du Toit, and then and there he decided to raze the old farmhouse to the ground. He phoned Joep de Jongh, the Humansdorp telephone technician and asked him to remove the telephone from the building. No sooner was this done than the old house was set alight and burnt to the ground. Joep, forewarned, had taken his camera with him and took a photo of the smoke beginning to rise. Many years later Joep gave me a copy of his photograph.

Hunt around amongst the crumbling foundations today and you may still find shards of pottery, odd pieces of iron and battered and rusted utensils, the last remnants of the old house.

* * *

The light of the setting sun burnished the waters of the Kromme and high-lighted the white walls of the modern town of St Francis Bay across the river. Situated on what once was the farm Goedgeloof, the town has all too frequently seen disastrous fires.

We packed away our cameras, restored our "treasure", the neck of a bottle strangely twisted by the heat of the flames, to where we had found it, and headed for home, bumping along the dusty farm track as the sun sank below the horizon.

James Backhouse and Hankey

We pick up our passenger in St Francis Bay. Open neck shirt, shorts and hiking boots, with a shock of white hair and strong, capable hands, good for gardening and making useful things, often for other people. He has a farmer's tan, although he is in fact a retired railway engineer: Godfried Potgieter, whose ancestors farmed in this area for centuries. Despite a heritage of which he is proud and the spelling of his first name, on which he insists, there has been an English influence in the life of this gentle Afrikaner who is known to everyone as Godfrey.

Godfried (or Godfrey if you so wish) is a passionate plant lover and one of the Custodians of Rare and Endangered Wildflowers (CREW[3]) team that have for several seasons monitored the area we are to visit. Today we plan to follow in the footsteps of an early botanical traveller, James Backhouse.

For a couple of centuries English gardeners from Cornwall to Yorkshire held the Backhouse name in high regard. Many gardeners bought not only their annuals, roses, trees and shrubs from Backhouse Gardens in York, but also Cape aloes, gladioli and mesems.

Lilium enthusiasts will know of how Robert Backhouse and his wife Sarah hybridised narcissi and lilies in their garden at Sutton Court in Hereford, while Ray Desmond's *Dictionary of British and Irish Botanists* lists 16 members of the Backhouse family involved with plants in one way or another, as nurserymen, horticulturists or scientists.

James Backhouse, 1794-1869, was a Yorkshireman and he and his brother Thomas established the York Gardens in 1815, the first English nursery to publish a catalogue devoted to Alpine plants. James, with a mop of unruly hair and a vast Victorian beard, was also a Quaker, and in 1831 he travelled to Australia where for six years he was involved in mission work. He returned to Britain by way of Mauritius and the Cape where he inspected the mission stations and, during a journey lasting 19 months and covering 9600 km, he collected seeds and bulbs and learnt to speak Cape Dutch. He also kept a detailed journal, which was published in 1844 and has ever since proved a valuable source of information for both historians and botanists.

Travelling eastwards from Cape Town in November 1838 he entered the Langkloof and followed the course of the Kromme River, noting the great beds of palmiet and bulrushes, some of which are still evident today, and how the hillsides

---

3. CREW is a citizen scientist initiative supported by the South African National Biodiversity Institute (SANBI).

were covered in waboom, while Knysna lilies dotted the stony places. He watched three Mfengu women eating the thick, fibrous roots of a cabbage tree or kiepersol and others eating the roots of blue water-lilies. Intrigued, he collected some of the flowers and recorded that they smelled like violets. Something, it seems, that no prior botanist had ever noted.

Further downstream he noticed the yellow-fringed flowers of *Villarsia capensis* and beside the river the blue flowering African lily, an aloe and some fine keurbooms.

He stopped off to look at Kruisfontein, to the west of present-day Humansdorp. Here the London Missionary Society (LMS) in Hankey were about to start an outstation. Tasked with reporting to the LMS on existing missions, the site of a proposed mission was obviously of interest to him. The outstation was eventually established a year after Backhouse's visit, in October 1839.

Today the venerable stone church remains in good condition, but the nearby former school is showing its age. Plots are advertised – "Just R55 000 plus house foundations" - and amongst the collection of houses old and new are a few of the old mission houses with their outside chimneys.

Backhouse now headed northwards and we drove on and up the hill following his route along a stony track to where there is a village named Die Berg. It is one of the oldest settlements in the area and is home to families – the Fleurs, Kettledases and Leanders, Dlaminis, Jubas and Matiwanes – that have lived here for generations. Some of their ancestors may well have watched Backhouse's wagon trundle up the hill.

As we drove along we came across a group of teenagers apparently practising a dance outside a hall. Our arrival brought the rehearsal to a stop. They ran down towards the school-bell – or was it a church-bell? – and quickly lined up from shortest to tallest and began a new routine which at first glance appeared to be somewhat salacious. Perhaps, we thought, some form of modern dance with which we were unfamiliar. We gave them the benefit of the doubt and drove on, passing stray cattle until we found a convenient parking place.

The walk up to the neck is steep, but as is the case with botanists, the slope was covered at a very moderate pace. With eyes to the ground, ever hopeful, we looked for that new species never before recorded.

At the neck there is an extensive view of the hills beyond and of the farm Honeyville, or Honeyvale, as Backhouse recorded the name. In the valley a wandering green line of foliage marks the course of the Swart, or Rondebosch River, on its way to Rondebosch farm and the sea.

The near slopes are covered in Australian black wattle. The first of these alien invaders may have been planted by the Kruisfontein community to supply firewood, but there is also the possibility that Wagner and Hippert, the tanners on Rondebosch, planted some trees. The tannin in the bark was frequently used in the 19th century to tan leather, but the trees were certainly not there when Backhouse stood at the neck.

The track down the hill was overgrown and the nearer we came to the river the denser the foliage, but the drift, through which Backhouse crossed, was clearly visible. He noted that common watercress was plentiful in the "streamlet", as the English nurseryman would have it. Perhaps that evening he ate some watercress together with a bread and cheese sandwich. Somewhere in the vicinity of the river he camped for the night.

In the very short time that Backhouse was on the farm, most of it spent asleep, he mentions, apart from the watercress he saw in the river, just seven species: fire lily (*Cyrtanthus angustifolius*), brunia (*Brunia* sp.), wild jasmine (*Jasminum inquinans*), scarlet geranium (*Pelargonium angulare*), ivy-leaved pelargonium (*Pelargonium peltatum*), carrion plant (*Stapelia grandiflora*) and the sweet-thorn trees (*Vachellia karroo* formerly *Acacia karroo*). Despite the loss of biodiversity that has already occurred in the Cape Floral Kingdom, we found it heartening to know that all seven species that Backhouse noted are still to be found on the farm.

Backhouse was up early the next day, the 1ˢᵗ of December 1838, before setting out for the mission at Hankey. He went by way of the farm Zuurbron, like Rondebosch to be devastated in 1869 by the Great Fire, and from there he cut across country to Wagendrift, where he crossed the Gamtoos only a kilometre or two from Hankey.

Backhouse was so taken with the work being done at Hankey that he later made a donation to enable the missionaries to buy a piece of land beside the Gamtoos River. To show their appreciation the LMS named the farm Backhouse Hoek. This name in the vernacular became Bakkieshoek. By 1983, when Johan Ferreira released the news that he had produced the first commercially successful crop of table grapes in the Eastern Cape on his farm, Bakkieshoek, the significance of the person James Backhouse had faded from memory.

Nowadays, as from 30 November each year, and while the season lasts, one can pick one's own strawberries on the farm. Throughout the year other berries - raspberries and blueberries - and also produce such as figs and mushrooms are available. But do not look out for Backhouse Hoek or even Bakkieshoek, but rather "Mooihoek". Backhouse, the old nurseryman, would not take offence at the change. As Shakespeare had it:

> *What's in a name? That which we call a rose*
> *By any other name would smell as sweet.*

* * *

Riding back home in the car Godfried turned to me with a twinkle in his eye. "Grief! I have just remembered that Backhouse was a teetotal Quaker. We won't be able to celebrate with a glass of wine this evening."

Well, Backhouse was once described as "an agreeable companion, and one with the marked gift of moving with friendly ease among all conditions of men", in fact just like Godfried. I believe that the genial, bearded Backhouse would have shrugged, and turned a blind eye to our failings.

Henri Dassonville snr at the wheel of his son Henri's 1902 Gladiator.

5.

Beside the Kromme: Dieprivier to Assegaaibosch

L arge areas of alien infestation, mainly *Acacia mearn-sii* have been cleared in recent years from the banks of the river by Working for Water teams. The Kromme River valley now resembles more closely the valley as seen by 19th century travelers, but still has a way to go!

Dieprivier

We leave Leeuwensbosch behind us, with the road winding up and out of the valley towards a copse of bluegums.

Lichtenstein came this way, travelling in the opposite direction, after following the course of the "Crooked" or Kromme River, through the Langkloof. There would not have been a bluegum in sight in 1803, and no land cleared for the Leeuwenbosch dairy herds.

Today the road from the Langkloof meets the R102 at Trifolia. In the 18th and early 19th century, with tracks rather than roads and with not a fence to be seen, wayfarers could choose their own routes. Most seem to have followed the left bank of the Kromme before crossing the Dieprivier and turning towards Leeuwensbosch.

We continue along the R102 towards Diepriviermond, the confluence of that river with the Kromme, near the head waters of the present day Mpofu Dam. Here at Dieprivier we come across more of the early European travellers, Thunberg, Sparrman, Paravicini di Capelli and Latrobe.

Carl Pehr Thunberg was at Dieprivier in November 1772. He was a Swedish doctor and today is regarded as the Father of South African botany. He studied at the University of Uppsala where he was taught by Carl Linneaus, the botanist, zoologist and physician, whose development of binomial nomenclature resulted in his being hailed as the Father of modern taxonomy.

During Thunberg's three year stay at the Cape, he travelled widely and took a keen interest in local natural history. He also studied the Khoekhoen way of life. Like Lichtenstein, but unlike the majority of Europeans, he tried to understand and find reasons for their customs and rituals. Europeans, for example, deplored the Khoekhoen custom of greasing their bodies with animal fat and were very vocal regarding their feelings. Thunberg, like his fellow Europeans was taken aback by the custom, but he came to realise that it helped the Khoekhoe protect their skin from the sun and insect bites.

While at Dieprivier, Thunberg questioned the local people about lions. He was informed that they were at times seen in the mountains, but no longer in the valleys where formerly they were to be found "in great strength". This would account for the name of the nearby river, to this day, the Leeubos, and of the nearby farm, Leeuwenbosch, where the Ferreira family impressed him, especially the cordial relationship between master and servant.

For obvious reasons the Dutch farmers made a point of harassing any lions that they came across, which explains why lions were always among the first animals to become locally extinct. The last lions south of the Orange River are reputed to have been seen between 1850 and 1858, although there are also reports of lions in the mountains near Cradock as late as the 1880s.

In recent years lions have been reintroduced to the Cape. In 2003 Kgalagadi lions were reintroduced to the Addo Elephant National Park, and a dozen years later to the Cradock Mountain Zebra National Park. Lions are also to be seen in various private parks, but you will not come across any in either the surrounding mountains or in the valley of the Leeubos River.

Thunberg's compatriot, Anders Sparrman, was at Dieprivier in November 1775. Like Thunberg he studied at Uppsala under Linnaeus, starting his medical studies at the age of fourteen. He arrived at the Cape in 1772, where he met James Cook and was taken aboard HMS *Resolution* as assistant naturalist. During the voyage they circumnavigated the world and became the first to cross the Antarctic Circle. Soon after his return to the Cape, Sparrman set out on the journey that took him, in November, to Dieprivier, where he came across five or six elephants and surmised that they had been driven there from the Tsitsikamma.

In 1816 the Reverend Christian Latrobe, while on a journey to inspect Moravian missions at the Cape, stopped at Dieprivier, where he saw no elephants, but was told that some half-dozen were seen regularly in the vicinity. These must surely have been the same ones that Sparrman had seen.

Lichtenstein, who we met earlier at Leeuwenbosch, was told much the same as Latrobe. That the elephants lasted as long as they did is quite surprising, for not only was their ivory sought after, but an elephant provided a large quantity of meat. Even the sturdy hairs of their tufted tails were used as pipe-cleaners.

Willem Bartholomé Eduard Paravinici di Capelli, like Governor Janssens, whom he served as *aide de camp*, was a high ranking army officer. One glance at his name is sufficient to surmise that he was of noble birth. In 1787 he started his military career as a cadet, aged nine, in the artillery and gradually rose through the ranks. Shortly before leaving the Netherlands for the Cape he married Justina van Oldenbarneveld, who accompanied him to southern Africa. Such a voyage in the early 19th century could hardly be described as a honeymoon cruise, but perhaps her stay at the Cape thereafter made up for the voyage.

Soon after his arrival, Governor Janssens set out to learn something about the Batavian Republic's new colony. He was accompanied by his *aide de camp*, but Justina stayed beside Table Bay. This was unlike Commissioner-General de Mist's 18 year-old daughter, Augusta Uitenhage de Mist, who, some months later, insisted on accompanying her father and Heinrich Lichtenstein on their expedition. What is more she kept a journal, which more than 200 years later is a very readable account of their adventures. .

One of Paravicini's duties was to keep a travel journal, which eventually ended up in the archives in the Hague. He wrote mainly about the Khoekhoe and missionaries, but was not blind to natural history, and when the expedition was at Dieprivier he recorded the sighting of an oribi.

These bright orange to rufous-brown small buck with white underparts, chin, throat and rump, are relatively common in east and west Africa, but far less so today in southern Africa. They prefer shortish grasslands and have declined with the spread of agriculture and competition with livestock. Oribi give a snorting whistle when disturbed and make off at top speed, but they have the curious habit of stopping after a short while to check on the cause of the disturbance. They will even on occasion return to have a good look, which must have proved to be the undoing of many.

Unlike Paravicini we have never seen oribi west of Port Elizabeth. We have spotted them at various times on Kasouga, near Port Alfred and on the adjoining farm, Barville Park, home of the Dell family, and where my father was born and spent his childhood.

Essenbos and the Du Preez family

Back on the R62 we continue westwards. It was one of the early travellers who described the area as unexciting, and little has changed. Rocky, low-lying rises, hardly koppies, dot the surrounding grasslands. Since Lichtenstein last travelled this way some 220 years ago invasive pines and some bluegums have made their appearance beside the road.

In places the narrow-gauge line is parallel to the road and close beside us. A white on green information board: "Kareedouw 20, Oudtshoorn 247." There is little traffic. We are reminded by signs at odd intervals that the speed limit is 100 km/h, to which the drivers of passing cars seem to pay little attention. A road-sign indicates a turn-off to Suuranys and Boplaas. Soon after passing it we drop down into a shallow dip and there is the farm, Essenbosch, not far from the railway siding of Essenbos. We drive in to the farm and even before getting out of the car see a bushbuck doe on the edge of the *bos* making her way down to the dam. She is undisturbed by our arrival, and, reaching the water, spreads her front legs and drops her head to drink.

It was the *bos*, the little wood nestling in the fold of the land that caught everyone's attention and in which there grew, and still do, Essenhout or Dog-plum trees (*Ekebergia capensis*). After the long haul through the grassland here at last was something different. Almost all of those early European travellers chose to spend a night or two here. It was an ideal camping place sheltered from the wind. A stream ran

93

through it. There was plenty of firewood, and from 1775 there was also some company, for in that year the farm was granted to Johann Friedrich Scholtz, a native of Hamburg, Germany, who had arrived at the Cape in 1761 in the employ of the Dutch East India Company. Now a free-burger, he had successfully petitioned for this farm beside the Essenbos, *"gelegen aan die oversijde van Attaquaskloof aan de Krommerivier"*. (The fact that Attaquaskloof lies some 260 km to the west of Essenbosch is an indication of how slight the knowledge of this area was back at the Castle of Good Hope.)

Then at some date prior to 1830 the farm was acquired by Hercules Stephanus du Preez and his wife Engela Jacoba, nèe Kritzinger, and the Du Preez family have been there ever since.

However the family is not there today. There is not a soul to be seen. The bushbuck, having finished drinking, moves slowly back into the undergrowth and disappears from sight. We try knocking on the door, but to no avail. The windows are all shut. We walk up towards the shed, but there too there is no sign of life.

During the Anglo-Boer (or South African) War the Du Preez family, although officially British citizens, were Boer sympathisers like so many of their kin-folk. One day a British patrol arrived at the farm commandeering horses. Gawie du Preez was in no position to refuse them, but he warned that they would be better off not taking one particular animal, a fine looking stallion. The soldiers laughed at him and said that he could not fool them. The stallion was to be their first choice. Just to be sure that it went with them one of the men would ride the horse, and a bridle was called for and fitted. A soldier then mounted the stallion and rode off bareback, but before reaching the gate the horse began bucking, the rider was thrown and broke his neck. Shortly thereafter there was a single rifle-shot and the stallion collapsed and breathed its last. Later, in the newspapers, the death of rider and horse appeared under the headline: "Incident at Essenbosch."

Gawie's sons were determined to get their own back for the loss of their horse. Later in the war a British patrol chose to camp on the farm. After the men had gone to bed the boys sneaked out and diverted the water in an irrigation furrow towards the campsite. Sometime later the Tommies were heard cursing and splashing around in the dark, much to the family's satisfaction. A sodden and weary group of men set out the next morning on their way to Humansdorp.

Corrie du Preez was born on Essenbosch and later married Christian Wagner of Rondebosch, a farm we visited earlier.

A photograph from the Du Preez family album shows Corrie, aged five, standing next to her younger brother. He, to judge by his expression, appears to be taking the whole experience in his stride. She on the other hand is scowling at the camera while clutching her favourite wax doll.

There is a story about the doll that involved the old Jewish shopkeeper at Scholtzbosch.

It was the custom at the time for the Scholtzbosch shopkeeper, once or twice a year, to travel around visiting his customers as he had done earlier in his *smousing* days. Coming to Essenbosch he laid out his wares and the family gathered around to see if there was anything that caught their fancy. The first thing that Corrie noticed was the wax doll. The shopkeeper, aware of this, said to her that she could have the doll so long as she kissed him on the cheek. First, said young Corrie, he must give her the doll. Only then would she kiss him. He gave her the doll, and she turned and ran off like the wind. Only after he had left the farm did she emerge from her hiding place. Said the old Jew before leaving, "There are very few people in this world that can *verneuk* me, but that five year-old has!"

Corrie was indeed bright and after school trained to become a teacher. In due course she taught at the farm-school on Essenbosch.

It was during a train-trip to a picnic, a journey on the narrow-gauge railway that passed the farm gate, that she met Christian Wagner of Rondebosch. He was smitten by the tall, dark-haired girl and would eventually take the train from Humansdorp every Saturday in order to spend the night at Essenbosch. Then it was back on the train on Sunday in order to be at work on Rondebosch on Monday.

At the time (1924) there was another suitor, Koos du Plessis, who regularly visited Essenbosch. Fortunately his visits took place during the week. He was of the "rich" Du Plessis family and usually brought Corrie chocolates, a luxury that Christian could not afford. Corrie would save the chocolates in order to be able to share them with Christian at the weekend, a sure indication of which way the wind was blowing.

When Christian first spent the night at Essenbosch he was prepared for the old custom of *boeke vat*. After supper Corrie's mother handed Christian the family Bible and asked the young man to choose the reading. Christian took the brass-bound book and announced that he had chosen to read from Proverbs 31, starting at verse 10: "How hard it is to find a capable wife! She is worth far more than jewels!" Corrie's mother, as Christian had hoped, was impressed. She later remarked to her daughter how suitable a reading her suitor had chosen. But, she added, Corrie still had lots to learn before she could consider herself to be a capable housewife. There followed two years of hard work, learning to cook, bake and do needlework. Only after a further year's engagement were Corrie and Christian able, in May 1928, to stand before the altar together at the church in Kareedouw.

* * *

There was still no sign of life on Essenbosch, and not a single traveller stopped at the farm. While waiting we pondered how many daughters would today postpone their wedding day for three months, let alone three years, in order to learn how to become a jewel of a housewife?

With the question unanswered, we climbed into the Isuzu and headed on down the R62 bound for Assegaaibosch.

1925 - Bathurst to CT: Chatty Knight and Joy Hofmeyr

A flurry of Frenchmen at Assegaaibosch

Slowing down to take the turn-off to the Assegaaibosch Country Lodge, formerly the Assegaaibosch Hotel, we pass an elderly man at the side of the road. He is neatly dressed wearing a faded windbreaker, open-neck shirt and grey flannels, with a small carry-all on the ground beside his scuffed brown shoes. He is holding a ten rand note, which he waves at us. Seeing the car's red brake-lights shining, he grabs his carry-all and takes a few steps in our direction before he realises that we are not stopping for him. In the rearview mirror we see him standing, still holding the ten rand note and looking aggrieved. How does one explain that one has reached one's destination and cannot help him? It is at times like this that I envy the early travellers moving around the country at the pace of an ox. Only then would it be possible to echo the Welsh poet WH Davis:

What is this life if full of care
We have no time to stand and stare

97

or to pass the time of day with an elderly man carrying a grubby black carry-all and bound for who knows where?

* * *

In the mid-19th century a most unlikely small group of settlers arrived in the Humansdorp Division of the old Cape Colony: they were Frenchmen who within a generation were completely integrated within the Dutch community. One of these, Henri Emile Dassonville, was for many years a resident of Assegaaibosch.

Our old friend, the late Jack Skead, who you may remember had family connections with the Cape St Francis lighthouse, told of how as a child, he stayed at the Assegaaibosch Hotel. He was intrigued by the plumbing and sanitary arrangements and could never understand why his mother objected to him describing them to family friends. "Fortunately," he would say, "times have changed, and I have reached the age at which I can talk about these things without any fear of bringing a blush to a maiden's cheek."

Today if our old friend visited the Assegaaibosch Country Lodge, he would surely have difficulty recognising his old haunts, and there is nothing about the plumbing and sanitary arrangements that would be of special interest to a small boy.

Metaphorically we doffed our hats to Jack Skead as we do so often whilst travelling in the Eastern Cape. Wherever we go we come across wonders, both natural and man-made, that fascinated him.

One of Jack's many interests was in the origin and meaning of geographical names; the science of Onomastics. In this regard he corresponded with experts Gabriel Nienaber and Peter Raper, both of whom he greatly respected. However he did disagree with them at times. A case in point was the origin of the name Assegaaibosch, first recorded by Hendrik Swellengrebel in 1776 in the form Assagajbos.

According to Peter Raper's *New Dictionary of South African Place Names,* (1989) the name Assegaaibosch came about as a result of an assegai being found in a bush-clump. He maintains that it has nothing to do with either of the plants commonly known as Assegaaibos, *Grewia occidentalis,* or *Curtisia dentata.* Both of these trees grow in the vicinity, and both are used for the shafts of assegais, hence their common name. Jack felt sure that whatever may or may not have been found in a bush, it was the presence of one or other of these trees that gave rise to the name.

* * *

Henri Dassonville was born in 1834 in Paris, if one subscribes to the idea that he was a commoner, or in Lille as Henri D'Assonville, if one prefers a man of aristocratic descent. Not only is the matter of his birth a mystery; little else is known of his early life. He enlisted in the French army and served in India where it is said that together with four friends: Deschamps, Leygonie, Teran and Chèze, he deserted and fled to British India. In due course the five deserters arrived in England. Then in 1859 they sailed to the Cape and shortly thereafter made their way to Humansdorp. Here Dassonville worked as a shop-assistant for a flamboyant character, Charlie Baker, and it was during his time as a shop-assistant that he courted and later, in 1864, married Aletta Frederika Terblanche.

Up the road from the shop was another of Baker's businesses, the Farmers Hotel (later the Grand Hotel). Particularly during *nagmaal* when farmers and their families gathered in the town, the bar of the hotel was a real money-spinner and it has been suggested that seeing this activity going on up the road from the shop decided Dassonville to look out for a hotel of his own. Was this actually the case, or did Dassonville already have some experience in the hospitality industry? And where did the money come from to enable a humble shop-assistant to dream of buying such a business? Perhaps even if there were no aristocratic connections, Henri Dassonville was the scion of a moneyed family.

In 1866, Gustav, the first of the Dassonville children was born, and shortly thereafter Henri Dassonville acquired the Assegaaibosch Hotel. However, he was still a French citizen and as such was unable to obtain a liquor licence. As a result the hotel was for a time licensed under the name of his Humansdorp attorney, Honoratus Maynier, who later became a magistrate and was remembered for the somewhat rough and ready justice of his court.

The Dassonvilles left Humansdorp for Assegaaibosch, and it was there that the rest of the children, Louisa, Maria, Armand, Henri junior, Victor, Jules and Constance (known as Malvina) were born. Before too long the question of schooling arose. The town of Kareedouw, only 2.5 km west of Assegaaibosch, did not as yet exist. A school at Humansdorp was the only possibility, and one by one the children were sent off as boarders.

Then, in 1872, Dassonville rented Assegaaibosch to his compatriot, François Deschamp, and, together with Aletta and the first five children, set sail for France. Once again this raises various questions, the most obvious being what sort of reception a deserter from the army was likely to receive in his homeland?

The family was away for a year and during this time the three eldest children, Gustav, Louisa and Maria attended school in Paris. Their younger siblings, Armand and Henri junior were baptised in the Roman Catholic Church, an indication that Henri senior, despite his marriage and new home at the Cape, had not entirely abandoned his upbringing and French connections.

During the return voyage from France the ship called at the Island of St Helena, and like so many other travellers at the time, the Dassonvilles took the opportunity to visit Longwood House, site of Napoleon's exile and death on the island. There beside his original resting place grew a weeping-willow from which Henri took a twig to plant at Assegaaibosch. He was neither the first nor the last to take away a souvenir.

In 1821, the year in which Napoleon died, Capt Robert Rubidge and his wife Hannah sailed for the Cape. They too stopped at St Helena, and the gallant captain was one of the early visitors to Longwood to come away with a twig of Napoleon's willow. They settled on the farm Gletwyn, near

Grahamstown where the twig was planted and flourished. In time, however, Rubidge decided, wisely as it turned out, that prospects in the Karoo were better than in the Albany District. They left for the farm Bloemhof, north of Graaff-Reinet, but they took with them a twig from their willow, which they planted outside their new home, which they named Gletwyn Cottage. There it flourished beside an irrigation furrow.

Some seven years after the Dassonville visit to Longwood House, a Mr O Townsend and his wife visited the Napoleon grave site and came away with a twig. I only know this because at one time there was a willow growing on the station platform at Cathcart on the line from East London to the north. Beside it there was a plaque which read:

This tree was planted by the wife of Station Master
O Townsend from a slip taken from the grave of
Napoleon at St Helena in November 1880.

Today all three trees are gone. The Dassonville tree was planted in front of the hotel and when it showed signs of old age a slip was taken and planted, but that too soon succumbed. The Townsend tree has completely disappeared, as has the plaque. On a visit to the town we asked after it and received the succinct reply, "scrap-metal collector." The Rubidge tree has also gone, but when a few years ago we visited Bloemhof and Gletwyn Cottage we were shown the rotten stump.

By the time the two youngest Dassonville children, Jules and Malvina, were of school-going age, the family had established contact with a Mrs Stewart on the farm Hendrikskraal who took on the responsibility of their education. She must have been a most remarkable teacher, for they went from Sub A to Standard 7 (Grade 9) in her capable hands. Only then did Jules move on to Marist Brothers in Port Elizabeth.

* * *

In March 1885 two unusual guests booked into the Assegaaibosch Hotel. Charles Hallack and Frank Girdlestone, riding

101

bicycles, were on their way to becoming the first cyclists to ride from Port Elizabeth to Cape Town. The journey of 560 miles (896 km) took them 19 days.

At the time their journey aroused a good deal of interest, not least in the Langkloof. Few believed that there was any likelihood of their arriving safely in Cape Town. Some of the local people had never before seen a bicycle. As Hallack remembered it they were well received, but their vehicles and clothing provoked astonishment. One old farmer's wife asked from whence they came, how old they were, and whether or not the bicycles belonged to them. She was also interested in the nature of their occupations. She doubted that the bicycles were solely a means of transport and wondered whether they were not some new kind of musical instrument.

At Krakeelrivier they were detained by "an oratorical Boer", but after escaping from him booked in at Teran's Hotel, run of course by Henri Dassonville's countryman. Wherever they went they were welcomed by enthusiastic crowds who gathered to stare at their machines and wonder at their adventures.

Meanwhile, with their schooldays drawing to an end it was time for the Dassonville children to prepare for life away from home. Father Dassonville arranged for a Mr Marks to teach the three eldest boys, Gustav, Armand and Henri the art of wagon-building. Their youngest sister, Malvina, also became involved. She had recently received a Singer sewing-machine as a birthday present, and was now roped in to sew the wagon tents. It was incredibly hard work for a teenager and must have resulted in an extraordinary number of blunt needles.

As the children, now young adults, moved off and married, so the family at Assegaaibosch gradually decreased. Gustav and Victor went off to become farmers in the Free State, which later led to adventures and heartbreak they never foresaw. Jules took an interest in photography and as a sideline became the local unqualified dentist, specialising in extractions. Perhaps as a result of this specialisation his sister, Malvina, no longer sewing wagon-tents, took measurements for false teeth which she sent off to England. Some months later the new dentures arrived back in the Langkloof for fitting. Understandably perhaps, we could find no records as to the satisfaction or otherwise of customers with their new smiles.

The year 1899 saw the outbreak of the Anglo-Boer (or South African) War. Gustav and Victor, as citizens of the Free State, were called on to do their duty to the Republic and rode off to join their commandos. Both were captured during the course of the war and were sent overseas as prisoners. During their absence Victor's farm was burnt to the ground and his stock destroyed. His wife and two children died in a British concentration camp. Gustav was more fortunate in that his farm, Eensgevonden, escaped destruction. Both young men returned to a very different country to that which they had left.

With the cessation of hostilities the boys' "little" sister, Malvina, back at Assegaaibosch, put false teeth measurements aside, and in 1901, married Gert van Rooyen of Krakeel where they opened a shop. Later Gert established the Royal Hotel in Kareedouw, and Malvina found herself back where she started, only a kilometre or two from her birthplace.

In the year after Malvina's marriage Assegaaibosch was visited by another record-breaker, Henri and Aletta's son Victor Dassonville. He, like Charles Hallack and Frank Girdlestone had an unusual means of transport, a Gladiator motor-car which he had collected off the ship in Cape Town. His journey from Cape Town to Port Elizabeth is believed to have been a "first". A photograph was taken to mark the occasion. Seated behind the wheel is Henri Dassonville senior, with his son, Henri, beside him. Who took the photograph? Jules with his interest in photography is an obvious candidate, but it might actually have been Victor: a minor mystery by comparison with some of the others surrounding the Dassonville family.

Incidentally, two other "record-breakers" that called in here were AP "Chatty" Knight and his fiancée Joy Hofmeyr. In 1925 they may not have been the first to ride a motorcycle, a

3½ horsepower Connaught, from Bathurst to Cape Town, but they must surely have been the first to complete the journey carrying a large suitcase. The journey, via the Langkloof, took three days. There were numerous drifts on the untarred road and after 150, they gave up counting the number of gates they had to open and close. "This involved cocking the bike up against the heavy suitcase twice for each gate," explained Mr Knight. Miss Hofmeyr then found her seat, the suitcase was lifted onto her lap, Knight climbed on the bike and they were off again to the next gate.

Henri Dassonville senior made one last journey to France in 1906. He was suffering from stomach cancer, and the visit was a final attempt to find a cure. There was no cure to be found and he died two years later back at Assegaaibosch.

His wife, Aletta Dassonville lived on. Eight years after her husband's death she moved in with Gert and Malvina at the Royal Hotel and stayed with them until her death in 1936 in her 102nd year.

In 1971 a fire destroyed all of the old section of the Assegaaibosch Hotel. All that was left that a Dassonville might have remembered was the pub. Those looking for some tangible connection with the Dassonville days will have to call in and speak to present owner Anton Gerber. Oh yes, and have a drink in the pub. Better still, book in for a night or two and explore the area.

* * *

What happened to the other Frenchmen? Teran we have already met running the hotel at Krakeelrivier.

Leygonie is said to have moved to the Suurveld, north of Humansdorp, after his arrival, but more recently two Leygonie brothers, Ceylestone and Paulin, were farming much nearer Humansdorp, Ceylestone on "The Burns" (the 1926 owner being none other than Frenchman Emile Deschamps) and his brother Paulin Leygonie on the adjoining farm, Swartrivier. Today Ceylestone's widow, Adeline, lives in Jeffreys Bay.

Some years ago we came across the name Leygonie in a completely unexpected part of the Cape. A dirt road leads north from Graafwater in the Western Cape to Vredendal. Thirty-two kilometres from Graafwater one reaches a stony hillock with a cave near the summit. Years ago someone gave it the name Heerenlogement, "Gentleman's Lodgings", and it is indeed an excellent camp-site and was used as such by numerous early travellers. Many of them "signed the visitors' book" by carving their names on the walls of the cave. Many well-known names adorn the walls, and many that have been completely forgotten. Two who signed in 1849 were J P Philip and L Leygonie. They went on to start carving *"Vive la France"*, but gave up halfway. At the time the names meant nothing to me. Then I happened to be reading the late Lawrence Green's *On Wings of Fire,* and there I came across the sentence, "Leygonie had been one of Napoleon's staff officers on St Helena". Whether or not Leygonie was the friend of Dassonville, I do not know.

François Deschamps, together with a Mr William Haskings, set up in business in Humansdorp as "Deschamps and Haskings, Produce Buyers and Direct Importers" in 1882. An advertisement states that they dealt in groceries, materials, gents clothing, first-class furniture, guns and ammunition. In bold print it was stressed that "Mourning Orders a Speciality". Attached to the shop was a bottle store which still operates as "Haskings Bottle Store" in the original building in Main Street.

Which leaves us with Chèze, about whom little appears to be known other than that he moved from Humansdorp to settle in Port Elizabeth. A search through "Red Book" directories produced a single entry for an A Cheze, living in Uitenhage. Resorting to the internet all that appeared was "Chèze – a commune in the Hautes-Pyrénées in south-western France".

How I wish that either the old man Henri Dassanville, or Aletta, his long-lived wife, had put down some facts about his younger days, the visit to France and life at Assegaaibosch. Much the same applies to the others. Surely they would have found Cape Town to be a more cosmopolitan and congenial place to settle? What was it that decided French-speaking

Catholics to dwell amongst Dutch-speaking Calvinists in Humansdorp, a village little more than a decade old?

If Jack Skead were still alive there would be many more questions, not least those concerning the plumbing and sanitary arrangements at the hotel during first quarter of the 20th century: so many questions with so few answers.

* * *

Driving back to the R62 we looked out for the old man in the windbreaker and grey flannels, the hopeful traveller, but there was no sign of him. Either he had found a lift or given up the attempt to reach wherever he was going; just another very minor mystery.

6.

Top: Pepper Tree Cottage as it was

Left: Pepper Tree Cottage - Jouberts Kraal, Nov 2020

An excursion to Jouberts Kraal and back on the R62 to Krommerivierhoogte

In the mountains farmers now grow honeybush tea, but for many years this was a subsistence-farming region. In the early 19th century some of South Africa's most grisly farming stories had their origin here, but it is now a peaceful and largely undisturbed natural area.

Jouberts Kraal

We are sitting on the veranda, or stoep, at Pepper Tree Cottage on Jouberts Kraal with the buzzing of the bees in the pepper tree loud in our ears and a large tortoise grazing beneath the jacarandas. It is warm in the sun, but there's a sneaky breeze that every so often lets us know that winter is not long gone. Down beside the river are a mass of old-fashioned roses, garden escapees that started off in the garden of which the jacarandas are also a reminder. The two enormous logs came to rest on the grass during the 2019 flood, the biggest flood since 2004. Swallows dip and dive on their journeys down to the river, collecting mud for the nest they are building attached to one of the rafters of the roof above us. Later we will go hunting for orchids, for there are questions regarding their pollination that require an answer.

Earlier, leaving Assegaaibosch, we resisted the temptation to take the road to the narrow-gauge railway station of the same name with its coaling facility and turntable; a magnet for steam-train enthusiasts. Instead we followed the winding dusty road into the Suuranys Hills followed by the spectacular drop down to the gorge of the Kouga River. At the bottom is a causeway, often underwater in times of flood. A white mark on a concrete marker indicates whether or not the water is sufficiently shallow to allow a safe crossing.

Halted beside the flooded causeway on one occasion, we watched a Divisional Council lorry come down the road. The driver gave us a cheery wave and a self-satisfied grin as the lorry plunged without hesitation into the mass of water flowing across the causeway. It emerged safely and began the climb up the other side, while we sat wondering when if ever we would be able to cross.

Today there is no problem crossing the river. Ahead is the long climb to the ghosts of Moordenaarskloof, Jammersfontein and the most haunted valley in South Africa, whose story I have told elsewhere[4], also the farm Rachelsrivier, but who

---

4. For more on Moordenaarskloof, Jammersfontein and Nooitgedacht see *Boots in the Baviaans*.

was Rachel? Finally, tucked right into the mountain is the Nortje's farm, Nooitgedacht. This is honeybush tea country, for which the farm is famous. *Cyclopia* sp bushes provide the leaves from which the tea is produced. I once asked the late Scheltema Nortje of Nooitgedacht whether or not he knew a Nortje of my acquaintance, knowing full well that they were cousins. He smiled and raised a quizzical eyebrow: "Your friend drinks spirits", he remarked, "and you seem to have forgotten that we are honeybush-tea drinking Nortjes. He is one of the brandy-Nortjes."

On this occasion, soon after reaching the plateau above the river, we turn off on the road to Sewefontein and Jouberts Kraal. The road is not good, it never has been, but the slow pace suits us, enabling us to keep an eye out for anything of interest beside the road.

Sewefontein is one of the oldest farms in this area between the Kouga River and Mountains. For many years it was farmed by the Potgieter family. When first granted it was given a number, 107, and the name Zevern Fonteinen. During the years that followed the number remained the same, but the name changed from Dutch to a mixture of English and Dutch before eventually settling down to Afrikaans.

The farm name Jouberts Kraal, adjoining Sewefontein, has on the other hand remained the same since it was first surveyed.

* * *

It was in 1821 that Ignatius Petrus Duprez (*sic*) applied for a vacant piece of land known simply as farm 109 in the Uitenhage District, as it was then. The surveyor sent out from Uitenhage to mark the boundaries of the farm was 40 year-old Johan Knobel, a German who had arrived at the Cape in 1803. Initially he took up a job as secretary to the landdrost of Uitenhage, but in 1813 was appointed a surveyor. By the time he travelled out to survey farm 109 he was a very busy man. He had recently drawn up the first map of the Lower Albany district and had subsequently allotted land to the British settlers of 1820. He was soon to be appointed Sworn

Surveyor to the Government, a post that preceded the later post of Surveyor General. His promotion would see him leave the Uitenhage District for Cape Town.

Knobel, on his diagram of the farm, filled in no name for the property, just the number 109, but close to an unnamed river is a dot beside which is written, "Jouberts Kraal". There is no indication as to whether the dot represented an actual kraal in which animals might be kept, or whether it was perhaps a house. Whatever may be the answer, the farm has remained Jouberts Kraal 109 ever since.

Also on the map are brief descriptions of the land and surroundings. Knobel wrote of the land, "Mountainous and Rocky Grazing Ground", which was sandwiched between "High Rocky Mountains" to the north, and "Deep Rocky Ravines" to the south. Not suitable for crops one would think. Despite this, furrows were dug to lead water from upstream on what is now marked on the maps as the Jouberts Kraal River, to lands where crops were planted.

Little is known of the history of the farm. Duprez was followed at a later date by the Kritzinger family, of whom a few lie buried in the small farm graveyard. Some of the graves are reminders of the prevalence of child mortality little more than a century ago:

Jacob Daniel Kritzinger
Was gebode 13 Oct 1906
Overleden de 25st Janiary 1907

It was during the Kritzingers' tenure that Jouberts Kraal hit the headlines with the discovery of the Kouga Meteorite on the farm, which is now to be seen in the Iziko South African Museum in Cape Town[5].

After the Kritzingers came the Strydoms. Recently a couple of Strydoms returned to visit the farm and delighted the owners with their reminiscences of growing up in the shadow of the Kouga Mountains.

---

5. See *Boots in the Baviaans*.

The present owners are Anton and Saskia Boonzaier who, after renovating and rejuvenating the house in which they live, took a look at other old buildings on the property. At, or close to the dot on the survey diagram labelled by Knobel as "Jouberts Kraal" was a dilapidated structure used as a shelter for stock. It was in poor condition with large vertical cracks in the walls and the corners disintegrating. On closer inspection however, it was quite obviously built as a dwelling and as such was the oldest house on Jouberts Kraal. Anton and Saskia decided to try and save the 200 year-old building before it collapsed completely.

Restoring any old building involves compromises of one kind or another. Buildings evolve over time. Repairs are made using materials not available to the original builders. Rooms are added, doors or windows bricked up. To which stage of the building's existence does one intend restoring it? To help with this and other problems, the Boonzaiers contacted green architect, carpenter and natural builder, Capetonian Dave Roberts.

The building was originally a simple, three-roomed farmhouse, to which on the front elevation and at some later date, a lean-to room or shed had been added. This much was clear, but the first job was to save the original structure by dealing with the cracks. This was done by cross-bracing the walls with steel rods. Loose plaster was then stripped from the walls and added to the mortar used for repairing damage to the walls. In the process a doorway, long since walled up, was uncovered and re-instated. At the same time a new opening was created to take a large sash-window to provide more light for the kitchen, and an interior wall was partially demolished to open up the inside. The mud-bricks obtained from this were carefully removed for use repairing the walls. Smaller repairs were done by applying a mixture of clay, sand and chopped straw.

A plaster of lime and sand was used for the outside walls. Lime was soaked in water for a few weeks in a sealed container. The water (calcium hydroxide) was then sprayed on the walls to act as a key before applying plaster. A rough cast plaster or harling was applied to the walls by "harling" (hurling) slaked lime and coarse aggregate onto the walls to achieve a weather-protective finish. As it hardened it was brushed to close any remaining small holes. The walls were finished with a traditional lime wash containing linseed oil and salt to make it more durable.

Inside walls were plastered with a mixture of lime, sand and cow dung and finished with a paint made from clay, fine sand and flour.

Meanwhile Anton was busy milling Blackwood felled on the estate for the interior joinery, also a massive beam for the roof, the ceilings, cladding for the interior walls of the lean-to bathroom (constructed from recycled corrugated iron from the roof) and the pillars and rafters of the veranda. This latter feature was built on the stone foundations of a previous structure.

Using stone from the estate Anton added dry stone walling to his accomplishments, producing stone walls of an exceptionally high standard. The floor of the veranda was then paved with flagstones obtained from an old kraal on the farm.

Anton went on to construct the bathroom and complete the plumbing and gas work for bathroom and kitchen, adding further items to his *curriculum vitae.* The original fireplace was adapted to take a wood-burning stove that keeps the cottage snuggly-warm on winter nights.

Not only did a large proportion of the materials come from the farm, but also the labour. Both Anton and Saskia were heavily involved, but two farm labourers also worked on the building, while receiving on-the-job training. For short spells when necessary a Humansdorp bricklayer and his assistant were brought in to assist with brickwork and plastering. All the finishing touches to the building and to its furnishing and appointments were done by the two Boonzaiers.

The result is a most charming small building that blends perfectly with its surroundings and which, at a glance, might easily be mistaken for an early 19th century farmhouse, which it is not. It is a compromise, and one of the best possible.

Back on the veranda with the orchid pollination problem still unsolved we sit back in our warm jackets to watch the evening closing in. The tortoise has moved on and the swallows have stopped their building work, their place being taken by a tumble of insectivorous bats setting out on an evening's hunting expedition. They disappear into a mist bank moving in from the south-east. It is chilly and time to go inside and pour a glass of Merlot. Whether or not we solve the orchid problem tomorrow remains to be seen, but we are confident that we will enjoy another carefree day amongst wild surroundings and that at day's end we will return again to this small, lovingly restored cottage.

Kareedouw

Back to the R62 and heading westwards towards Kareedouw. If one is not careful one drives through Kareedouw before realising one has reached the town, excepting on Fridays when the main street is packed with people doing their weekend shopping.

When it comes to the meaning and origin of the town's name, most but not all of the experts agree that so far as the "douw" is concerned it is the Khoekhoen for a pass.

The writer TV Bulpin states boldly that the name Kareedouw means ;"Pass of the Karee trees", the karee being known botanically as *Rhus lancea*, which taxonomists recently, after due consideration, changed to *Searsia lancea,* but try not to let this further confuse you.

Peter Raper, while agreeing that this is a possibility, offers alternatives. He notes that so far as the mountain of the same name is concerned, Kareedouw comes from the Khoekhoe *//hari!hau* meaning "Cutting-stone". Or the name may have come from a local tribe, the *"A"Caree.* He also mentions the possibility of it meaning "white gorge".

Is it any wonder then that the local people favoured another and I believe simpler origin? Not only local people, but also the late Dr Jack Skead pointed out that by far the most popular home-brewed drink in the Langkloof/Tsitsikamma area is *karibier* (or just *kari*). What is more the active agent is the root of a common succulent plant of the genus Trichodiadema, known locally as *kiri-* or *karimoer*.

Bulpin and Raper, noted Skead, did not know their botany. The *Rhus* (or *Searsia*) species does not occur locally, not favouring local fynbos conditions, unlike the *Trichodiadema*, or *karimoer*. The chances of the pass being named after a plant that does not grow in the area are slim indeed.

The drink *kari* is found not only locally, but in many other areas in South Africa. In the Kareedouw district the principle ingredient is honey, but to get things going the brewer introduces the finely chopped roots of the *vetplant*, Trichodiadema. While to local brewers the plant is *karimoer*, it is known elsewhere within the boundaries of the old Cape Colony, and even to farmers' wives elsewhere, as *moerbossie*, the yeast-like properties of this plant being used not only to brew beer, but also to bake bread.

The name *kari* may be local, but the drink is an ancient and cosmopolitan one. To some it was honey-wine or beer, to others mead or metheglin. With rice added to the honey it was brewed in China, while in Scandinavia it was the drink of the Norse gods.

Whenever one can lay hands on some honey it is possible to brew *kari*, but the best time is in the Spring when there is plenty of pollen in the honeycomb. One first has to locate a swarm of bees in a rocky overhang or in a hole in a tree. The comb is then extracted, an operation that can prove to be the most difficult and painful of the whole process. Honey in the comb is available from some beekeepers and as a last resort you can visit your local supermarket. Dedicated *kari* drinkers regard this as a desperate measure and only to be contemplated in an emergency.

Method

The comb is pressed into a calabash (more often in these days a plastic container) and topped up with water (preferably from a mountain spring).

> *The finely chopped roots of a moerbossie, together with some lees from the last brew are put into a Springbok pipe-tobacco sakkie or cotton bag (Springbok pipe-tobacco bags being hard to come by in the 21st century).*
>
> *Leave for eight hours, then pour through muslin to remove sediment. Add some of the lees to the tobacco bag for future use. (The moer is best kept in the kitchen chimney until next needed.)*
>
> *Allow to stand until there is no further bubbling. It should be a golden-yellow colour (the more yellow it is, the more powerful the brew).*
>
> *You now have, according to Hjalmar Thesen, "a cauldron of witches' trouble complete with floating bees' knees and whiskers fit for any mountain man".*

This may be considered a traditional recipe found throughout the Langkloof and Tsitsikamma, but there are as many variations as there are brewers. Further to the northeast the Xhosa brew *iQhilika*, which is basically the same drink excepting that prickly-pears are used instead of honey.

> *Peeled pears are boiled up in about five litres of water and allowed to simmer for an hour or two until the mixture has turned a light yellow.*
>
> *A kilogram of brown sugar is added together with a cotton bag of chopped moerbossie.*
>
> *Allow to ferment for about 18 hours.*
>
> *(Note that other fruit such as pineapples or oranges may also be used in place of prickly pears.)*

The brewing is usually done by women and most of the drinking by men. Perhaps, as a result, the brewers always insist that one should drink *kari* "responsibly". A Mrs Nel of Bellville, a regular brewer of *kari*, writes, "If you are not careful *kari* can make a person *maldronk,* but there is no better drink with traditional foods" - such as Tsitsikamma-burgers, of course!

* * *

115

The Kareedouw Pass has been a route down to the coast from the Langkloof for centuries. For decades timber from the Tsitsikamma forests was carried over the mountain to the station at Assegaaibos. The Tsitsikamma farmers too made frequent use of the pass and after delivering their produce to the station or collecting agricultural machinery, many would call in at the Assegaaibosch Hotel.

The road from the town and over the mountain goes on to cross the N2 and continues to the ocean. There, stretched out along the coast, are a number of holiday cottages or fishing shacks, many in the "Boer baroque" style of architecture. One owner, with the admirable intention of disguising a long, blank, concrete retaining wall has covered it with *faux* garage doors. It was among this moneyed community that Prime Minister and later State President Balthazar Johannes Vorster chose to have a holiday home.

Politicians are a necessary evil. While we cannot do without them, I can quite easily count the number of those whom I admire on the fingers of one hand. However, having a prime minister in our midst meant that we were reminded every so often of his presence when a military helicopter flew down low along the coast, or there was a heavy security presence at the nine-hole Hankey golf-course. And whatever his failings, John Vorster (as he preferred to be called in later years) was, as Helen Suzman described him, "flesh and blood" as opposed to his predecessor, the diabolical Verwoerd, or successor, PW *"Groot Krokodil"* Botha. Vorster had a sense, albeit perverted, of humour. Neither of the other two would have greeted visiting foreign dignitaries with the remark, "Welcome to the happiest police state in the world", as did Vorster.

Vorster, as Minister of Justice, oversaw the Rivonia Trial of Nelson Mandela, and was Prime Minister at the time of the Soweto Riots and the Steve Biko crisis. He had the dubious distinction of having been himself detained. During the early years of the Second World War he became a founding member of the pro-Nazi Ossewabrandwag, and rose rapidly through the ranks. As a result he spent some 14 months during 1942-43 at the Koffiefontein detention camp. He later claimed that he, being anti-British rather than pro-Nazi, played no part in the acts of sabotage orchestrated by his organisation.

Every country, so it is written, has the government it deserves, in which case we the citizens may be deemed as much to blame for the state of the country as our political leaders. So it surely would be wiser for those of us who hold politicians in low esteem, to rather try and improve the quality of our leaders. This view is strongly supported by the majority of revolutionaries. The problem is that so very few revolutionary leaders turn out to be upright, morally responsible politicians.

In 1983, aged 67, John Vorster died in disgrace. Two scandals, the Information and Muldergate Scandals, had muddied his name even within his own National Party. Still, despite his failings his family, as was only to be expected and many of his friends travelled across the pass of *moerbossies* to attend his funeral at the elegant Kareedouw Dutch Reformed Church. And there too he was buried.

We no longer have military helicopters flying on a regular basis to and fro along the coast.

The church beside which Vorster is buried is a handsome building with a traditional rooster atop the weather-vane on the steeple. The rooster at one time leaned sideways at a jaunty angle, but we were always assured that this had nothing whatever to do with *kari*. In recent years the rooster has been straightened, perhaps to emphasise the sobriety of the congregants.

From the church we drive westwards along Keet Street and turn up Buitenkant Street to reach the Tenax Private Nature Reserve. There we meet with local veterinarian Maarten Bootsma and his wife Karen. The ground across the fence from their home is the old Kareedouw commonage, bounded on the west by the Pass. It is now the Tenax Reserve.

This area was frequently visited by Henry George Fourcade of Witelsbosch in the Tsitsikamma, a remarkable man of whom there will be more to record later in our journey. (See chapter 15). For the moment it is enough to say that in 1941 he produced a checklist of plants from the southern Cape. In his walks over the mountains and across the veld he came across 3 000 species which he identified himself or with the help of Louisa Bolus of the Bolus Herbarium in Cape Town. All this despite the fact that he was not by profession a botanist!

The Bootsmas are well aware not only of Fourcade, but also of the botanical treasures in the reserve. Some are threatened by alien invaders or by *muthi* collectors. There is wildlife, both great and small, birds and reptiles. Knowing this, the Bootsmas worked diligently to have the old commonage declared a private nature reserve, and are now its unpaid custodians.

The lower slopes of the mountain are covered in alien pines (as well as some of the higher reaches on the western side beside the Kareedouw Pass) but once through this the lower part of the reserve is covered with fynbos and proteas. Amongst these we found, not unexpectedly, the low growing *Protea tenax*, from which the reserve takes its name.

Tenax, the Tenacious sugarbush, as it is commonly known, is unusual in that while one will never walk into it, as one might the better known sugarbush – *Protea repens* – one may well walk on it. This ground-hugging, low trailing shrub is pollinated, because of its manner of growth, not by birds or insects, but by rodents, attracted to the flowers by their yeasty smell. The flowers may be found at any time of year, but are most likely to be seen from May to September. The seed is dispersed by the wind, which accounts for the scattered plants found in isolated populations on hill and mountain slopes in the southern Cape. On our mountain walks we frequently come across this humble little protea. It is little threatened by rampant plant invaders, collectors, agricultural development, mining or civil engineering works. The red list of South African plants classifies Tenax as being of least concern. Long may this remain the case.

Another find was the delightful, little yellow-flowered *Liparia hirsuta*. At the time we took no special note of this, but some weeks later we were delighted to hear from Tony Dold at the Schonland Herbarium in Grahamstown that our pressing of the plant had filled a long-standing gap in the Herbarium records.

As we climbed the slopes, a blue sky arcing above us, so more and more grasses appeared amongst the fynbos, stretching upwards towards the rocky Table Mountain sandstone of the Kareedouwberg. Behind us the town assumed Lilliputian proportions and one became aware that there was more to it than a short stretch of the R62, which in the town is known as Riebeeck Street.

We sat in the shade of an alien pine to eat our sandwiches, but despite the alien at our backs, our view was of veld largely undisturbed and unthreatened. Sparrman and Thunberg and all the other early travellers would have witnessed scenes such as this, although probably at more of a distance, for they all tended to follow the windings of the Kromme.

One who after reaching this gap in the mountains chose not to continue beside the Kromme was a 27 year-old German pharmacist, Christian Ferdinand Friedrich Krauss. The apothecaries of the day all had an interest in plants, and Krauss was no exception. He came to the Cape to collect plants and there is no doubting his dedication, for on his return to Germany after a year at the Cape, he took with him 66 crates of specimens.

It was in 1838 that Krauss made his way up from the Langkloof and across the Kareedouwberg to Koksbosch (today Clarkson). The reason for the detour was simple, Krauss was on the lookout for a bed for the night and some friendly German faces, and the missionaries at Koksbosch provided both needs. While on the mountain he came across "lovely red everlasting flowers, Helichrysum, some Ericaccae, Indigoferae and other Leguminosae [Fabaceae]".

We too, among the many species recorded, have come across *Helichrysum felinum* and *Erica sparmannii,* but to our delight we also found an Indigofera, the humble, little *Indigofera hispida.* It is only known from seven localities and is declining in numbers due to alien plant invasions. As a result of this, it is facing a high risk of extinction, so is classified as vulnerable.

Was it this species of Indigofera that Krauss found? We had no way of knowing, but felt that our discovery deserved a celebration. *Kari* was the obvious drink with which to toast our find, but having none with us; a mug of coffee from our flask had to suffice.

Lichtenstein at Jagersbosch

Martin Karl Heinrich (or Hinrich) Lichtenstein, whom we have already mentioned, was aged 22 when he arrived in Table Bay in 1802, but had been fascinated by the Cape from an early age. He qualified as a medical doctor at the University of Helmstadt and shortly thereafter learnt that General Janssens of the Batavian Republic needed a doctor to accompany an official party to the Cape. Janssens was also looking for a German tutor for his son. Lichtenstein, considering himself to be suitably qualified for both positions, applied and was accepted.

Before departure Lichtenstein travelled to Brunswick where he was instructed by entomologist and botanist Count van Hoffmansegg in the correct collecting and preservation procedures for natural history specimens.

At the first possible opportunity after his arrival at the Cape, Lichtenstein set out to become acquainted with his new surroundings. Although impressed by the natural beauty of the Peninsula and the massive array of new plants and creatures that he came across on his walks, Lichtenstein found his official duties as doctor and tutor to be less congenial than he might have wished. He dreamt of an adventurous life as a naturalist leading an expedition into the depths of the continent.

Then in October 1803 he was given permission, as medical officer, to accompany Commissioner-General Jacob de Mist on a journey to Saldanha Bay and from there eastwards to the Great Fish River. During the journey he kept a diary or journal, which was later rated by both De Mist and Janssens as a highly valuable document of special interest to the Colonial government. It included information concerning climate, topography, soil fertility, birds, animals and plants, insects and seeds, cultural practices of the Khoekhoe, San and Xhosa peoples, and the activities of farmers, hunters, traders, missionaries and government officials.

Towards the end of the year 1803 the party headed eastward into the Langkloof and eventually followed the course of the Kromme River to Jagersbosch, the farm of a Mr P Ferreira. It was raining heavily, but they were able to shelter in the house. However, their wagons only arrived the next morning, so they went to bed with empty stomachs and with no beds or bedding.

The next day they met their first Xhosa: five men and three women of Chungwa's (or "Conga's" as Lichtenstein called him) Gqunukhwebe people.

A board was set up at which the men threw their assegais, with the colonists offering a red cotton handkerchief as a prize for the most accurate throw. Lichtenstein goes on to describe their shields, "kirris" and manner of fighting. They also sang and one of the women demonstrated how they made rush baskets tightly woven enough to hold milk.

Lichtenstein and the Dutch travellers were not free of European prejudice. He and his fellows regarded their visitors as "savages", yet he admired their dexterity, praised the woman's "uncommonly neat" handiwork and noted that the rush basket did "great honour to the inventor". And when it came on to rain again the Gqunukhwebe visitors were invited to share the Dutch party's dry accommodation for the night.

The following day Commissioner-General de Mist was called on to settle a dispute between a Khoekhoen woman and a colonist. She claimed that her former employer had withheld from her a cow and a calf which she had earned. De Mist took the opportunity to exhort the colonists to be especially careful in their conduct towards those that behaved well in their service. He made it a rule, he said, as did General Janssens, in all cases where there was an element of doubt, to

121

favour the servant rather than the Christian master. "This", as Lichtenstein comments, "had a good effect upon the behaviour of the colonists."

Later, on the 5th of January 1804, the party arrived at Leeuwenbosch, the farm of Michael Ferreira. Lichtenstein was impressed: "The man and his wife were quiet pious people, and seemed to lead a most happy life in their solitude, surrounded by a number of fine children, and by a company of faithful slaves and Hottentots: both the latter appeared really and warmly attached to them."

During the afternoon Lichtenstein walked in the veld and came across a large snake hunting a field-mouse; very likely a four-striped field-mouse. The young German was fascinated and watched for some minutes. He noted how the mouse became at one stage seemingly "palsied with terror", before the snake snapped up its prey and disappeared into a bush. What, he wondered had caused the mouse's paralysis?

Nowadays Leeuwenbosch is known for its dairy, but we remember it because Heinrich Lichtenstein once spent the night there, and was impressed by the Ferreiras' "purity and simplicity of heart . . . which made the frugal meal they set before us doubly agreeable". Perhaps a part of Lichtenstein's charm was his ability to recognise the merits of others, whoever they were and whatever their station.

It was Lichtenstein's accounts of the people and natural surroundings and creatures that so impressed Janssens and De Mist, and which more than 200 years later make Lichtenstein's two volume *Travels in Southern Africa* still such interesting and entertaining reading.

In 1812 Lichtenstein's book was translated into English by Anne Plumptre (or Plumptree, according to the title-page of the English edition). Anne and her sister Annabelle were the daughters of Dr Robert Plumptre, the President of Queens' College, Cambridge. They were two noted blue-stockings and members of the Enfield Circle, a local group of *literati*.

Anne was a novelist and a translator of French and German works. She was largely responsible for introducing her fellow countrymen to the works of German dramatists, which may explain why she chose, or was chosen, to translate Lichtenstein's *Travels* from the German. There is however, no indication that she had a particular interest in the Cape.

She did have a special interest in France and lived in that country for three years. While there she became an ardent supporter of Napoleon Bonaparte, and in 1810 declared that she would welcome a French invasion of her native land. Napoleon would, she felt sure, do away with the British aristocracy and establish a far better government.

No doubt she was also an admirer of Jan Willem Janssens, who although of noble descent, played his part in the revolutionary wars that signalled the establishment of the Batavian Republic (later a part of the French Empire of Napoleon Bonaparte). Likewise Jacob Abraham de Mist, but she may have cooled towards him after his return to the Netherlands when, in 1807 he accepted the Knighthood of the Order of Union, followed by a further knighthood in 1812, of the Order of the Reunion.

She died aged 58 in 1818, by which time the Cape was firmly in British hands, a colony administered by British governors who were themselves members of the British aristocracy. Anne would not have approved.

Krommerivierhoogte

Travelling westwards from Kareedouw we follow the route taken by the early travellers beside the Kromme. Much of the area has been cleared, thanks to the Working for Water initiative, of the alien vegetation that previously covered its banks. So once again one sees the valley as did Thunberg, Sparrman, Masson and all the others. Well, almost as they did, if one ignores the tarred road, the railway up to one's right, the fences and farm-buildings, the weirs in the river, the power-lines and the odd aliens missed by Working for Water.

Climbing gradually from the valley we reach the farm Hendrikskraal, where that noteworthy teacher, Mrs Stewart, once taught Julius and Malvina Dassonville of Assegaaibosch from Grade one to Standard seven. Hendrikskraal is one of the earliest farms granted in the Kouga district. It was on the 20th of October 1826 that Cornelis Rademeyer senior was given title to the land against an annual payment of £1-2-6. By 1850 there was a Cornelis Rademeyer junior farming Hendrikskraal. Nine years earlier he had married Maria, whose maiden name, Ferreira, singled her out as a local girl, for we are on our way to the cradle of the Ferreira family. But who, I often wonder was Hendrik?

Hendrikskraal remained a Rademeyer farm for 144 years. Then in 1970 it was bought by a Dr van Staden and shortly thereafter his son-in-law, a Zondagh, another well-known Langkloof name, was the farmer.

The original house built by the senior Rademeyer in the 1830s consisted of a single row of rooms; kitchen, living room and bedroom, a typical early Langkloof house. The original chimney disappeared when an extension was made that converted the house into an L-shaped building. The former kitchen then became a second bedroom. Several yellowwood floors and ceilings dated back to the days of the elder Rademeyer. Some years ago the old house was destroyed by fire and a notable link with the first Dutch farmers in the area has now disappeared.

Those intrepid cyclists, Charles Hallack and Frank Girdlestone, while pedalling to Cape Town, came across the Rademeyers towards the end of March 1885 when they stayed at Rademeyer's Hotel at Compagnies Drift, the farm adjoining Hendrikskraal. The next day they faced the long, uphill grind to Kromrivierhoogte, the name nowadays shortened to Heights, the true start to the Langkloof.

At Heights there is the turn-off to the Onder-Kouga, but before heading out on that road, we turned towards the former Heights Station situated on the old farm Elandsfontein. The farm has been worked by Ferreiras since 1806 when Petrus Hendrik Ferreira, one of several generations of Petrus Hendriks, was granted the land. He became *Veldkornet* for the Lower Langkloof ward of the old George Division. His wife, Martha Johanna, became famous, or infamous depending on one's point of view, because of a quarrel with Coenraad de Buys. We were to come across her again while in the Onder-Kouga, Today various Ferreira cousins farm the land.

The original house on Elandsfontein, built by Petrus Hendrik, burnt down after he and Spoorbek, Heinrich Schorbeck of Spoorbek-se-erf, had an altercation. The prophet and *towenaar* then cursed the building. As a result the Ferreira house was destroyed in a subsequent fire, but, so it is said, Spoorbek's own thatch-roofed outside room was untouched by the blaze.

We drove past the oldest existing white-walled house, built by Thomas Ignatius Ferreira, grandson of Petrus Hendrik and Martha Johanna, in 1860, and onto an almost equally venerable building to meet George Ferreira, honey-bush tea producer, plant-lover, cat-owner and photographer. As is often the norm on old farms, the kitchen door did service as the front door, and there we were met by George, his cats, a rooster and a hen. After negotiating the animals and putting the door on the hook to prevent the chickens eating the cats' food, we sat down at the kitchen table to drink coffee and discuss plans for a botanical "bioblitz" on the farm.

George, with dark hair and a beard flecked with grey, bespectacled, tall and lean, bustled around preparing the coffee while Anne, the cat, climbed on the table to make our acquaintance. Then with everyone at the table, the botanical library was brought out and we settled down to plan the campaign, with Anne (of Green Gables, explained George) showing a keen interest in all that was going on.

* * *

After the arrival of the narrow-gauge railway at Heights in 1910, a bustling small settlement developed with a shop, church and school, a solidly built station-master's house beside the station and further on, and on the opposite side of the line, the small houses of the labour force.

The general-dealer's establishment was of course the central point of the village where all the local inhabitants met.

Little remains today. The station-master's house is still there, but with broken windows. Shacks have gone up beside the line and when I approached, two dogs were let out to see me off. The general-dealer shut the shop years ago. Here an "informal settlement" or shanty town is developing, a familiar South African problem and common enough on the outskirts of our cities and towns, but in our experience uncommon in the depths of the *platteland.*

George remembers the days when there was a daily gathering at the shop to await the arrival of the train. He remembers the day when old Mrs M tripped over a can of paraffin and landed on the floor with her skirt over her head and, so George told us, "All you could see was Snowflake".

For the benefit of the younger generation one has to explain that half a century or more ago Snowflake flour was marketed in white, cotton bags emblazoned with the name of the product. There were many country-folk that used the material for making their underwear. We for example, remember Katie's bra factory. On sunny afternoons Katie sat, busy with her needlework, outside her small house. On Saturdays her customers came to call, some for measurements to be taken, others to collect their orders. Bras would be brought out by Katie and customers would retire discreetly to try them on. To judge by the numbers that called, and especially the fact that we could recognise some as repeat customers, Katie turned out a good product. This, long before "recycling" and "ecology" became buzz words, was a pleasing example of someone making a living while helping to save the planet. One wonders whether or not the millers of Snowflake were ever aware of their contribution to the South African garment industry.

* * *

We spent most of the first day on the southern side of the farm beside lands covered with Honey-bush tea plants - *Cyclopia* sp. - and in the adjoining Formosa Nature Reserve. There we went orchid spotting, splashed through the reed-shrouded Kromme and walked on the slopes of Peak Formosa amongst the fynbos and proteas. We returned by following roughly the course of the river until, down a series of spectacular water-falls, it plunges down from Heights and into the valley below and the farm Krugersland. Perched on a rock at the edge of the chasm we had the waterfalls to our right and in the dis-tance to our left the traffic on the R62, crawling ant-like up the incline from Kompanjiesdrif.

Returning to George's house we passed a small, white-washed cottage with hollyhocks framing the front door. Out-side the garden gate was parked a shiny, cream-coloured car. George explained that the car belonged to the daughter of the woman who lived in the cottage. "My cousin and his wife real-ised that the daughter had talent and ability and ensured that she was able to complete her schooling. From there she went on and now works for a big dairy business."

Do not judge Heights solely by the squatter-camp at the former station!

The next day we tackled the southern side of the farm and there, amongst the renosterbos and with not a protea in sight George pointed out how we were driving along the original "road", a track really, through the Langkloof. It wavered from side to side and there were off-shoots where, in wet weath-er, travellers had sought drier ground. While it is often diffi-cult to pick out these 200 year-old tracks at ground level, it is easy enough on Google images of the area. Amongst them we found further botanical surprises tucked away among the bushes.

Later, while sitting at a lay-by beside the R62 waiting for the others to climb through a fence, I made a surprising dis-covery of another kind. There on the table, were four unblem-ished spark-plug boxes containing four obviously well-used plugs. It seemed that some traveller decided at precisely that point that the car's spark-plugs needed changing, a road-side repair that could be completed in a matter of minutes. The job done, he put the old plugs into the boxes that had con-tained the new spark-plugs and placed them neatly side-by-side before driving on to Joubertina. Or do you have another explanation?

The next day we left the farm. George stood outside the kitchen door with Anne tucked under one arm and the rooster under the other. When we were safely on our way he put the two down and gave us a wave.

We left with a bag of Honey-bush tea, and only then did it strike me that during our stay on this Honey-bush tea farm we had drunk only coffee.

* * *

Hallack and Girdlestone, having toiled up the hill to Heights, had a reasonably easy ride to Twee Riviere, where they stayed overnight at Shepherd's Hotel, a name that South Africans who served in the North African campaign during the Second World War associate with Cairo rather than the Langkloof. No sign of the Twee Riviere Shepherd's still exists, and we could find no one in the village today with any idea where it was situated.

This quaint village of small, stone-built houses and winding lanes is reminiscent of Europe rather than Africa. The cyclists' "hotel" must surely have been what today is referred to as a BnB establishment.

Mr Wessel Olivier showed us around. Clad in open-necked shirt and shorts and with slops on his feet, he looked more like a holiday-maker heading for the beach than the local land-owner. The building he believes to have been the oldest house now serves as a shed attached to what may have been the second oldest house. Some of the houses are one-roomed with low walls and a great chimney at one gable-end. Many of these are now used as sheds and those that are still inhabited are no longer A-frames, but have had the walls raised, flattening the pitch of the roof. Originally of thatch, most if not all of the roofs are now of corrugated iron. Red roofs with white walls and beige surrounds to many of the doors and windows is the predominant colour scheme.

For more than two centuries Twee Riviere has been associated with the Olivier family. In the middle of the 19th century Michiel and Ockert Olivier were registered as inhabitants. By the 20th century there was Michiel "Giel Bokkie" Olivier who, according to local legend, established an unenviable reputation in the Onder-Kouga.

By comparison with the farmers of the Onder-Kouga, Giel Bokkie Olivier was a man of some substance. Apart from anything else he owned a threshing machine and the steam-engine that provided the power to drive it.

The Onder-Kouga farmers to a large extent practised subsistence farming. They had cattle, sheep and goats, fruit orchards, vegetables and on the plateaus between the rivers, known to them as *vlaktes*, they grew wheat and oats. These were reaped by hand, but to thresh the harvest they hired Olivier's thresher and steam engine, and with great difficulty dragged these machines from Twee Riviere and across the Kouga River to their farms.

The Onder-Kouga farmers and their families were unlikely to ever go short of food, but having sufficient cash to develop their farms or buy goods from outside the area was another matter. Before the advent of the narrow-gauge railway line to Port Elizabeth, taking their produce to market was at first well-nigh impossible and even after that, never easy. They discovered however, that Olivier was willing to give them loans which they could repay in produce and many of them became deeply in debt to him. According to the farmers' descendants Olivier, who died in 1928, never wrote receipts for these transactions. Rightly or wrongly the Onder-Kouga farmers believed that Olivier frequently cheated their fathers.

"Neither a borrower nor a lender be," was one of my father's maxims, and anyway we were on our way to find the source of the Kromme, so forgetting for the time-being the Olivier family, we, together with other members of our botanical group, went in search of Rodger Smith who was to be our guide.

On the outskirts of Twee Riviere, we found Rodger sitting on the stoep of a farmhouse that was surrounded by a rough-cast stone wall. While we parked in the shade of a tree he came down to meet us; medium height, broad-shouldered and burly. He was dressed in a short-sleeved bush-shirt hanging loose at the waist, and khaki shorts and was bare-foot, with a green-brimmed, khaki baseball cap on his head. He looked the sort of man one would like to have with one when stalking a wounded buffalo. Perhaps the cigarette between his fingers and the lighter grasped in his hand indicated that Smith did have some insecurities; he was more than just bush-craft and brute strength.

It took some minutes before everyone was ready. Cameras and rucksacks were collected, together with notebooks and plant-lists, water-bottles and walking-sticks. Rodger tapped his shirt pocket to make sure he had his cigarettes and we were ready to go.

Progress up the mountain was slow. There were burnt patches and scratchy fynbos, but those with botanical interests tend to walk with their heads down, and to stop at frequent intervals anyway.

On the way up to the first rocky outcrop we found a solitary *koringkriek* – wheat-cricket, *Acanthoplus discoidalis*. These fearsome looking creatures are omnivorous, but acquired their common name as a result of the damage they cause in wheat lands. However, despite being heavily spiked, and exuding some foul liquid when attacked and of being capable of a nasty nip, they are flightless and easily gathered by those protecting their crops. In fact it has been suggested that they should be used as a high protein chicken food. We left this particular example of the species in peace.

Nearing the source the mountainside becomes far more interesting with rocky outcrops resembling an assemblage of tombstones, and a greater variety of plants including disas, both *Disa porrecta* and *D. tripetaloides,* also redhot pokers – *Kniphofia* sp.

We reached the stream, little more than a trickle, which would eventually become the Kromme. It ran from one pool to another; most of them shallow, but one with a rock wall that dammed the flow of water sufficiently to form a swimming-pool.

At this stage Rodger borrowed someone's hat and was able to catch a small – about 10 cm – slender, silvery, fork-tailed fish, which he informed us was a *Galaxias*, one of the most widely distributed freshwater fish in the world. However, until quite recently they were unknown in South Africa, though common in New Zealand, Australia and South America. We gathered around and admired the small creature, far more appealing than a *koringkriek*, and cameras were produced to record this ichthyologic object of interest.

At this point one of our party, Ron, a keen fisherman, with camera poised for a photo, stood on some slime and disappeared quickly yet gracefully into the pool while holding his camera aloft. Willing hands pulled him out in an instant. He had just enough time to look at his camera and start to say something when he slipped in for a second time. Once again he and his camera were rescued. This time, however, the spectators, aware that there was nothing wrong with Ron, although there were doubts about his camera, were unable to contain themselves. There were roars of laughter.

We set out on the return-journey in a cheerful frame of mind. Even Ron recovered sufficiently to see the funny side of his misadventure. And a few days later he was able to reassure us that the camera was none the worse for its dunking.

Opkoms, May 98

7.

Onder-Kouga, Langkloof, Voorkloof and Bo-Kouga

It was once the haunt, according to a 19th century government official, Col Collins, of tax-evaders and other nefarious characters.

Onder-Kouga: the cradle of Ferreiras and Gerbers

Following in the wheel-tracks of Giel Bokkie Olivier's threshing machine we set off from Twee Riviere bound for the Onder-Kouga. Leaving the R62 at Heights, we turn onto the dirt road heading at first in a north-north-easterly direction, travelling through apparently dry brown veld, despite overnight showers. Then we begin to wind down towards the Kouga River. There the river is flowing and we pause for a while to enjoy the shade of the willows and the gurgle of water. To some the river is a boundary that divides the Onder-Kouga from the rest of the Langkloof; however as we soon find out, there are as many opinions as to the location of the Onder-Kouga as there are farmers in the area.

In 1850 Uitvlugt was farmed by Johan Daniel Strydom and his wife Anna, née Kritzinger. Despite living in what was then the Onder-Langkloof Ward of the George Division, they did not regard themselves as being a part of the Onder-Kouga. That lay further north they said, beside the Kouga River. They described themselves instead as *niemandlanders* belonging to neither Kouga nor Onder-Kouga.

More than 150 years later there are still those, the present writer amongst them, who are unsure as to the exact boundaries of the Onder-Kouga. Perhaps the most extreme claim being that the Onder-Kouga stretches from Hoeree in the west to Jammersfontein in the east.

The Ferreiras of Opkomst, however have no such doubts. Hoeree, they claim is far to the west of the Onder-Kouga, while their farm, just north of Uitvlugt, lies on the furthest eastern boundary of the area. For the sake of peace we have decided to accept the Gerber/Ferreira view that the Onder-Kouga consists of the original four farms running from east to west: Opkomst, Braamrivier, Brandhoek and Kleinrivier.

Opkomst (without the "t" on modern maps) was first granted in 1772, to Jacobus de Buys, ca1737-1826, and his wife, Catharina née Pienaar. Jacobus was the uncle of the famous or infamous, depending upon your point-of-view, Coenraad de Buys. A number of De Buyses and others followed Jacobus in quick succession; all to a greater or lesser degree related, until finally, during the rule at the Cape of the Batavian Republic, 1803-1806, Coenraad de Buys was granted the farm.

De Buys, described as being close to seven feet (±2m) tall and possessed of immense self-confidence, had led a wild and adventurous life. For some time he lived near the frontier, cattle-raiding and causing general mayhem. Then in 1798 he was banned from the colony by the British authorities. He took up residence at the homestead of the Rharhabe leader, Ngqika. There he became consort to Ngqika's mother and adviser to her son. He also at this time became friendly with the London Missionary Society's Dr Johannes van der Kemp of Bethelsdorp, and acted as his interpreter when Van der Kemp visited Ngqika.

During Batavian rule at the Cape, De Buys, having been pardoned his past sins, was back in the Onder-Kouga, and on 12 December 1803 at Avontuur in the Langkloof, he met Commissioner-General J A de Mist and fellow traveller Heinrich Lichtenstein. De Mist granted De Buys the farm, "d'Opkomst over de Cauga". Both De Mist and Lichtenstein were favourably impressed by De Buys. Not so his Ferreira neighbours. The main bone of contention appears to have been his relationship with people "of colour".

In 1812 he married Elizabeth, born *in het land van de Makina, achter de Tambookes*, a move which did not go down well with the Ferreiras. Then during the so-called "Black Circuit" of 1812-1813, he gave evidence for the prosecution in a criminal matter against the accused, *Kwaai* (Hot-tempered) Martha Ferreira. This for the Ferreiras, was a step too far, and shortly thereafter De Buys, his wife and half-caste children left the Onder-Kouga for the north, where about 50 km west of present-day Louis Trichardt they settled at a place now named Mara.

After his wife's death in 1821, De Buys once again set out on trek, never to be seen again. He is believed to have succumbed to malarial fever at some unknown spot somewhere between Mara and Inhambane in Mozambique. Today his numerous descendants, the Buysvolk, are still to be found at Mara, nor is he forgotten in the Onder-Kouga.

With the departure of De Buys, much to the satisfaction, no doubt, of the Ferreiras, Opkomst was taken over by Johannes Theodorus Ferreira and his wife, Johanna Jacomina née Prinsloo, Ferreira being the son of *Kwaai* Martha, who must have savoured this triumph over her old enemy. Thus began the long association of the Ferreira family with the farm.

* * *

Crossing the causeway over the Kouga, and following the course of the Opkomsrivier, we climb the gravel road up-stream towards the small settlement of Opkoms. However, should you wish to visit Opkoms nowadays you will need to know someone with a key to one of the locks on the gate. A word with the first Ferreira you meet might do the trick.

Geographical factors that influenced the early settlers' choice of land were the rugged terrain with high mountains and deep valleys, and the fertility of the soils derived from the Bokkeveld formations, by comparison with those derived from the Table Mountain Sandstone. Likewise the fact that these farmers, all recent descendants of European founding fathers tended to follow European customs when choosing their sites. The result was small settlements of houses sur-rounded by farm land. This also made sense when considering the remoteness of the area settled by these pioneers, whose only source of help in time of need were their neighbours. The result is that small groups of farm houses and sheds beside the rivers with houses facing the road may still be seen.

The folk of the Onder-Kouga were a close knit community with local values and a similar world-view which included the value of land. Thus sons followed in their fathers' footsteps. There was little incentive for other young men to venture into these communities, for other than as *bywoners,* or squatters there were few opportunities for them to go farming. As a re-sult there were very few surnames. Opkoms, where we were headed was Ferreira territory, while at Braamrivier the Ger-bers held sway. At Brandhoek there were both Gerbers and Ferreiras, but at Kleinrivier solely Ferreiras. New blood was provided by young females from outside the area.

A disadvantage of the land being passed from father to sons was the constant subdivision of land, which meant that in time farms became smaller and as a result, uneconomic. Only after the mid-twentieth century did this situation begin to change as young people started to leave the Onder-Kouga in search of opportunities in the outside world.

So today one is able to drive through an area of great scenic beauty; the rolling foothills of the Kougaberge with their peaks to the north, Tsitsikamma Mountains to the south; steep-sided valleys and wide vistas, while enjoying the opportunity to observe settlements and a way of life little changed from what they were two centuries ago.

We now drove towards Braamrivier on the river of the same name and to Brandhoek on the Schrikkerivier. Normally the road is covered with dust as thick as cream, but the overnight showers had not only settled the dust, but in the early morning light bejewelled the roadside bushes.

As is so often the case we were on the lookout for a plant, *Freylinia crispa,* the Kouga *klokkiesbos,* bell-bush, with its attractive, hanging, bell-like purple flowers. This slender shrub has leaves with margins that are slightly thickened, ragged and crisp, hence the species name. It is currently Red Listed as Vulnerable, being a rare and restricted endemic known from only two sites in the valley of the Kouga. It was first found by Ernst van Jaarsveld in November 1984 north of the Kleinrivier.

The chances of finding a rare plant from a moving vehicle, even when it is a shrub that reaches a height of two metres, are fairly slim. Despite this we travelled slowly along the road in second gear. Suddenly Caryl called for a stop, jumped out of the car and ran back a few metres. "Here it is!" she called triumphantly.

It ticked all the boxes. Not only did it resemble the photo we had of it, but the location on an east-facing, dry, rocky slope, surrounded by Passerina bushes, together with the height of approximately two metres, purple, bell-like flowers, crisp-edged leaves and growth-form were all as described by Van Jaarsveld. Our excitement resulted in behaviour that might have amazed any passing Ferreira or Gerber, but no one drove by. Cameras were taken out and in the low light the purple bells with a dusting of rain drops made for some exceptional images. We eventually went on our way as happy as five year-olds with ice-creams.

Driving beside the Braamrivier we come across a house we photographed some years ago. It is sad to see how its condition has deteriorated. This is happening throughout the *platteland* as people move to the towns and cities hoping to find better paid work, and indeed safety at this time of farm attacks. Change is inevitable, but it is depressing to come across farmhouses, once loved homes cherished for a century or more that are now going to rack and ruin.

* * *

With the second British occupation in 1806, the Cape became a British colony and the inhabitants of the Onder-Kouga, British citizens. This made little difference to their way of life until the outbreak of the Anglo-Boer War in 1899 when, like many of their fellows, their sympathies lay with their fellow Cape-Dutch speakers in the Transvaal and Orange Free State. The advent of guerilla warfare in the latter part of the war and with it the arrival in the Cape of Boer commandos, resulted in a variety of acts regarded by the British authorities as treasonable.

Johan Andries Gerber's activities on Braamrivier were more criminal than treasonable. He hid food in a *bakkrans* on the farm and then claimed that it had been stolen from the farmhouse by British soldiers. As a result he was hauled off to Uniondale and in due course spent some time in the Uniondale gaol.

Far more exciting was the news that on the 11th of August 1901 the Gideon Scheepers Commando clashed with the 10th Hussars at Wanhoop, a farm just west of the Baviaanskloof and to the north of the Onder-Kouga. So far as the Boers were concerned it was a successful encounter, with one Hussar killed and four wounded.

The commando now headed south towards Misgund, and at Krakeel a group led by Pieter van der Merwe captured the local Justice of the Peace (JP), Jacobus van Niekerk and eight others. Shortly after this they added to their tally by capturing Mr Cloete, the magistrate, a Lieutenant Markotter of Haarlem and five men of the Uniondale District Mounted Troop (DMT). They followed this up on the 18th by burning to the ground Van Niekerk's house at Misgund. Van Niekerk and the other prisoners, having been marched ahead of the commando to Misgund, were now forced to witness the spectacle.

The Boers then moved to the east with the intention of replenishing stores at Humansdorp. However, near Twee Riviere they came into contact with the Uitenhage DMT under the command of Lieutenant Bonnin Hobson. The Boers were forced to backtrack with the DMT hard on their heels. In Humansdorp the Town Guard manned the trenches unnecessarily.

On the 16th the commando was back in Misgund where they set alight to Pace's Bar and Stone's general dealership.

Stirring stuff, and two young men that were stirred were Daniel Gerber of Braamrivier in the Onder-Kouga and his friend Pieter Kemp who was probably a *bywoner* on the same farm. They joined the commando and set out on an adventure that proved to be far harder and less exciting than they probably ever imagined. They did, however, survive the war and laid down their arms in June 1902 at Hopetown.

There was some initial excitement. With the Hussars close behind them, the commando reached Avontuur where they ransacked the shops and post office, before Scheepers headed for Dysseldorp in the west, and the inhabitants of the Langkloof and Onder-Kouga were left to pick up the pieces of their disturbed lives.

* * *

In April 1999, archeologist Dr Johan Binneman of the Albany Museum in Grahamstown was scratching away at the floor of a *bakkrans* up the Schrikkerivier from Brandkraal when he found a stone with painted figures. He recognised this at once as a gravestone, and with a paint brush he spent two days delving a little deeper. There under a layer of sticks and *gifbol - Boophone disticha -* leaves, he found a well preserved set of toes. A little more work and a complete skeleton in foetal position was revealed, together with beads and seashells around the head.

The find prompted a good deal of interest in both scientific and local communities. Despite Binneman's assurance that the "Kouga Mummy", as it came to be named, would be treated with respect and dignity, John Witbooi of the local Khoekhoen community feared that the grave-site would be destroyed and the remains displayed as a freak show.

"Bokka" du Toit of Humansdorp announced, to the surprise of many, that gunshot holes in the skull reflected recent aggressive history.

In order to set peoples' fears at rest Binneman met with interested parties in the Langkloof. Among those attending were the Permanent Secretary for the Department of Sport, Arts and Culture, Lindiwe Msengana-Ndlela, members of the Khoekhoen community and local farmers. Binneman gave a short history of events since the discovery, and what little was known to date about the Mummy: it was estimated to be at least 2 000 years old; its remarkable state of preservation – the *gifbol* leaves had played an important part in preserving the body – and future plans for the remains.

Binneman addressed his closing remarks to those farmers and their wives who were at the meeting: "The landowners are the most important people in my life, and the farmers in the Kouga and Bavianskloof are the friendliest bunch of guys – I've only been shot at once in 18 years."

Despite this meeting, wrangling continued not only between the scientists and Khoekhoen representatives, but also between rival Khoisan groups, the Inqua and the Gonaqua: to which group did the body belong? Local farmers also had their say as to on which farm the cave was to be found. Three years after the discovery National Government refused both Binneman and Maryna Steyn of the University of Pretoria permission to present information concerning the Mummy to their peers at international conferences.

Binneman was quoted as saying, "Disputes are deterring archaeologists from exploring the Kouga Mountains site further." To which he might have added; for the benefit of Onder-Kouga farmers, the Khoekhoen community, National Government and indeed the whole of humanity.

* * *

From Brandhoek one can drive the winding, rolling road to the R62, passing Kritplaas – possibly so named because sodium nitrate, an essential ingredient of gunpowder, was once mined there – to the turn-off to the Vosloos' farm, Hoeree. It is believed that while the commandos were in the area, Gideon Scheepers spent some time resting on Hoeree. Was this the first sign of the ailment that ultimately led to his capture by the British and later his execution? From there it is not far to the tar road. However, before traversing this section we chose, after leaving Brandhoek, to turn off and take the long road into the mountains and to the Ferreira farm of Kleinrivier.

Today Kleinrivier, under the name Kouga Wilderness, is besides being a working farm, a tourist destination, but when we first visited Nico and Melodie Ferreira on the farm, tourism lay in the future. Nico showed us around the *opstal* before his young son, Righard, who had recently completed matric, took over to show us more of the farm.

"Has your bakkie got four by four?" He asked. "Not? Well never mind. Climb into ours. It hasn"t either, but there's only one really bad bit. If we get up enough *voomah* we'll make it."

So we did, and when the bad bit came in sight he told us to hang on tight. We did so as the bakkie hurtled down the hill and bounced up the other side.

"Made it!" exclaimed Righard. "Man, if you can get a Toyota bakkie going fast enough you can get through almost anything." We believed him.

That evening we sat with Righard and his father. Righard talked of his ideas regarding adventure tourism for adrenalin junkies: climbing, abseiling, a giant *foefie* slide (today known as a zip-line) and similar stomach-churning activities. With Nico talk revolved not only around everyday farming activities, but also his ancestry, one of his antecedents being none other than Kwaai Martha Ferreira.

Then Melodie called us to the table. "This is a real Onder-Kouga meal: everything is from the farm," she said. We found our places at the table and admired the steaming dishes before us.

"*Ogies toe*," said Nico, and we bowed our heads while he said grace. And then we set to and ate enough for a week, or so it seemed.

That evening before drifting off to sleep I thought of the Kouga Mummy and Kwaai Martha and Coenraad de Buys and of all those others who over the centuries have lived for a while in this small paradise.

Joubertina, Krakeel, Louterwater and Misgund

A soft white duvet of cloud tumbles off the Tsitsikamma Mountains as we turn off the R62 into Joubertina to deliver an order of travel books to Office Solutions. Our destination comes as no surprise to us after reading on a local website that coffins were available from the hairdresser and fresh milk from a hardware store.

The majority of small country towns have a centre situated around the church, or a shopping and business area, or a combination of both, but not Joubertina. Here, besides a relatively large number of empty stands, one finds the church up the hill in P J Retief Street, towards the R62, some of the shops near the now disused narrow-gauge railway line in Hoofstraat, while others are scattered around the town, or beside the R62, to catch passing traffic. Joubertina is obviously a town of rugged individualists.

Not having obvious tourist attractions, its setting between the mountains is nevertheless appealing and the town has a charm and friendly atmosphere that grow on one the more one comes to know it.

Redclyffe Hotel, Misgund

It is a comparatively new town, having been founded in 1906, when the narrow-gauge railway arrived in the Kloof. It was named after W A Joubert, well-loved dominee of Uniondale from 1878 to 1893.

Isaac Schryver was the first, in 1689, to make written mention of what he called the *lange Kloov*, an indication that other Europeans had travelled this way before him. Then in 1773 the British plant collector, Francis Masson, noted that there were only seven or eight farms in the entire valley, and that they were subsistence farms, because the nearest market, in Cape Town, was too far away.

During the Batavian governance of the Cape, Commissioner-General De Mist and Heinrich Lichtenstein travelled along the Langkloof from Avontuur in 1803, and after crossing the Waboomsrivier met a colonist named Kritzinger rebuilding his house, which had been destroyed in the war of 1799. This was on the farm Onzer, a long-time Kritzinger property, probably farmed at the time by Jan Jacob and Johan Andries Kritzinger. The town of Joubertina is now situated on a portion of the farm.

De Mist and Lichtenstein then travelled on for a few kilometres to the next farm. There they met the owner, "a certain Olivier" who had not long before returned to his farm. As a result of the recent war he was so impoverished "that he had scarcely even bread and mutton to sell us". There was little of Olivier's house still standing, so De Mist and his party were forced to spend the night under canvas. Olivier was of course of the family we met earlier at Tweeriviere. The original house, or what remains of it, is now a shed.

* * *

With cloud continuing to cascade down the northern face of the Tsitsikamma, we turn in towards the village of Krakeel. Striding out purposefully along the road are two women, *doeks* on head, brightly coloured tops, and one wearing a black skirt, the other black track-suit pants. Black skirt has arms folded across her chest and a belligerent expression on her face. Black track-suit pants has obviously a lot to say, but appears less grim. They have marched from the RDP houses beside the R62 and appear to be on their way to the village. Black skirt unfolds her arms for a moment in order to shake a fist in the general direction of the village. We decide that now is not the time to offer them a lift.

Krakeel you may remember was where Pieter van der Merwe of the Scheepers Commando and his men captured the local JP, Jacobus van Niekerk and eight others. From here Van Niekerk and his fellow prisoners had little to eat and slept on the ground or on a table if they were lucky. They also had to walk, but unlike the two women on their way to the village, the men were forced to keep ahead of the mounted commando, and it was all of 24 km to Misgund.

Krakeel is a village similar to Tweerivieren; one that grew spontaneously and, unlike Joubertina, in the days before town planners and a multitude of rules and regulations. Just as in Tweerivieren, there are several small A-frame houses, but also two houses of special interest. The original farmhouse, which later became the hotel granted in 1770, is T-shaped, but the gables were added later. With the exception of some Graaff-Reinet buildings, the 18th century *trekboere* were seldom tempted to copy the *holbol* gables of the Western Cape.

A second house is dated about 1830 and is made up of three parallel, elongated but unconnected sections. Both houses are built of stone with yellowwood floors and ceilings.

The two 1885 cyclists, Frank Girdlestone and Charles Hallack, called in at the hotel in Krakeel. This, no doubt, was at the behest of Henri Dassonville of Assegaaibosch, for Monsieur Teran, who ran the hotel at Krakeel was Dassonville's old friend and compatriot. Charles Hallack in his record of their journey makes no mention of the French hotelier, but he does comment on their meeting a tiresome and "oratorical Boer" known by the name of "Klein Boel", who delayed their departure for some time. Somewhere in the Langkloof today there must be someone who knows of a Strydom, or perhaps, but less likely, a Kritzinger or Rademeyer, a talkative fellow who was nicknamed Klein Boel.

We continue on to Louterwater, a settlement that developed with the advent of the railway. The name comes from the river of the same name, meaning "pure water". It has been known by others: Apies, Groot Aapies, Klippendrift and Klipriviertjie. Should you stop beside an illegal roadside fruit seller and ask him from where his apples come, you may hear some other names. They never ever, so it seems, come from farms in the immediate vicinity.

Amongst all the Dutch names, the farm Somerset's Gift comes as a surprise. It was apparently granted to a Ferreira by Governor Lord Charles Somerset for his services during the fifth war on the Cape eastern frontier (1818-1819). It is by no means the only farm in the Cape with the same name. It seems that the Governor was keen to ensure that others were aware of his generosity.

* * *

Today the Langkloof is renowned for its apple and pear orchards. Seventy years ago when my English mother first saw the Langkloof in spring, she found the countryside breathtakingly beautiful. At last she had found somewhere in Africa that rivalled in her mind the soft green appeal of her native land in the spring. (In the years to come she grew to appreciate more the delights that were on offer in Africa.) To find how other Europeans reacted to the land, I went to the accounts written by some of the early travelers.

In April 1752 Ensign August Beutler travelled the length of the Langkloof on his way, amongst other things, to shoot elephants. Coming in from the west he noted at a point somewhere to the north-west of present-day Avontuur, that grazing was difficult to find as there was little grass, but plenty of *renosterbos – Dicerotthamnus rhinocerotis*. Nineteen years later Carl Thunberg, writing of the same area, found otherwise: "the land in the Lange Kloof is bare and without any shrubs and bushes, but abounds in grass."

Then came Anders Sparrman in October 1775, where he recorded from "Brak River", the start of the Langkloof so far as he was concerned: "In the Langkloof they made great complaints about piss-grass . . . though nobody could with any certainty point out any particular herb coming under that denomination."

It was the Englishman, John Barrow, in December 1797 by which time the blossom would have been over, whose description best fitted my mother's reaction: "Lange Kloof abounds with streams of water and good pasturage. The ground consists throughout of a fine rich soil." He goes on to mention the gardens and orchards and the mountains covered with snow in winter.

There are various mentions of fruit, often citrus, and orchards in the old accounts of the Langkloof, but with the difficulties involved in taking it to market, almost all of it was consumed in the valley. It took a canny Scot to recognise the possibilities.

In 1903 Alexander Baldie and his wife, Annie, née Wright moved from Port Elizabeth to the Langkloof, having bought the old Rademeyer farm, Misgund. Alexander brought with him 3 000 apple trees he had bought in the Western Cape. It was the start of commercial fruit-growing in the Langkloof. By the time the trees were established the narrow-gauge railway from Port Elizabeth was up and running. The transport problem had been solved and in time other farmers realised the opportunities offered by fruit farming. With the help of Alexander Baldie and the nursery he had established at Misgund, the orchards were starting to spread along the Kloof. The spring would never be quite the same again.

Alexander Baldie was succeeded by his second son, James, the start of a succession of James Baldies at Misgund, the next being James Alexander Baldie who married Joan Elizabeth Taute, a surname that will crop up again as we travel from the Langkloof and down the Voorkloof.

Today the Misgund orchards are still a Baldie family enterprise. After the death at a tragically early age of the fourth, James Wayne Baldie, his youngest brother, Robin, stepped up to the mark and together with other members of the family, including his mother doing the books, now oversees an enterprise more than a century old. The orchards, together with 250 head of cattle, provide work for 340 permanent staff and 120 seasonal workers. Over the years a happy working relationship has developed on the farm and in some cases generations of a labouring family have matched the generations of Baldies at Misgund.

Born and bred on the farm, Robin has never been afraid to get his hands dirty. His aunt, Kay Basson, tells the story of Robin and her son, Vernon, who nowadays is also a farmer near Humansdorp. The two young boys had been cooped up for days because of rain. When at last the rain stopped they begged to be allowed out to play. Seeing the mud outside the door she warned them to be sure not to get their clothes muddy. Sometime later they reappeared at the kitchen door with dirt from head to foot.

"Just look at you!" exclaimed Kay. "Mud everywhere."

"Yes," agreed the boys, "but not on our clothes," as they stood there proudly in the nude. *"n Boer maak "n plan!*

* * *

The long stone-walled building about five kilometres west of Misgund is an eye-catcher. Today it goes by the name of the Klip Hotel Country Store, Restaurant and Farm-stall. It, like the apples of Misgund, has Scottish connections. It was in 1926 that Glaswegian Harold Bayldon Smith bought the property.

Harold Smith arrived in Port Elizabeth at the age of three, completed a part of his schooling in England and, having qualified as a surveyor at the Cape, returned to Glasgow to become an architect. He was the son of George Smith, senior partner in Port Elizabeth of Smith, Sons & Dewar, Architects and Government Surveyors. In 1904 the firm sent Harold Smith to work as a surveyor on the narrow-gauge line to Avontuur. There he dreamt that one day he might own a Langkloof farm. Finally, in 1926 he was able to buy the ground which he named Redclyffe.

The impressive building that exists on the farm today was designed and built by Smith. At the time the main Port Elizabeth to Cape Town road ran through the Langkloof. However what with opening and closing gates, fixing punctures and dodging ruts and potholes, the best distance that most motorists could manage in a day was about 200 km. As Misgund was only a little more than that from Port Elizabeth, Smith envisaged a comfortable hotel for travellers.

He started levelling the site by quarrying the stone needed for the building. Only local, mainly unskilled labour was used to quarry stone and to build the hotel. Work started on the building early in 1932 and was completed 18 months later.

Every bedroom had a basin with running water and also a telephone; an unheard of luxury in a country hotel at the time. (The basins are still there.) In addition there was a tennis court and a swimming-pool. Smith, having weathered more than one hailstorm at Redclyffe, thoughtfully provided undercover parking for visitors' cars.

One thing was missing, a liquor licence. Smith refused to apply for one fearing that the availability of alcohol might result in hardship for his labourers and their families. Local legend has it that after dark it was amazing to see the number of motorists that visited their cars, having forgotten some essential item.

After the building of the National Road along the Garden Route and the introduction of petrol rationing during the Second World War, business tapered off at the Redclyffe Hotel. It was used briefly as a convalescence centre for wounded servicemen, but by that time Smith had already sold the hotel. He nevertheless retained his fondness for the Langkloof, visiting his old hotel just four months before his death in December 1962.

Smith incidentally was also very much involved with the historic cottage at No 7 Castle Hill, Port Elizabeth, close to where this journey began. The house was completed in 1827, one of the oldest surviving buildings in the city, and was once the home of the Reverend Francis McClelland, Colonial Chaplain in Port Elizabeth.

When, in 1938, Smith heard that the house was to be demolished, he immediately made an offer for the building, which was accepted. It is now a cottage museum where visitors are able to experience what life was like in the Settler City nearly two centuries ago.

Sitting enjoying a cappuccino on the stoep of the former Redclyffe Hotel we look out across the valley towards the border between the Eastern and Western Cape. This is a view that Harold Smith must often have enjoyed, perhaps sitting just where we are now.

"That's where the road-markings start," comments Andrew, who brought us our coffee, "there where you go into the Western Cape."

More importantly that is where Ongelegen is situated and the source of the Kouga River, but a visit to the source will have to wait for a while. At the moment we are tracking Boer commandos and cyclists.

* * *

Haarlem, Avontuur, Molenrivier, Eenzaamheid and Schoonberg

Approaching Haarlem we meet up once again with Charles Hallack and Frank Girdlestone on their bicycles. There are those that tend to overlook the extraordinary nature of their ride from Port Elizabeth to Cape Town. After all, even taking into account the poor state of the roads in 1885, the two cyclists were only travelling some 750 km (as the crow flies), a distance that today no accomplished mountain bike rider would find particularly daunting.

Hallack and Girdlestone, however, were forced because of bad weather and muddy roads to walk, pushing their bikes, for 240 km. People forget too that Hallack and Girdlestone were proud riders of "Huckling of Maidenhead" penny-farthing bicycles. The so-called "safety bicycle" which we ride today only appeared in Britain in the year of their ride.

The safety bicycle, with front and back wheels of the same size and with a chain drive from pedals to the back wheel, was known as such because one was far less likely to go over the handlebars. If one did strike an obstacle and go over, there was less distance to fall than when perched atop the big wheel of a penny-farthing.

Hallack, in his record of their trip omits to mention the number of "headers" they took during the journey. They also of course, wore no safety helmets, and must have been aware that headers were at times fatal.

The two young men had never before heard of Haarlem and were astonished by the well-kept cottages and "the prosperity pervading it". They stopped to speak to "a fine looking old (Khoekhoe) man" who told them some of the history of the settlement and sent them on their way with a gift of apples from his orchard.

Haarlem dates back to 1856 when Mr J C Taute, a well-known name in this district, established a township, with missionary work in the area being conducted by a Congregational Church minister. Four years later the mission was

149

transferred to the Berlin Missionary Society under Friedrich Prietsch who renamed the mission Anhalt-Schmidt, a name that never took on, particularly as the village remained Haarlem. Several of the widely spaced houses date from this period.

In 1865 a combined church/school building was erected, which with later additions, remains in use today as a school. In 1876 Prietsch returned to Germany and was succeeded by Howe, who in 1877 began work on the present church, which was completed in 1880 and which 140 years later remains practically unaltered. This applies not only to the exterior, but also to the church furniture, the stinkwood and yellowwood pews, the 1882 Gruneberg organ and the three elegant brass chandeliers. Architecturally, the church at Haarlem is one of the treasures of the Langkloof.

All rugby enthusiasts are aware of Haarlem's other claim to fame as the birthplace of August Frederick "Oubaas Mark" Markötter 1878-1957, the third son of German missionaries Christoph and Mari Markötter.

From starting school August showed an above average academic ability, but he also thoroughly enjoyed games of soccer with other boys from the village. It was while he was at school that he acquired the nickname "Oubaas", which stuck with him for the rest of his life.

At the age of 15, young Markötter lost his father: killed by a horse-drawn carriage in Humansdorp. The next year, 1893, having matriculated, he was enrolled at the Victoria College in Stellenbosch (later Stellenbosch University) where he was introduced to the game of rugby football. He was hooked for life. He qualified as a lawyer, but his heart remained on the playing fields of Stellenbosch where in due course he became the rugby coach.

During his rugby career he was a South African player, selector and Stellenbosch coach from 1903 to 1957. Fifty Stellenbosch players coached by the Oubaas were awarded Springbok colours, and 150 won Western Province colours. Eleven of the 1906 Springboks in the United Kingdom tour were from Stellenbosch. In addition it was he who created the position of 8th man and introduced the swing pass.

Back in his school days everyone at Haarlem recognised that young August was destined for great things. No one at the time imagined that he was to become a rugby legend. Perhaps in later years a few of his contemporaries thought wistfully of what an asset he might have been to the Haarlem soccer players.

* * *

Arriving at Avontuur from Haarlem, Hallack and Girdlestone looked for the hotel. Perhaps they enquired at the post office and were directed by Mr McIntyre, the postmaster at the time, to look behind the building where they met a "daunting dog" with "an awful projecting row of lower teeth". They were saved by the publican, a Mr Howell, who rushed out and explained that the teeth were as a result of an accident in its youth.

When next morning the two young men set out they took not the road to the west leading to George, as they had intended, but that to the south; the Prince Alfred Pass completed by Thomas Bain in 1867 and officially opened two years later. This was done on the advice of a local – Mr McIntyre? Mr Howell? – and is to some extent surprising. This route to Knysna is downhill practically the whole way, but it was just this type of road, steep and possibly rutted and rocky, that penny-farthing riders feared. It was on these roads that they were most likely to take a header. Some even went to the length of riding with their legs on the handlebars, so that if they did strike an obstacle they would then fly off feet first.

It is here that we say goodbye to the two young men. No mention is made in Hallack's record of any mishaps in the Prince Alfred Pass.

They were eventually met, on 10 April 1885, on the outskirts of Cape Town by members of the Cape Town Bicycle Club with whom they rode into the city. There followed newspaper interviews, telegrams and toasts "drunk in bumpers of champagne". They climbed Table Mountain and visited Robben Island, and went on excursions with the Club.

Soon after completing their momentous ride and returning to Port Elizabeth, the two young men left separately for the Witwatersrand. There, two years later, Charles Hallack died "tragically" in Johannesburg. Frank Girdlestone, in reporting the death of his friend, gave no further details.

* * *

Turning off the R62 and into Avontuur almost the first thing one sees is the impressive entrance to the farm, *Matt Zondagh Landgoed – Avontuur*, in black on white. The farm was granted to Matthys Zondagh in 1765, and has been in the family ever since. It was here that Commissioner-General De Mist and Heinrich Lichtenstein met Coenraad de Buys, and numerous other travellers also visited the farm.

The road into the settlement is immediately opposite the entrance to the farm. Along the way one passes a narrow-gauge steam locomotive on a plinth; other than for rusty, overgrown rails and rusting sheds, the only reminder of what once was the narrow-gauge railway terminus. A fence topped with razor-wire surrounds the locomotive. Copper piping has been replaced with brown plastic hose; a sign of the times.

Perhaps the old post office was once in the vicinity. After all, the presence of the locomotive seems to indicate that this is or was the centre of the village. In fact the present post office is less than fifty metres away, but it turns out that they cannot help us.

* * *

On the 27th January 1901 the Boers rode into Avontuur unopposed. They ransacked the post office and destroyed the contents of 11 mail-bags before riding off with the horses used on the Avontuur to Willowmore postal route.

In August the Scheeper's commando was in the area. Before their entry into the village, Van der Merwe and his men stopped on the farm Welgelegen. There Mrs Andre Meyer was shocked to see the condition of the prisoners, some with their shoes coming apart, dirty, hungry and exhausted. She spoke to Van der Merwe who agreed, after the prisoners had given their parole, to allow her to give the prisoners a meal and a bed for the night in her comfortably large farmhouse. As a result the prisoners, including Jacobus van Niekerk and the two Knysna Scouts, T Monk and John Rex captured at Haarlem were in much better condition when they finally arrived in Avontuur. They watched as the Boers not only burnt the mail, but also destroyed the premises. This probably explains why nobody knew of the whereabouts of the old post office when we asked a century or more later.

One thing that Van der Merwe apparently did not destroy was the telegraph-key. Mr James Burchell, the telegraph linesman was, so to speak, mentioned in dispatches. It was reported that he "displayed great courage and at great personal risk maintained telegraphic communications in his section of the coastal route" during the presence of the Boers.

* * *

A man sitting on a plastic baker's tray with a khaki cap and blue overalls is obviously interested in our presence, so we go and ask him about the old post office. He shakes his head but refers us to a man with a red beanie, black jacket, jeans and Chinese takkies, but he too has no idea. This comes as no particular surprise. Is anyone else likely to know? They shake their heads. How does one go about finding the location of a building destroyed more than a hundred years ago?

Driving out we pass the first and only woman to be seen in Avontuur that morning; a young mother and child. For an instant I think about stopping to ask her, but then drive on.

* * *

The commando, still shepherding their captives ahead of them, now set out into the Voorkloof to the west of Avontuur intent on burning those farms they believed belonged to *veraaiers* - traitors.

Approaching Molenrivier, the Taute family farm, they were spotted by young Charlie Taute. He at once grabbed a

153

horse and galloped to Herold where he knew there was a column of British troops. He was questioned by an officer, but then told to "cool off under a tree". The British refused to believe that Charlie had seen the Boers in an area where there was no road shown on the map.

Matthys "Thys" Taute of Molenrivier was later asked to form a troop of local volunteers to be based at the top of the Montagu Pass to help defend the town of George. This he did, one of his recruits being his son, Charlie. They went under the name of Taute Scouts. Commando leader General Jannie Smuts came into contact with them later. He was not impressed by their fighting spirit and regarded them as renegade Dutchmen.

Meanwhile Van der Merwe and his men went on their merry way burning farms, one of which was Molenrivier. The next door farm, Eenzaamheid belonging to C E Guest who became a member of Taute Scouts, was also put to the torch. A fortnight before the house and farm buildings were destroyed, Stephen, brother of C E Guest had joined the Scheeper's commando. Not all the Voorkloof farmers were, as Jannie Smuts declared, "British-inclined".

Having dealt with the "khaki-supporters" to his satisfaction, the men under Van der Merwe together with their prisoners proceeded on their way towards Herold where they ran unexpectedly into a British column. The Boers turned and fled leaving their frightened and weary prisoners behind. No doubt they were all delighted to be free once again, but for Monk and Rex there still lay ahead a long walk to Knysna on bare feet, for the British, of course, were heading in the opposite direction.

In October Charlie Taute had a personal meeting with Smuts, the famous Boer leader. The Taute Scouts, massively outnumbered by the 200 men of the Smuts Commando, fled from Dieprivier to De Plaat, where they over-nighted at the farm, Mount Hope. Next morning they were surprised by the arrival of the Boers. Thys Taute gave the order to saddle-up and ride for their lives. In his haste, Temple Pulvermacher, a friend of Charlie Taute, dropped his rifle and asked Charlie to pick it up for him. Charlie was having a problem with his horse. By the time he had handed it to Pulvermacher the Boers were almost upon them. They abandoned their horses and fled for the stoep of the house, where they fired a couple of shots at the Boers before going inside and locking the door. There they were joined by a third Scout, Danny Deneyson. It was not long before the attackers smashed the front door. The three Scouts decided to surrender. Charlie found a woman's white *kappie* and was about to stick it out into the passage on the end of his rifle, when his friend, Temple, ran out of the door. A shot rang out and Temple fell to the floor bleeding profusely, with a bullet through his thigh.

Smuts's right hand man, Ben Bouwer, advanced down the passage. He was furious. He accused Temple Pulvermacher of firing on them after he had surrendered and thrown down his rifle. He ordered the three to be lined up against the nearby fence to face a firing squad. Pulvermacher was incapable of standing. While the three waited with pounding hearts beside the fence, Smuts rode up and demanded to know what was happening. Ben Bouwer explained and various other Boers had their say.

Smuts then spoke to the prisoners. Having heard both sides of the story he told the three Scouts that as not all of the men that witnessed the event were in agreement as to what had happened, he was going to give the three the benefit of the doubt. However, he added, he hoped that in the near future he would meet them again and be able to shoot them all.

Pulvermacher was then handed over to the Boer "doctor", Carl Möller, a 25 year-old University of Edinburgh medical student, who could do very little for the young man. The bullet had severed an artery, and three hours later Pulvermacher died.

* * *

Petrus Johannes Taute bought the farm Molenrivier in 1815 from his wife's uncle, who was on the adjoining farm, Eenzaamheid. At different times there were various mills on Molenrivier, hence the name. (For a time in the mid-19th century

155

it was known as Mill River.) The oldest mill was a *Norsmeule* or Norwegian Mill, such as the one used by Spoorbek beside the Kromme.

For many years Molenrivier was a well-known stop-over on the route from the coast to the interior, particularly Graaff-Reinet. Governor Sir Harry Smith on his famous ride from Cape Town to Grahamstown in 1835 changed horses at Molenrivier.

General Smuts, two months after Pieter van der Merwe and his men destroyed what they could of the farm, spent three days on Molenrivier before heading for Mount Hope, and his meeting with Charlie Taute.

Later still the famous South African author, Pauline Smith, a friend of the Taute family, stayed on the farm which she described in *The Beadle*, a work acclaimed not only in South Africa, but by such critics as Arnold Bennett and William Plomer.

The opening line of the book reads: *For close on forty miles, from west to east, between the Aangename* [Kamma-nasie] *hills and the Teniquota* [Outeniqua] *mountains ran the straight grey road of the Aangename valley.* Standing at Molenrivier while reading the line it is easy enough to relate to the scene described.

Back to March 1901 and the arrival on Molenrivier of men of the Scheepers commando under Pieter van der Mer-we. Edith Taute, warned that they were coming, fled together with her daughters Edie and Millie, son Arthur and the recently arrived English governess, Miss Gayne, to Mill House (near the road). The Boers looted the house and shop, shot all the pigs and dogs, and broke the necks of all the poultry. They smeared the interior walls of the house with lard, emptied bottles of ink, unravelled cotton reels and poured condensed milk over the furniture. Next morning they smashed furniture and piled it up and soaked the curtains in paraffin before setting it alight. Fortunately it began to rain and at about the same time the 10th Hussars rode up and the Boers galloped off. The house, although badly damaged, was saved.

In the 1960s Ms Barbette Taute took on the job of restoring the original building. Repair work done immediately after the Anglo-Boer War had perforce been of a hasty nature. Now Ms Taute sought the advice of another family friend, the famous South African architect, Norman Eaton, who had been responsible for the restoration of Reinet House in Graaff-Reinet. Eaton and Taute spent hours discussing the project, and the architect drew up plans for the work, but before work could begin Eaton was killed in a car crash.

Barbette Taute nonetheless went ahead with the restoration of the oldest - for P J Taute had added to an already existing building - and most pleasing house in the southern Cape.

An interesting and ingenious small feature is the semi-circular fanlight over the front door. Few people give it a second glance, but look carefully; it is made up of half a wheel that first saw service as a part of the mill machinery.

Eenzaamheid is a part of the original land grant, which included Molenrivier, to Pieter Terblans, who is reputed to have been a miller. It is a fine example of an early Langkloof house, consisting of one long row of rooms, with reed ceilings in some of the rooms, an oven built into the kitchen and with a thatched roof. It is reputed to have been built in or about 1785 and is another architectural treasure of the area.

Roughly 17 km further down the road we turn in to Schoonberg, yet another farm with an interesting history. During the middle years of the 19th century the farm was owned by Peregrine Bertie Richardson, whose names immediately put one in mind of a character from the humourous writings of P G Wodehouse. Richardson however was a serious minded man who was particularly concerned for the material and spiritual welfare of the 70 men, women and children on his farm. He envisaged a village rather than a mission where the inhabitants, both of Khoekhoen and European ancestry, could both work and worship together. For this purpose he donated land and also money.

In December 1848 Bishop Gray of the Anglican Church in Cape Town met Richardson at Schoonberg. Gray was suitably impressed by the man and his ideas. Richardson expressed the wish to be able to build a church, and Gray after his return to Cape Town had his wife Sophy, an amateur but noted church architect, draw up a suitable design for Schoonberg.

Services at Schoonberg started in May 1850, and Gray, passing by on his way back home after a visit to Port Elizabeth, was involved and stirred by his experience.

On the 10th of March 1854 the church opened its doors, and the *Cape Monitor* reported: "(The) Sabbath was one much to be remembered by the people who worshipped together without distinction of class or colour." The following year Gray again visited Schoonberg to consecrate the church and purchased land in order to give the village a start.

You will not find the village there today, but Sophy Gray's delightful Church of St John the Baptist is still in good order and regular use. In 1982 the entrance porch was destroyed by fire, but a stone transept in keeping with the rest of the building took its place. The church is not only an architectural gem, but a suitable memorial to a remarkable man well ahead of his time, Peregrine Bertie Richardson.

Bo-Kouga and Uniondale

The introduction of the people of Uniondale to the trials and tribulations of warfare first occurred on the 20th of January 1901 when men of the Scheepers' Commando rode unopposed into the town. The local telegraphist, Ernest Dugmore, to judge by his letter home, rather enjoyed the experience. He wrote of the "tremendous excitement" when the Boers arrived and how they pulled down the Union Jack and ran up the Free State flag. They then turned their attention to the post office, by which time he had managed to hide four large mail bags and the cash box in the jailer's house. As he returned to the office the Boers marched in and demanded the latest telegraphs, which he told them he had sent to Cape

Town. They left unaware that the telegrams were rolled up in the blind above their heads.

Dr R Morrow had arrived in town as a locum only ten days earlier. Prior to his arrival he worked at a Prisoner of War camp and had purposely chosen Uniondale as being as far as possible from the war. He described how many white families fled, but "the Coloureds sat at home as silent as death. They knew that to Scheepers their lives were of little value". He met Scheepers at the Royal Hotel and watched him read letters taken from the post office. Scheepers also warned the hotelier not to serve drink to any Boer without special permission. Morrow also met Scheepers' second-in-command and good friend, the 25 year-old lawyer Hendrik "Henry" Hugo. Morrow, who instinctively distrusted Scheepers, found Hugo far more approachable and described him as "educated, genial and kindly disposed".

Later, when news arrived of an approaching British column, the Boers left Uniondale in a hurry, but not before looting the shops of Messrs Bernstein, Cellarius and Shear & Ryan, smashing the telegraph and burning the Magistrate's Court records. Then, having commandeered food and forage from the hotel, they locked the Rev E Matson together with the magistrate and the jailer into a cell and went off with the key. It apparently was "a terrible business" trying to free the three men.

Scheepers rode off towards Avontuur, but the people of Uniondale did not immediately see the end of his commando. Some days later some 30 Scheepers men, led by Piet van der Merwe, while riding for Dysseldorp, encountered a group of Hussars near Uniondale, and there was an exchange of fire, of which the Boers got the better.

When things calmed down Dr George Washington "Ben" Smith, the Boer doctor with the commando, was found by British troops bandaging one of their wounded officers. Smith finished what he was doing and was allowed to rejoin his compatriots.

Later two junior British officers under a white flag approached the Boer camp. With them they brought an invitation for Smith to pick up a field medical kit in Uniondale. Suspecting treachery, Scheepers was unwilling to allow Smith to go, but eventually did so after keeping a *rooinek* hostage until Smith's safe return. Smith came back the following day with not only a complete ambulance medical-kit, but also a supply of Players Navy-Cut cigarettes, which were much appreciated by the smokers.

More than a century after the event one is tempted to wonder irreverently whether or not the Brits were trying to kill the Boers by kindness.

* * *

The farm Rietvallei was originally allocated to Matthys Zondagh in 1765, but by 1856 the farm comprised of two portions, one owned by a Mr J A van Rooyen, the other by Mr A L du Preez. In that year Van Rooyen established a village he named Hopedale on his land. Four years later his neighbour also decided to lay out a village, which he named Lyon. By that time there was already a post office on Hopedale. No doubt Van Rooyen felt that this amounted to official recognition, which Lyon lacked. One gathers that there was a certain amount of tension between the few residents of the adjoining villages. The Dutch Reformed Church stepped in to cool fevered brows, and in 1865, to mark the reconciliation, named the united and attractive village Uniondale, laid out beside the Kammanasie River.

The work on the Dutch Reformed Church building started in 1878, and was finally completed in 1895. It is a fine light brown stone building with a tower, which caused problems and further differences in the community. Not that long after it was built, the tower collapsed. This gave rise to both alarm and discord in the ranks of the faithful. It was Dominee W A Joubert, the well-loved shepherd of the Uniondale flock from 1878 to 1893, and after whom Joubertina is named, who brought the situation under control.

Meanwhile the Anglicans were also busy with plans. It was in 1857 that Bishop Gray sent a young missionary, Edward Glover to serve the community of Schoonberg and other scattered Anglicans north of George including those at Hopedale and Lyon. The Bishop first visited Uniondale in the year of its union, and noted in his journal that there were about 300 souls there. Four years later he was back and bought an erf on which to build a church, for which of course his wife Sophy drew the plans. The church, a charming white-washed, thatch-roofed building, was eventually consecrated in 1876 by Gray's successor, Bishop West Jones. Sadly neither Robert Gray nor Sophy ever lived to see the little church completed.

There are several other old buildings in and around the town which add to its charm, including a mill and a Boer War fort. The mill was built by James Stewart over a period of two years starting in 1852. The wheel alone, the second largest in the southern hemisphere, must have taken much of the time. The mill remained in use for almost a century, closing down in 1950. The fort was one of several built during the war and has a commanding view of the town. The two buildings have an unusual connection, the renowned Afrikaans author Dalene Matthee.

Dalene Scott was born and brought up in Riversdale and it was there that she met and married bank clerk Larius Matthee. Every few years Larius was moved to another branch. While they were in Oudtshoorn Dalene studied music at Van Zyl's Music School and in Graaff-Reinet she achieved her licentiate in piano. She also took to writing short stories for Afrikaans magazines and had a half-day job as curator of the Hester Rupert Art Museum. This contact with the Ruperts led to her becoming one of Dr Anton Rupert's restoration team working on Stretch's Court, once the homes of emancipated slaves and today a part of the Drosdty Hotel.

In 1971 the Matthee family - there were by now two daughters - moved to Uniondale where Larius took over as manager of the Standard Bank branch. Dalene soon found herself making use of the skills she had acquired in Graaff-Reinet, restoring both Stewart's mill, and also the Boer War fort.

Larius, as a result of ill-health, was forced to take an early retirement in 1978, and the family moved to Hartenbos. It was there that Dalene settled down to write the "forest" novels for which she is famous. We were to come across her again later in our travels.

Besides the churches, mill and fort there are various other interesting old buildings in the town, many of them dating back to the 1870s. A walk around is not only worthwhile from the architectural point of view. We discovered too, that shops in Uniondale, like those in Joubertina, often serve a dual purpose. A butcher we visited had a sign up indicating that while placing an order for a leg of lamb, a Christmas turkey or a kilogram of sausages, it was also possible to be measured for a coffin, or take a chance and buy one off the shelf. We felt that the association of butchery with coffin-making was perhaps unfortunate.

* * *

Uniondale does not automatically spring to botanists' minds when plants are discussed, but it nevertheless has a strong botanical claim to fame. Two of South Africa's most notable plant collectors worked in the district during the 1860s, while a third collected there in the 1930s and 40s. None of the three were professionally qualified, but all three were later to receive honorary doctorates from South African universities. All three were from Western Europe and yet developed a passion for Cape plants.

In 1850 Harry Bolus arrived at Algoa Bay from England and moved to Grahamstown. Some years later he married Sophia Kensit, his boss's daughter, and moved to Graaff-Reinet where he established, together with his brother Walter, a general dealer's business.

A son, Alfred, was born to Harry and Sophia, but in 1864, aged six, he died of diphtheria. Harry was persuaded to take up botany to take his mind off his son's death, for which he blamed himself, having apparently not taken the sick boy's condition sufficiently seriously. In his diary he recorded collecting his first specimen on the 30th of April 1865.

After a very successful business career and notable scientific contributions, he bequeathed to the University of Cape Town his South African home, Sherwood, together with £21 000 to provide scholarships for needy students, his herbarium and botanical library, together with an endowment of £27 000 for their upkeep.

Peter MacOwan, a science teacher, emigrated to South Africa in 1862 to become headmaster of Shaw College in Grahamstown. It was during this time that he used his beam balance to ascertain the specific gravity of the stone from Hopetown that came to be known as the Eureka diamond.

In 1869 he moved to Gill College in Somerset East as science master. It was only in 1881 that he decided to devote the rest of his life to botany and left Somerset East for Cape Town to become the director of government botanic gardens and curator of the herbarium. By that time he had already published his *Catalogue of South African Plants* and stayed with Harry Bolus in Uniondale, perhaps at the Royal Hotel, before they went out together to tramp the veld and search for rarities.

Sir William Thiselton-Dyer in 1897 wrote of MacOwan and Bolus that they were the two who "will be forever memorable in the history of South African botany".

You may remember that we first met the third and later plant-collector, Henry Fourcade near Kareedouw. We will meet up with him again while on the Garden Route. Suffice it to record here that he too, like Bolus, was a general dealer at the time he investigated the Uniondale veld, and like Bolus bequeathed money and more to the University of Cape Town.

The opening sentence of Bolus's 1886 *The Flora of South Africa* would have rung true not only for MacOwan and Fourcade, but also for countless others: "Ever since the time of its first settlement the Cape has been a constant source of pleasure and delight to the botanist and the gardener."

* * *

We set off for Avontuur, leaving the Boer War fort on our left and after the crest of the hill, dipping down towards the river with the meticulously worked dry-stone walling of Thomas Bain's road on our left.

The Uniondale to Avontuur link was initially regarded as a minor road. It was completed by Bain in the 1860s while working on the Prince Alfred's Pass. The route he chose across the Gwarina (valley of the eland) involved some steep gradients and a river crossing, acceptable for a secondary road, but hardly up to standard in the 20th century.

In 1928 a new road was completed by a Mr Hawke. It was by and large an improvement, but the river was crossed by a bridge that meant right-angled turns having to be made on each side. This gave rise to profane language, especially by those in charge of ox-wagons, not yet in 1928 an entirely archaic form of transport, and the crossing became known as Hawke's Folly.

It was only in the 1960s that the offending bridge was removed and the road re-aligned, which involved considerable blasting, and excavating. At the same time the road was tarred.

The pass with its glimpses of the convicts' stone-work raised under Bain's direction is a reminder of all those who worked a century and more ago to make travel easier. And let us include Mr Hawke who did his best in difficult circumstances and whose Folly has since disappeared.

There have been floods and wash-aways since then, but basically there has been little change to the 10 km road that snakes through weathered red and orange cliffs with splashes of yellow lichen (of special interest to MacOwan) and which in season are decorated with scarlet-flowered aloes and brightly coloured mesembryanthemums (of interest to all three men).

At the Avontuur end of the road, some 300 m before one meets the R62, there is on the right a long, low building with a corrugated iron roof, but which was once thatched. It closely resembles a 17th century Middle German "all-in-one" farmhouse, with both living-quarters and stabling/cow-byres in one long building. As the founding father of the South African Zondagh family, Matthias Sonntagh was born in Wüstenwetzdorf in Turinge, now Germany, it is possible that the building dates back to shortly after the first occupation of the land by the family in 1765. Perhaps it is of later origin, but take a good look at it for there are today very few such buildings left in South Africa of a design that originated in northern Europe.

Remains of an Attaquas Kloof fort

8.

Three Outeniqua passes

Whether travelling from east to west or the reverse, the rugged and forested Tsitsikamma was an impassable barrier on the coastal route. The only alternative was to cross the Outeniqua Mountains. Thomas Bain not only conquered the mountains, he also pioneered a route through the Tsitsikamma.

Attaquas Kloof

We could hardly believe our eyes: pounding along the line between Holgate and Camfer was a mighty "Gammat", a GMAM 4-8-2+2-8-4 Garratt locomotive pulling a water tanker and a string of coaches. I was instantly transported back through the years to the start of school holidays and the two-day journey home. Of course at the end of the holiday there was also

166

the return journey to school, but memory plays tricks, and in my mind 70 years later it is always the start of the holidays.

We reversed into a farm-gateway, and hurried back on our tracks to Camfer and were in time to watch the crew complete taking on water before it set out again with a load of ardent steam *aficionados* in the special excursion train. The great locomotive passed us by, leaving behind a whisper of white steam and wheezing great gusts of grey smoke.

A special excursion in an out-moded form of transport; does anyone go on ox-wagon excursions on passes over the Outeniqua Mountains?

Camfer is situated close to the top of the Montagu Pass, but we were on our way to the oldest of the passes that carried travellers from the coastal plains to the east by way of the Langkloof, the pass named after the Khoekhoe inhabitants, the Attaquas.

We drove back towards Holgate Siding and along the R28 towards Oudtshoorn. Then back on to the dirt and via Wolwedans, what a wonderful farm-name, to Mount Hope, the farm which in 1901 belonged to Peter Heyns, a Western Province rugby player. It was at Mount Hope that Temple Pulvermacher died of a thigh wound, and where Charlie Taute and Dan Dennyson almost, but not quite, thanks to General Smuts, faced a firing-squad.

From there we drove beside the dusty bed of the Doringrivier, along which the commandos also rode to its confluence with the Kandelaarsrivier. The confluence also happens to be the intersection with the tarred R328 to the Robinson Pass and Mossel Bay, which is a good spot for a word of advice before we head further south towards the mountains.

The Attaquas Pass is only passable with a 4x4 vehicle or on foot. Whichever you choose, there are locked gates and permits are required for entrance into the Nature Reserve. Before planning a trip one should contact Bonniedale Holiday Farm at: +27(0) 44 695 3175. Nico Hesterman at Bonniedale, a sun-tanned, white haired and grizzle-bearded former game warden, has a treasure trove of information concerning the area, which he will deliver if asked, together with a twinkle in his eye and a delightful sense of humour. If your interests include back roads, natural history, together with a history of the San, Khoekhoe and early European travellers and farmers of the Swartberg, Outeniquas and elsewhere, Nico is your man. Give him a ring!

The northern end of the Attaquas Pass is at the farm Safraanrivier, but the first four farms at the northern end were only granted in 1756.

First mention of the Attaquas was by Lieutenant Hieronymous Cruse in 1668. He was at Mossel Bay on a trading mission during which he contacted the Attaquas who lived in a "mountain valley". The first Company official to make use of the valley to reach the interior was Ensign Isaac Schrijver in 1689, and in 1729 the first farm south of the pass, aptly but unimaginatively named Voor Attaqua Kloof, was granted.

Ensign August Beutler was perhaps better educated than the rank and file of Dutch East India Company officials. His father was a Lutheran pastor and his mother the daughter of a doctor of medicine. This may well account for his being chosen by Governor Ryk Tulbagh in 1752 to undertake an expedition into the interior to investigate the possibilities of developing the eastern regions of the Cape. So it came about that in March of that year a total of 71 persons with 11 wagons, one of which carried a boat, set off to climb the Attaquas Kloof Pass.

Beutler's expedition marked the beginning of regular traffic through the pass. Carl Thunberg, the Swedish traveller, sent his wagon up it in October 1772, and was back again, together with Francis Masson, who collected plants for Kew, the following year. Two days later Thunberg's countryman Anders Sparrman used the pass. By the turn of the century as many as a dozen wagons a day made their way up or down Attaquas Kloof and it had become an integral part of the *Groot Wagen-pad*, later to be known as the Colonial Highway, or *Kaapse Wagenweg*.

The opening of the Montagu Pass in 1848 marked the death knell of the Attaquas Kloof Pass, but with fewer and fewer wagons passing through, it nevertheless remained open for wagon traffic for some years. By the end of the century it was no longer in use.

The remains of a toll-house are still to be seen beside the road and, despite its no longer being in regular use at the time, the ruins of a fort erected by the British during the Anglo-Boer War. Those sent to man the fort must have hoped at times for a little action.

We walked the pass on a hot day when horseflies were a problem, and Nico the natural-historian was quick to inform us that slapping horseflies aggravates the problem. Squashing a horsefly releases pheromones that attract others of their kind. Rather shoo them away, preferably before they have sunk a proboscis into your flesh.

When Nico Hesterman is not telling you about horseflies or how to spot caves once inhabited by stone-age people, by the plants growing immediately below the *bakkrans,* or of the 26 leopards living in the mountains, of which neither he nor you are likely to see a solitary example, get him to tell you the story of Gerrit Johannes "Bloubaard" Swanepoel.

In short, Swanepoel was a violent man. He had already served a two year sentence for flogging a Khoekhoen servant maid and was suspected of far worse crimes. While serving his two year sentence he met Willem Viljoen who, after his release, joined Swanepoel on his farm and became involved with Swanepoel and his misdeeds. One of these involved the disappearance of a certain Jan Willemse whom it was believed had been murdered by Swanepoel with Viljoen playing a supporting role. Justice Menzies investigated but found the evidence implicating Swanepoel and Viljoen was merely hearsay. He released the two. Viljoen however, now sued Swanepoel for unpaid compensation, which Swanepoel denied that he owed. In the course of events Viljoen spilled the beans about the death of Willemse. In March Swanepoel was found guilty of the murder by Mr Justice Cloete and was sentenced to death. On the 28th of April 1856 Swanepoel was hanged in Pacaltsdorp, the last public hanging in the George district. His wife Catharina collected his body, placed it in her horse-drawn spider, and took it home to the farm, where she buried her late husband not far from their home.

There is a good deal more to the story than appears here. It is best told by Nico Hesterman beside Swanepoel's grave with a wind soughing through the leaves of the nearby bluegum. At night with a waning moon and scudding cloud would be even better.

* * *

Just six kilometres to the east of the Attaquas Kloof Pass, is the modern Robinson Pass. One of Thomas Bain's master-pieces, it was opened for traffic in 1869 and named after the Chief Inspector of Public Works, Mr Murrell Robinson Robinson. However, it was the Montagu Pass, which was opened for use in January 1848 that from that date became the preferred route for travellers to the east coming from Swellendam or Riversdale.

Montagu Pass

The story of the Montagu Pass actually starts in 1811 with the establishment of George Town, today just George. From the start it was apparent that there was a need for a route over the Outeniquas from the new town. Landdrost Adriaan van Kerwel was keen to see the new town succeed and drew up a report noting that he had found a route for such a road. What was more he offered to construct the pass for just 5 000 rix-dollars. (At the time 5 000 rix-dollars was the equivalent of £1 000 sterling - £120 000 in today's money [R2,4 million]. In December 2020 an 1830 40 rix-dollar note was on sale in Johannesburg for R4 000.)

Governor Sir John Cradock accepted Van Kerwel's report and work began almost at once, in February 1812. The pass was to be nine kilometres long and climb over a thousand metres. Much to the surprise of the local inhabitants the road was completed to Kerwel's satisfaction two months later. Despite it having been named Cradock Kloof in honour of the Governor, there were soon complaints that reached gubernatorial ears. Sir Charles Bunbury, the geologist and botanical collector wrote: "The road over Cradock Kloof certainly deserves its reputation, being the most formidably bad, if not of all the roads I ever saw, assuredly, of all that pretend to be passable by wheels."

The replacement, the Montagu Pass, was only completed in January 1848 at a cost of £71 598 and the use of an average 250 convicts at any given time. It was built under the supervision of an Australian surveyor and roads inspector, Henry Fancourt White, who also had a road in central Port Elizabeth, Whites Road (now John Kani Road) named after him. The pass, however, was named after John Montagu, the Colonial Secretary at the Cape. As opposed to the three days that it took an ox-wagon with two teams of oxen to climb Cradock Kloof, an ascent of the Montagu Pass was possible in three hours with a single span.

When White set out to build the Montagu Pass he first set up a construction camp on the approach to the mountains. This became known as Blanco, a play on his surname, and he built a house, later to become, thanks to his son, Ernest Montagu White, a mansion, which the son named, "Fancourt". It now forms a part of the Fancourt Hotel and Golf Estate, and is a provincial heritage site.

Work began on the pass in 1844 and still visible on the old pass are the toll house ,with its massive stone walls, and about halfway up the scattered stones of a more temporary building, the former blacksmith's workshop.

The pass was designed not just with ox-wagons in mind, but also with horse-drawn vehicles, Cape-carts and spiders. This being the case the surveyor, Dr William Stranger, saw to it that no gradient was steeper than 1 in 6 and it was reckoned that for much of the way horses could trot.

Bishop Robert Gray and his wife Sophy walked the pass in "just an hour". She was much taken with the road and the

171

views it offered of the surrounding countryside, and during one journey along it made six sketches "of the magnificent pass", and was deeply impressed by the beautiful wild flowers.

Among the views to be seen today is one to the east that includes the route of the former Cradock Kloof Pass, marked by white painted cairns. They give some idea of the steepness of the old Cradock Kloof Pass. Look to the west and you see the gentle gradient and sweeping curves of the Outeniqua Pass, completed in 1951.

After leaving George, the railway line winds its way slowly upwards, passing the siding of Power and coming ever closer to the road. By car one negotiates a sharp bend to drive beneath the stone bridge that carries the line shortly before it reaches the siding of Topping. From there on it was easy going for the steam locomotives until they reached Camfer.

The first car to traverse the Montagu Pass was a 1902 Darracq owned by Dr Owen Smith and Donald McIntyre. It reached the top with only one slight hold-up along the way, when a passing horse was required to assist over a short, difficult stretch. The pass remained the main route to the north from George until 1951, but was never really suited to motor traffic.

On one of our trips down the pass we met, radiator to radiator, a large German 4x4 with outsize wheels. It seemed that there was no possibility of passing, but the driver of the German vehicle indicated that he would pull right over against the mountain. He proceeded to do so with the tyres of the 4x4 in the gutter at the base of the cutting. By pulling in the left side mirror, we were just able to inch past. We stopped and went back to thank him. Meanwhile he started up and tried unsuccessfully to extricate his vehicle from the gutter; the wheels being firmly jammed in. At this point another difficulty arose; he could not leave the cab as his door was too close to the mountainside. Nor could he climb out of the passenger's door as there was some obstruction between the front seats. Eventually a cell-phone call to George had to be made to ask for help.

Do not let this deter you from taking a drive up or down one of the most spectacular of the Cape passes.

Prince Alfred's Pass

We leave Avontuur in early morning sunshine and head due south for the Zondaghsberg, following around a section of its skirt before starting the steep descent. Ahead lies a blanket of cloud with here and there island peaks that breach the rumpled white bedding.

I am reminded of a trip many years before and travelling in the opposite direction. On that occasion too I had left early, but from Knysna, and under lowering grey skies. Long before reaching the halfway mark the regular thump of the windscreen wipers had become the accompanying soundtrack to the journey. During the final climb they were clearing sleet and then snow from the screen. Shortly afterwards the VW Beetle slid to the side of the road and efforts to dislodge it ended in spinning rear wheels.

Amidst the snow and slush and ankle-deep mud I used an enamel plate to dig a way out and filled the track with fynbos. It worked and I was on my way again. I heaved a sigh of relief approaching Avontuur.

Just outside the town police were setting up a barricade. One came across to the car.

"Where have you come from?" he asked.

"Knysna."

"Don"t you know the road is closed?" he said as, shaking his head at my stupidity he pulled the drum aside to let me through.

Today there is no barricade and despite the cloud lower down we anticipate no problems.

* * *

Travelling inland from Knysna during the middle years of the 19th century involved either travelling via George or Pletten-

173

berg Bay. The road to George was of "a fearful ruggedness", according to Andrew Geddes Bain. One was then faced with the rigorous climb up the Cradock Kloof or later the Montagu Pass. If going via Plettenberg Bay one had the terrors of Paardekop. As the Reverend Latrobe wrote in 1816: "With the help of our men, bearing the wagon upon either hand, as the slope of the road required, and suffering our cattle to rest every two or three minutes we at length surmounted every difficulty and got safely across this dreaded mountain". This decided Andrew Geddes Bain, father of Thomas, that a new, direct road should be built from Knysna over the mountains to the Langkloof. He and his son set out in 1856 to locate a suitable route. Battles in Parliament as to the route and the money required to build the pass were still to come, but were eventually fought and won. Work eventually began in 1862 from the bottom of the pass and reached Avontuur four years later.

* * *

With the cloud gradually clearing and the sun's early rays warming the air, we travel slowly down the mountain with frequent stops to admire the view. Spectacular as it is, it is possibly more beautiful when the declining sun tints the rocks with a variegation of rose and gold. Yet even now, with every gully and fold thrown into deep shadow, the form of this ancient landscape stands out in massive relief.

On a tight left-hand bend above Voogtskraal (or Fuch's Kraal as it appears on the old maps) we stop for a cup of coffee. Someone at sometime planted poplars here, which now have reached a great height. Although aliens, they do not appear out of place here; rather standing out as markers on the long climb up the mountain, or providing a shady nook on the way either up or down.

Nearby there is a show of indigenous vegetation amongst which we spy stokroos or African hemp – *Sparrmannia africana* – with its heart-shaped leaves. Its pretty white flowers have within a dash of gold and red to emulate the rocky heights above. Botanically it is of course named after the

Swedish traveller, Anders Sparrmann, who introduced the plant to European horticulture in about 1778. The English common name of African hemp dates back more than two centuries to when it was thought that it might prove to be a viable alternative to Indian hemp for the production of ropes and sacking. It was found to be unsuitable, but in Europe this bush or small tree remains a popular conservatory plant, lighting up the grey northern skies as it did our poplar-bower.

Voogtskraal is situated in the section of the pass that was the most difficult to build. Assistant Chief Inspector of Roads, Mr Murrell Robinson Robinson, was doubtful as to the line chosen by Bain, and as to whether or not the road would ever pay for itself. Robinson also suggested that the convict station be moved from its original position at Yzer Nek (today Ysternek) to De Vlugt by July 1863, and that the inspector and district engineer should also move so as to be always available on site. This last remark must have been hurtful to Bain who was known for his close supervision of the work in hand. When finally Avontuur was reached Robinson made amends for his earlier criticism:

> *I inspected the whole of the undertaking and I have to express my great admiration of the ability displayed by Mr Thomas Bain in its construction. . . the work itself is, I believe, at least equal to work of the kind in any part of the world.*

Just beyond our coffee-stop is Reed's Poort (now Rietpoort), where the work was particularly difficult, with some of the dry-stone retaining walls being more than 15 metres high. The road crosses the Voogtsrivier seven times, and much blasting was required. It was also necessary to cut grooves in the rock to hold the stinkwood beams supporting the bridges. It was only in 1930 that the stinkwood beams were replaced with reinforced concrete. Beyond Reed's Poort lies De Vlugt and an alternative route to the west linking up with the Langkloof road.

The move to De Vlugt was made early in 1863. Accommodation for 100 convicts was erected together with housing for the visiting doctor, chaplain and magistrate, stables for horses and mules, a magazine and a house for the Bain family, which still stands in good condition. On a 1904 railway-map, the convict station, east of the river, appears as the Village of Edmonton.

Two incidents clouded the lives of the Bain family during their stay in the lovely but lonely valley of the Keurbooms River at De Vlugt. Their daughter Alice, born in the July before the move to De Vlugt, was knocked off the high stoep of the house by an irate turkey. She lingered for some weeks, but died at home, for where could they possibly take her? Her father carved her gravestone and she was buried in the garden. Johanna Bain went on to have more children, in fact her twelfth (and last) was Constance' born in 1878.

The second incident involved Thomas's father, Andrew Geddes Bain, who had taught his youngest son to be a *padmaker.* While in Britain the elder Bain suffered a heart-attack and returned at once to Cape Town arriving in October 1864. The Bains at De Vlugt received a telegram regarding the old man and of his being in no condition to continue his journey home. Thomas Bain immediately applied for leave to visit his father. His application was turned down on the grounds that no one could be found to act for him. In due course another telegram arrived announcing the death of Andrew Geddes Bain on the 20th October 1864.

Despite these trials, Georgina, the fourth Bain child, in later life remembered the years at De Vlugt as one of the happiest periods of her life. There were picnics and expeditions and she and her siblings all learnt to ride. Their mother taught them to read and write while their father taught them about the rocks and plants, animals and stars. Nights spent in the house at De Vlugt with her mother, Johanna, singing while her father played the violin or concertina. And there were the visitors, some of them famous, such as, in 1867, Prince Alfred, Queen Victoria's second son, in the forests to shoot an elephant. The Prince took home with him a map her father had drawn and a walking-stick he had carved for the Prince to give to the Queen.

At Dieprivier there is a picnic spot. Many years ago some-one planted lemon trees here and some have survived, but it is not often that one sees a lemon ripe for the picking: the baboons usually beat one to it. There beside the road is a me-morial plaque unveiled on the 150th anniversary of the birth of Thomas Bain.

To honour the memory of
Thomas Charles John Bain
(1830-1893)
to whose dedication and
skill as a road engineer
the people of South Africa
owe this fine mountain
pass and several others
in the Cape.

Not far further south is Kruisvallei where the road to Plettenburg Bay by way of Paardekop, Kransbos and Wadrif-shoogte winds its way eastward.

The original convict station was built at Yzer Nek (now Ysternek), with the usual convict accommodation, plus hous-ing for constables, overseers, blacksmiths and odd-job men. There were workshops and stables, all of wattle-and-daub construction with thatched roofs. The entire settlement was destroyed by fire in 1860 and the replacement was built from wood and corrugated iron. Many of these buildings were lat-er moved to De Vlugt.

It was at Yzer Nek that Bain's work as a roadmaker really began. Up to this point the most important task had been the removal of trees; forest giants up to 21 metres high. It held up the actual pass-building and worried Mr Robinson. It seemed that no real progress was being made, but Bain knew what he was about. The 70 km of road that he built was not only completed on time, but at a total cost of £10 632, roughly £4 000 under budget.

A few kilometres further south brings one to the Forestry Station of Diepwalle. The rugged passes together with rolling

177

farmland are now behind one as one enters the forest proper of stinkwood, yellowwood, assegaaibos, ironwood and witels. Here too one might come across *een van die ou grootes* – one of the famed Knysna elephants that once frequented this area.

Diepwalle was also once the terminus of the South Western Railway Company line from Kysna. The possibility of extending the line to Avontuur was once mooted, but nobody took that too seriously. Work on the 35 kilometre line started in 1904 and the rolling-stock consisted of four locomotives and wagons for carrying logs and a single passenger vehicle, a home-built caboose, sufficient for a few passengers. The timetable showed three trains a week leaving the Knysna terminus at The Recreation Ground and stopping at Templeman's Mill, Park Station, Brackenhill, where Thesen's Mill was situated, and finally Diepwalle. Surprisingly the little train carried a good number of passengers going off to see the forests, and with some luck perhaps an elephant. This was especially the case during the summer holidays. However, it was not enough to pay the bills, and on the 4th of April 1949, the little train with its battered wagons made its last journey.

One reaches the N2 opposite the turn off to Noetsie. This marks the end of the pass named after Queen Victoria's second son Prince Alfred. The entire drive from Avontuur to the N2 is an experience that has never failed to impress travellers.

Those inveterate travellers, Bishop Robert Gray and his wife, Sophy, went up the unfinished pass in 1865. On horseback they reached De Vlugt, where they left their horses with the Bain family and completed the journey to Avontuur on foot. During the course of the walk they were soaked to the skin. Four years later, with the pass now complete and officially open; they ventured down "the lovely pass" and were once again caught in heavy rain. On neither occasion so it seems, were their spirits dampened.

Attaquaskloof to Bartlesfontein

Bouncing down the dirt road from Attaquas Kloof to Herbertsdale pulling a veil of dust behind us and with a clear blue sky above, I begin to wonder, as I so often do, about the name of the small dorp we are approaching. What was Herbert, so quintessential an English name, doing here among the *boere* of the southern Cape?

The town itself, to judge by the tarred main road, the clean streets, the well-maintained houses and shops and the 20th century Dutch Reformed Church, is prosperous. Surrounding the town are green farm lands dotted with occasional bluegums. Herbertsdale is the sort of country town that many city-dwellers hanker after in the first quarter of the 21st century.

It was relatively easy to find out that the town, founded in 1865 on the farm Hemelrood, was named after James Beeton Herbert, part owner of the farm. Now the work began: what brought him to this part of the southern Cape, and where did he come from? Not all the answers to my questions could be found.

In 1813, 26 year-old master mariner George Herbert, James's father, arrived in Cape Town aboard the *Hope* from Portsmouth. At different times George captained various ships sailing between England and the Cape, but also the coasters *Young Phoenix,* between Cape Town and Plettenberg Bay, and the *Iris,* between Table and Algoa Bays. In March 1820 he became a founder member of the Commercial Exchange and ten years later entered into partnership with John Thornhill. The ship chandler business of Herbert & Thornhill, with premises at No 17 Heerengracht, one of the best addresses in town, flourished.

Two years after his arrival George Herbert married Christina Johanna Middelkoop. Their offspring were thus half English and half Dutch; the boy who became the man after whom Herbertsdale was named being their eighth child.

At the time there was a growing coastal trade between Cape Town and Algoa Bay, with ships also calling at Port Beaufort, Mossel and Plettenberg Bays. George Herbert was very much involved in this trade, which may have resulted in his son moving eastwards to represent his father's interests.

Whatever the reason may have been he soon found a good reason to stay, in the guise of Johanna Wilhelmina Bland, the daughter of Daniel du Plessis Bland, a member of the Legislative Council at the Cape.

Johanna's paternal grandfather, John Bland, had come from England to the Cape to seek his fortune and he too had married a local girl, Cecilia du Plessis, and gone on to become a successful businessman and farmer in the Riversdale district.

Today the Bland family is commemorated in Bland Street, one of Mossel Bay's foremost thoroughfares, and James and Johanna Herbert's children, Cecilia, George, Amelia and Anna, despite their names, would have been more Dutch than English.

* * *

Driving out of Herbertsdale we are still on tar and heading across the coastal plain for the waters of the Indian Ocean, passing green fields and placid dairy herds. These are followed by patches of stunted coastal shrubs. The road winds its way through low hills for some kilometres and we pass two overall-clad men sitting on the guard-rail to watch what little traffic there is go by. There are turn-offs to Heuningklip and Cooper, but not an antelope nor an ostrich to be seen. At long last we see in the distance the flames of burning waste gas at the PetroSA (formerly Mossgas) plant at Bartlesfontein Siding.

Bartlesfontein is another unusual name to find in this area, but its origin is easier to explain, being the result of careless work by a clerk. The farm on which the siding is situated is Bartelsfontein, Bartel being a Dutch/Afrikaans name. The clerk in transcribing the name either made a spelling mistake or assumed that the siding was named after former

Cape Governor, Sir Bartle Frere 1877-1880. The line, a successful private venture by the New Cape Central Railways, only reached Mossel Bay from Worcester in 1907, so it was probably the former rather than the latter error that the clerk made.

It was only in 1925, that this private railway line, one of the very few that ever made a profit from start to finish, was incorporated in the South African Railways.

During the Cretaceous Period, 65 to 145 million years ago, oil and gas were formed from ancient marine organisms and trapped beneath rocks that now lie under the ocean off the southern Cape coast. In 1970 the Placid Oil Company, of Dallas, Texas, drilled a borehole 85 km south of Mossel Bay on the Agulhas Bank. Gas was found but not in payable quantities. It was ten years later that Soekor, a South African government-owned corporation established in 1965, drilling just three kilometres from the original Placid strike, found sufficient gas to warrant further exploration. On the strength of their results the decision was taken to build an oil from gas plant beside the railway line at Bartlesfontein Siding.

Then in 1990 a viable reservoir of natural oil was discovered 45 km from the original finds, and in January 2020 Total Oil announced the discovery of their *Brulpadda* – bullfrog – oil field, the first in the Outeniqua Basin, 175 km off the coast. Will this prove to be an economical source of oil and/or gas, sufficient to keep the flames burning on the stacks at the PetroSA plant?

We stand and look, though hardly admire, this sprawling industrial complex perched on the plain. Of course, it does serve a useful purpose, but it is hardly a thing of beauty, and what will happen to it once the available reserves of fossil fuel are gone?

With our backs to the plant we instead take a photo of the forgotten siding name-board before climbing into the Isuzu. Using PetroSA fuel no doubt, we drive to the N2, and amongst the traffic to which we have become unaccustomed, travel the last five kilometres into Mossel Bay.

Angra dos Vacqueiros - Bay of the cowherds

We stand on Cape St Blaize looking out over Mossel Bay. Not far beyond the harbour is the spring where the early seafarers filled their water-butts, and the milkwood in which, in 1501, Joao da Nova tucked despatches into an old shoe for delivery at some arbitrary date in the future, if and when they were discovered by a friendly "postman". Further down the slope is the cave visited in 1601 by Paulus van Caerden. He reported that it was full of mussel shells and so named the bay Mossel Baai. In 1804 Heinrich Lichtenstein climbed up to the cave and he too found mussel shells, but we saw no sign of them.

It was the Portuguese that named the area beside the ocean, *Aguada de Sao Bras* – the watering place of St Blaize – and so the outcrop on which we stand became Cape St Blaize. It is now crowned with a squat, totally white lighthouse. We were pleased to discover that the lighthouse was connected with our old friends, whom you may well remember, Captain Francis Skead, of the Seal Point Light, and Inspector of Public Works, Mr Murrell Robinson Robinson, who was so impressed by Thomas Bain's work on the Prince Alfred Pass, and who also visited the site of the Seal Point Light.

Here, as at Seal Point, Captain Skead was called on to select a site, remembering that the Mossel Bay light was built more than a decade before that at Seal Point. His choice of site was, to our eyes, the obvious one, but we were pleased to read that it "met with universal approval". What was more there was a quarry at hand that "proved equal to the most sanguine expectations", producing very durable sandstone.

The lighting apparatus was ordered from England and Captain Skead drew up the sailing directions and sent them for publication.

In 1862 Mr John Goodman was contracted to build the living-quarters and the tower for £927 and no less a personage than the Governor, Sir Philip Wodehouse, was called on to lay the foundation stone. There was a proposal that the light should be named after him, but nothing came of it.

In March the first keeper of the light, Mr John Armstrong, "being of good character" was appointed. He was to receive £90 per annum and free quarters.

Not long after the light was lit there were complaints that it was not, as was stipulated, visible 15 miles (24 km) from the shore. Mr Robinson was called on to investigate when next he was in Mossel Bay. This eventually resulted in a new lamp being installed by Mr Joseph Flack, also associated with the Seal Point Light, and whose mortal remains now rest in the Humansdorp cemetery.

Lighthouse keepers were given strict instructions regarding the upkeep and maintenance of not only the light, but also the buildings under their care. The floor and base of the lighthouse were not under any circumstances to be used for "domestic purposes". Cleanliness both inside and outside the building was to be ensured at all times, and "no dogs, poultry or other animals" were to be allowed inside the buildings. Despite this, an inspector of the Public Works Department visiting the Cape St Blaize Lighthouse in 1880 noted that although the accommodation, tower and light were satisfactory, "goats must not be kept in the quarters".

Pauline Smith, whom we first encountered on the Tautes' farm, Molenrivier, writing her classic book, *The Beadle*, also visited Mossel Bay, which in another of her books, *Platkops Children*, she referred to as Zandtbaai. She describes how one of the duties of the keeper of the light was to keep a lookout for the weekly steamer to and from Cape Town:

An' when he sees it he puts a ball on a cross-stick to let the hotel man an' all the other people in Zandtbaai know. An' the nearer the ball gets to the middle of the stick the nearer the steamer is to Zandtbaai. An' when it's right up to the middle, there the steamer is right in the bay an' the launch goin' out to it with passengers from the jetty.

(Unfortunately Paoli, the little girl writing the description of the keeper's duties, together with her father, Dr Smith from Oudtshoorn, missed the boat due to the "hotel man" over-sleeping.)

Did the lighthouse keepers witness the wreck of the *Mary*? I presume they must, but have found no mention of it. This British, 547 ton teak-built ship, while on a voyage from Madras to London with a cargo of indigo and dye-stuff, put in to Mossel Bay on the 9th of July 1824 to take on fresh water. She went aground and was a total loss.

Even if the keepers by some chance missed seeing the wreck they would have noticed the daily beach-walks of a former British sailor known locally as "Mossel Bay Jack". Jack scraped together a bare living by collecting sea-shells that he sold, at three rix-dollars for the equivalent of a wagon load, for lime-burning. Occasionally he added to this by collecting oysters at low tide. The wreck of the *Mary* added substantially to his income in the form of "treasure" chests containing indigo and dye-stuff, which he exchanged with a local trader for groceries and bottles of "Cape smoke". While this bounty lasted Jack lived like a king.

The quarry produced stone not only for the lighthouse but for many of the buildings in the town. The stone was considered to be long-lasting and relatively easily worked by the Scottish and other stonemasons who erected public and commercial buildings, banks, churches, schools and houses. To judge by what is still to be seen today, they were correct in their suppositions.

During the ostrich feather boom, many of these buildings were erected with feather money, but fortunately the Klein Karoo was a source of not only feathers, but a good deal of other agricultural produce. Still, the feathers certainly made a difference. In 1910, during the feather boom, South Africa exported 869 281 pounds (394 300 kg) of feathers from Port Elizabeth and Mossel Bay. By 1920, when the bottom had fallen out of the feather market, less than a half of that amount was sent overseas.

Despite the fact that many of the old stone buildings have been demolished, there are still a number to be seen, mostly in Bland and Marsh Streets, which run parallel to one another, and also in Church Street at right-angles to the other two, leading up the hill from the harbour and Dias Museum.

In 1902 the Mossel Bay Boating Company built two stone warehouses together with offices and stables for horses and mules. Gradually these interesting buildings were taken over by, first of all, the Cape Government Railways, and after the liquidation of the Boating Company in 1917, by the South African Railways & Harbours. On the sea-side of the building there is a slipway which enabled cargo to be dragged up and into the building.

On the corner of Marsh and Mitchell Streets we have a reminder of two other regular travellers that we have come across on our journey: Bishop Robert Gray and his wife Sophy, the talented church architect.

Robert Gray first visited Mossel Bay in September 1848, the year in which the town of Aliwal was founded on the shores of Mossel Bay. Governor of the Cape at the time, since the 1st of December the previous year, was none other than the swashbuckling Sir Henry "Harry" George Wakelyn Smith, hero of the Battle of Aliwal in India; hence the name of the town. However, there was another Aliwal on the banks of the Gariep in the north-east Cape. To distinguish between the two the names were changed to Aliwal North and Aliwal South. The residents of Aliwal South did not care for the name and never used it, so the town kept the name of the bay, Mossel Bay.

In 1850 ground was granted by the government for the building of a church and school. Four years later building began, coinciding with arrival of the first Anglican priest, the Reverend Thomas Sheard. By the time of the Bishop Gray's next visit, in September 1855, he could record that the "exceedingly neat" building was finished and he hoped that it would serve "for a few years the double purpose of School and Chapel".

No proof exists that it was built to a design by Sophy Gray, but as she produced the plans for eight other similar school/chapels, it is in all likelihood another of her creations. The building continued to be used as a school for many years, becoming known later as the All Saints Mission Chapel. It is now the St Peter's Parish Hall, with the Anglican Rectory alongside.

At the time of the opening, in 1855, Bishop Gray expressed the hope that when the congregation was large enough and rich enough they would be able to build "a good stone church". A block away in Marsh Street you will find the good stone church of St Peter's.

In 1875 a Mr Hudson donated ground for the church, and a part of the original Government grant was sold to help pay for the new building. It was completed in 1879 to a design by John Welchman. The building is in the neo-Gothic tradition, of which Sophy Gray would surely have approved, and has an interesting hammer-beam roof and a striking stone spire, added in 1906, which in this country is probably unique. However, neither Robert and Sophy Gray, nor Thomas Sheard lived to see the completed church.

When Heinrich Lichtenstein visited Mossel Bay as a member of De Mist's party, they of course called on the Government Post-holder, a young, unmarried Dane named Abue who lived alone in a small house, formerly a watch-house beside the present harbour. De Mist was put up in the house and the rest of the party slept in the Magazine, built by the Dutch to store wheat awaiting shipment to Cape Town, but empty at the time of their visit.

No sooner had they arrived than Lichtenstein went off to see the cave and among his finds discovered some unusual lichens. He asked the young Dane to send some on to him in Europe, but they never arrived. Lichtenstein himself set about collecting plants; he mentions among others "*zygophyllum, pelargoniums* and *royena*", and also insects and small birds. Thereafter he prepared his collection for their journey in the ox-wagon.

That evening Abue, whatever his later failings regarding lichens, treated them to a sumptuous meal of foods from the nearby bay, the highlight of which were the oysters. Lichtenstein declared them to be more finely flavoured than those gathered near Cape Town, but although tasty, some were too large and fat. They were obliged to divide them as they were too big to swallow "at once".

* * *

Near the spring and postal milkwood we sat in the Isuzu while I went through my notebook working out what to do next. It was difficult to decide and thoughts of oysters kept intruding. Finally we decided to stop work for the day and rather look for a fish-food restaurant.

Pinnacle Point

Gauis Plinius, 23-79 AD, more commonly known as Pliny the Elder (he had a nephew whom he adopted, hence "the Elder") was a Roman soldier, administrator and naval commander with a particular interest in natural history. Today he is remembered for his multi-volumed *Natural History* which remained a standard work until the 17th century. One of its more memorable quotes is still apposite today: *Ex Africa semper aliquid novi* – Out of Africa always something new. This applies especially to recent discoveries regarding the development of the human species.

African origins:

- In eastern Africa the earliest hominin remains dating back more than five million years are to be found. This area has been dubbed *The Cradle of Humanity.* The idea that humans evolved in Africa was first put forward by Charles Darwin in 1871.
- In 1947, at Sterkfontein in what is now Gauteng, Robert Broom and John T Robinson came across a fossil skull later to be known as Mrs Ples and to be dated at 2.3 million years old. Subsequently the fossilised

remains of numerous other hominins have been found at the Sterkfontein Caves complex, now a World Heritage Site known as *The Cradle of Humankind.*

- Archaeological work along the Cape south-east coast began in the 1920s. In 2010 Professor Curtis Marean from the Arizona State University started work at Pinnacle Point leading a team

Pinnacle Point Archaeological Site, Mossel Bay, South Africa

of up to 40 scientists from all over the world. Based on artefacts indicative of cultural development, Marean and his team found evidence of occupation by cognitively modern humans going back 164 000 years. This was supported by the important discoveries of Chris Henshilwood at Blombos Cave near Still Bay, to the west of Pinnacle Point. Meanwhile, in East Africa and in Morocco, evidence has been found of anatomically modern humans dating back to 300 000 years.

At Pinnacle Point, by road roughly seven kilometres south west of central Mossel Bay, there exists evidence of a Middle Stone Age group that survived here some 120 000 to 190 000 years ago. They were cut off from the rest of Africa by an ice-age that produced desert conditions to the north that effectively blocked them off from the rest of the continent. Their existence depended upon a temperate coastal climate, thanks to the warm waters of the Agulhas current, and an abundant food supply. The ocean provided fish, particularly shell-fish,

while on land plants, especially bulbs, but also grysbok, bushbuck and other small animals, were readily available.

Living in the caves at Pinnacle Point, these early modern
humans overlooked a vast plain, the Paleo-Agulhas Plain,
there thanks to the drop in sea-level brought about by an ice-
age. At the height of this glacial period the plain was the size
of Ireland, and contributed greatly to the diversification of
the Cape Floristic Region. As Curtis Marean and his co-work-
ers argue in their 2020 paper[6], it provided a most productive
foraging habitat for the cave-dwellers. There were nutritious
grasslands, savanna-like floodplains and wetlands, while to
the north were fynbos and shrublands. Both were cut by meandering rivers with extensive floodplains, wood- and grasslands. Here humans had access to large ungulates in addition
to the coastal resources and plant foods.

The most important discoveries at Pinnacle Point have
been made at Cave 13B, where the earliest evidence of the
use of marine resources has been uncovered. Among the
shell-fish found were:

- alikreukel or giant turban (*Turbo sarmaticus*)
- brown mussel (*Perna perna*),
- pear limpet (*Patella cochlear*),
- periwinkle (*Littorina littorea*),
- siffie (*Haliotis spadicea*) and
- goats-eye limpet (*Cymbula oculus*).

The shell-fish, together with cast-ups, resulted in an
abundance of food from the sea, especially of shell-fish that
provided a high quality protein diet containing omega-3 fatty
acids.

Living where they did, up to ten kilometres away from the
seashore, they had also learnt about the tides and the best
time to visit the rocks to collect shell-fish. Noting the phases
of the moon and establishing a connection between these
phases and the tides is an early example of careful scientific

---

6   Curtis Marean, Richard Cowling and Janet Franklin. The Paleo-Agulhas Plain:
    Temporal and spatial variation in an extraordinary extinct ecosystem of the
    Pleistocene of the Cape Floristic Region.

observation. In addition, speech as a means of communication was sufficiently developed to enable them to pass on this information to others. .

Plants were also an important source of food. Vegetable materials at the site that have been identified include:

- Baroe (*Cyphia digitata*) – still used by Khoe-Saan as a source of carbohydrate. The artist Thomas Baines (1820-1875) – not to be confused with the pass-builder Thomas Bain (1830-1893) – recorded eating a breakfast of baroe on his way from Grahamstown to Port Elizabeth. A companion on the trip, probably of Khoekhoe origin, came across some of the plant beside the road and stopped to dig it up. They ate it then and there.

- Watsonias – the corms have to be carefully prepared before cooking, but so long as they are kept dry, last for a considerable time in storage.

- Kaneeltjie (*Pelargonium triste*) – the tubers were eaten, but also require cooking.

- Veldkool (*Trachyandra ciliata*) – the young flowers of which may be eaten raw, and which in season we have as a green vegetable.

- Palmiet (*Prionium serratum*) - The young stems are still used today by the Khoe-Saan as a suitable food for infants.

- Taaibos (*Searsia glauca*) – One can hardly make a meal of the small fruits, but they were probably eaten as a snack while out gathering or hunting.

- Bobbejaantjies (*Babiana* sp.) – They too may have provided *padkos* as one can eat the corms raw.

There were, of course, also land animals, some of which, now extinct, were of immense size: giant eland, zebra, hartebeest and buffalo. Hunting animals such as these required cooperation and advanced cognitive skills. The ability to track animals and make assumptions regarding the animal and its recent movements is another example of the early use of scientific methods.

In addition, there was also the need for suitable weapons, of which many had sharpened stone heads. These not only had to be manufactured, but also attached to a shaft with some form of mastic. This would have involved a good deal of trial and error and possible curing before a suitable substance was found.

Silcrete was used for cutting and scraping tools, arrowheads and spear points. In order to be able to knap silcrete it must first be heated and multiple complex steps were needed to produce the finished tool or weapon. How was this discovered, and how was this information passed on to subsequent generations? Obviously these humans were capable of reasoning and had developed speech sufficiently to be able to pass on information.

The weapons that were used to hunt animals could also be used during conflict with other groups. From earliest times we have been an aggressive species. However, it was while living on the south-east coast of the Cape that our early ancestors also learnt the equally important benefits of cooperation: a lesson that we still have not entirely internalised. .

This comparatively small group of early modern humans lived in what was, by comparison with the greater part of Africa at the time, a relative paradise. A benign climate and readily available food made this possible. It also allowed for brain development that resulted in the discovery of skills and the ability to pass these on to succeeding generations. It was here on the Cape south-east coast that intellectual development first took place 120 to 190 thousand years ago and not in Europe 20 to 30 thousand years ago, as was previously believed.

With the skills that they acquired, together with improved weaponry, *Homo sapiens sapiens* was able, when climatic conditions were suitable, to move away from the Cape coast and out into Africa, and from there into Europe and Asia. The world had become their oyster. (And as Shakespeare went on to add: *Which I with sword will open,* serving as a reminder that besides learning the importance of cooperation there was still an aggressive side to our nature.)

191

* * *

A coastal path, The St Blaize Hiking Trail, runs along the cliff tops and shoreline from the cave at Cape St Blaize, passing Pinnacle Point before ending at Dana Bay. However, to visit this Provincial Heritage Site, the Point of Human Origins, contact 079 640 0004 to book a mind-expanding 90 minute tour setting out from the Pinnacle Point Estate to hear the story and visit the home of some of the earliest ancestors of our species.

20/20 Places

Knysna Lagoon

Prince Alfred Pass

Nature's Valley from Marine
Drive, Bloukrans

Groot Rivier at Nature's Valley

Pepper Tree Cottage

Van Stadens Bridge

Opkoms

Montagu Pass

Klasies River Archeological Site

20/20 Creatures

A young lynx

Epauletted fruit bats - proud mother and child

Bushbuck doe

Porcupine

Greater Collared Sunbird pollinating
Brunsvigia litoralis

Bokmakirrie

Spotted eagle owl

Crowned Plover and chicks

Cape Robin

Thickknee with
chicks

20/20 People

Bartle Logie at
Bartlesfontein

Jack Skead and daughter
Peggy in a howling
south-easter at
Seal Point Lighthouse

Brian and Ann Snaddon

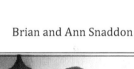

Rosie the dairymaid and friend

Dave Wilson aboard
Grace at Port St
Francis

Anton Boonzaier -
farmer, surfer and
restoration expert

Hoffie Williams with members
of the Fourcade Botanical Group

Maria Daniels,
road maintenance,
Bloukranspas

20/20 Plants

Hectares of Watsonias in flower on the farm Honeyville

Erica chloroma

Waboom, Onderkouga

Left: Aloe Striata.

Right: Gazania krebsiana

Brunsvigia gregaria

Boophone disticha

Carpobrotus edulis,

Moraea spathulata

Satyrium Halackii

Mossel Bay holiday makers a century ago

9.

Voorbaai to George

Voorbaai, Hartenbos, Klein- and Groot-Brak

The sky is overcast and there is a chilly wind from the west. There is not a soul to be seen on Santos or Pansy beach, not even a fisherman or surfer. But as the *Cape Colony Today* noted in 1904, "The beaches [of Mossel Bay] attract great numbers of country people who travel long distances by road and rail and camp out, till the whole sea-shore looks like a great camp." The beaches today, more than a century later, are still packed over the summer holiday.

Recently we read of a 19th century farming family from Beaufort West that was among those that made, by ox-wag-

201

on, the annual summer pilgrimage to Mossel Bay. Along the way they would outspan beside a particular river and before leaving the next day would place a crate of beer in the water, hidden by reeds. They were always sad when the beach-holiday came to an end, but knew that there would be cold beer awaiting them at the outspan. This cheered their spirits and made the leave-taking more bearable.

We leave town by way of Voorbaai, the industrial area. Progress is slow and we are caught in a long line of vehicles: people are going to work. Fortunately we are in no hurry, there is no beer waiting for us in some wayside stream.

The first recorded inhabitant of Voorbaai, known at the time as De Seven Fonteine, was a Scot, John Murray. He arrived during the first British Occupation, 1795-1803, and stayed on when the Cape reverted to Dutch rule under the Batavian Republic. He had a brig in which he sent firewood to Cape Town, which gives one some idea of what had happened to trees in Table Mountain *klowe*, the forests at Hout Bay and even the bush on the Cape flats since the arrival of Van Riebeeck in 1652. The brig returned with a cargo of cloth, hats, silks, glass and ironware for a general dealer's business he had established on the farm.

The day after their fish dinner, Lichtenstein and the Dutch party called in at the shop. "We were glad to supply ourselves with many little things that we wanted, and which we found of great use in the remainder of our journey." But he noted that the prices were very high.

Riding on towards Hartenbos Lichtenstein commented on how, "The influence of the sea air, united with the low situation of the country, upon the vegetation, is very striking . . . The *arduina bispinosa*, several beautiful sorts of *zygophyllum, pelargonium, royena, rhus*, and others, grow wild promiscuously among each other: some of considerable size, and the leaves quite a fresh bright green."

From our car in the line of traffic we could see factories, railway carriages and wagons, paper, plastic and cardboard litter, bill-boards, overhead power and telephone lines, traffic-lights, concrete and tar. There was almost no natural bright green visible, most of the foliage seemingly being of various shades of grey. The times they are a'changing, or perhaps it was simply because of it being a grey day with lowering skies, a cold wind and our state of mind.

With the traffic thinning out, we pass the Afrikaanse Taal en Kultuurvereniging (ATKV) camp at Hartenbos. Both the camp and the adjacent river are named after the farm Hartenbosch, which in turn was named after the "harts" or antelope that once were found here. The farm was granted to Engelbrecht Meyer in 1730, and Lichtenstein mentioned in 1804 that there were more "Meiers" in the area than any other family.

The Dutch travellers were given breakfast by Klaas Meyer who provided them with "cold provisions, admirable fruit, and wines which might justly be called costly". (To those of you who raise your eyebrows at the thought of wine for breakfast, remember that during the same period English public school boys were, as a matter of course, served beer for breakfast.)

However the greatest attraction was not so much the food and wine, as it was "the attractiveness of the female part of the family". Klaas's 18 year-old eldest daughter stood out above all the rest. "[We] really separated ourselves with reluctance from so lovely a creature."

The travellers pressed on towards the Klein Brakrivier. Lichtenstein makes no mention of the vegetation; perhaps his thoughts were still with Klaas Meyer's lovely daughter. But lunch-time was approaching and they were expected at Rheboksfonteyn on the far side of the river.

We too, turning off from the road to Thomas Bain's Robinson Pass and Oudtshoorn, crossed the Hartenbosrivier and headed for the Klein Brakrivier and Rheboksfonteyn.

Two hundred years ago the owner of Rheboksfonteyn was the widow Terblanche. Just as today a farmer and his wife might run a bed and breakfast establishment on the farm to bring in much needed extra income, so in 1804 the

203

widow Terblanche provided meals for passing travellers. Her farm was renowned for its good food and she made a point of serving her guests a greater number of dishes than even the *bon vivants* of Cape Town ever saw. As was to be expected, Lichtenstein was very appreciative. He claimed that she was the only South African who could make a cream cheese dessert properly, and noted that she was justly famed for this dish.

Today there is a large sea-side development of holiday and retirement homes situated on Rheboksfonteyn. No doubt the widow Terblanche would be amazed to see it, but we wondered whether or not she would approve. She might well, considering her own success in the tourism industry.

In 1835 a Cape Town businessman with Grahamstown links, C S Pillans, wrote a "schedule" to assist travellers between the two centres. He noted that in the southern Cape there was invariably a kindly welcome for travellers, and charges were moderate. Usually the only charge made was for forage for one's horse.

Among other matters he recorded farm routine with an eye to when those arriving on the farm might expect some sustenance: "Coffee early; breakfast at eight; dinner at twelve; supper between seven and eight; bed immediately afterwards: tea, commonly, the whole day through."

He went on to suggest that hungry travellers arriving between meals should hint politely about their condition, stating that *Botorom,* i.e. bread and butter, would be very acceptable. This would almost certainly lead to not only buttered bread, but also biltong, eggs and cold meats.

It was automatically assumed of any wayfarer asking if he might spend the night that he would also require an evening meal, and his supper would appear as a matter of course.

While the food offered to travellers in the southern Cape was almost always varied and ample, accommodation was rather more Spartan. French traveller, ornithologist, writer and artist, François le Vaillant was not happy about the beds provided. One was lucky if one was shown to a room with a buffalo skin fixed to posts at the four corners. As for the houses, he scathingly described them as being of wickerwork daubed with mud. This form of construction, more commonly referred to as wattle and daub, is still common not only in South African country areas, but also in Europe, and when coated with a white-wash made from burnt sea-shells is weather-proof and lasting.

It was John Barrow, as secretary to Governor Lord Macartney, who observed the whitewash on houses in the Klein/Groot Brak area. Barrow later married a Cape Dutch woman, Anna Maria Truter, but he did not have a very high opinion of the Dutch farming community. Still, in this instance his remarks concerning the stark simplicity of farmhouses were rather kinder than those of Le Vaillant. He also noted the striking exception to the general rule: the spacious, sturdily-built home of Klaas Meyer of Hartenbosch, and, like Lichtenstein, he singled out the widow Terblanche of Rheboksfonteyn for the warmth of her hospitality.

The Great Brak River was for many years a major obstacle to travel. At the best of times it was only possible to cross at low tide, but occasional floods were also a hindrance. During the 1840s there was a good deal of road-building in the southern Cape and it was at this time (1846) that Richard Searle and his wife Elizabeth, together with three children, arrived at the Cape from Plymouth, England. Within four days Richard and Elizabeth had found employment, he as a kitchen gardener and Elizabeth as a domestic servant.

In 1850 the family moved to Great Brak where Richard was employed by the Central Road Board as "person in charge of the causeway" over the Great Brak River. After the completion of the toll at the causeway, Richard became keeper of the toll at a salary of £75 per annum. Then, in 1856 he bought several erven in Blanco, the village founded by Henry Fancourt White at the bottom of the Montagu Pass, and the following year Richard, Elizabeth and family moved to the new village.

Then in January 1859, Richard's younger brother, Charles Searle, together with his wife Pamela and their four children, arrived in Port Elizabeth from Liverpool. Earlier, Charles had written to his older brother, "I shall leave it to your judgment to appoint that for me which you think will be best," and Charles was installed as toll-keeper on the Montagu Pass in July until the end of the year, when he and the family moved to take up a similar position at Great Brak River. This signalled the start of something entirely new: the toll became the centre of an ever-expanding circle of activities and the establishment of a Khoekhoen community, and a teetotal one at that.

Charles started with a store on a portion of the farm Voorbrug. He began gradually to buy up land in the area and in 1875 started a water-mill. Two years later he set up a woolwashery, but in 1884 sold the business to his sons. This gave him the capital to establish a boot and shoe factory and tannery and in no time there was a village of 2 500 souls.

There was also a Temperance Hotel, for Charles Searle and his successors stood steadfastly by their principles. Visitors were mightily impressed by the model village with its school and churches, social activities, care for the infirm and aged, and the "factory in a garden". The Searles may have been benevolent dictators, but there was a real sense of community with everyone attending the same church and their children, initially, being at the same school.

By 1910 a new generation of Searles was in control and things were beginning to change. The Salvation Army was unable to hold a meeting in the town because of an unruly element in the crowd. The next day the Searles' workers were gathered together and told that a repeat of such behaviour would result in their expulsion.

In 1949 Searles Holdings was listed on the Johannesburg Stock Exchange and in 1980 it was bought by footwear manufacturers Douglas Bolton. Today (in 2020) the factory first established by Charles Searle in 1867 is still, together with factories in Oudtshoorn and Cape Town, producing shoes, although no members of the Searle family are involved in top management. The population of the town, the halfway house between Mossel Bay and George, is now more than four times what it was in 1884, and Great Brak is not so much a manu-facturing centre as a holiday destination.

Blanco

The first road to be built by a qualified surveyor between Great Brak River and Blanco was that of Henry Fancourt White in the 1840s. In the previous decade he constructed Whites Road, now John Kani Road in Port Elizabeth.

White, born in Yorkshire in 1811, came to the Cape with his parents in 1820. They were allocated land near Riversdale, but soon moved to Assegaaibosch, just east of the Langkloof. In 1836 White left for Australia where he became a surveyor and road-builder and in time was appointed Assistant Surveyor to the state of New South Wales. There followed an altercation with the authorities that in 1839 led to his dismissal, despite considerable support for him from local settlers. White then returned to the Cape.

At the time Colonial Secretary John Montagu had begun an extensive road-building programme using convict labour. One of the roads being constructed was that over the mountains from George to the Langkloof, known today as the Montagu Pass. Work had started under the supervision of a Mr H O Farrel, but it became evident that he was not up to the job, and Montagu appointed White to finish work on the pass.

White completed the pass successfully and it was officially opened in 1847 and named after the Colonial Secretary. It was Montagu who suggested that the road-camp at the base of the pass should be named after the surveyor, and suggested the name, "White's Village" or "Whitesville". Subsequently, however, this was changed to "Blanco", a play on the surveyor's surname.

Richard Searle, elder brother of Charles Searle of Great Brak River, was for some time toll-keeper on the Montagu Pass. With the establishment of the village at the former road-camp he bought several erven and started planting oak trees around what was now a village.

For just on a century the Montagu Pass was the preferred route from Riversdale and Mossel Bay into the Langkloof and from there to the Eastern Cape and Border. Blanco lay on this route and as a small town it flourished. By the time White was buying plots there were already 12 cottages and a hotel, a cabinet-making business and an elementary school. There was even talk of a "lock-up" to cope with any "unruly characters" that might arrive in the hamlet. A post office had been established during the road-camp days, but there was now sufficient business for William Dudley, the schoolmaster, to lodge a successful application for the position of postmaster. He apparently found the change from school-mastering to be congenial, for he stayed in the service, later moving to Uniondale and later still to Avontuur.

James Murray was neither an unruly character nor a fly-by-night. After moving to Blanco in 1859 he became Inspector of Roads for the George Division and stayed there for the rest of his life. He lived next door to Richard Searle, with their orchards separating the two houses. In due course there were Searle/Murray marriages.

Searle operated a bakery from his house on the corner opposite the post-cart station. From his shop he sold bread, Bath biscuits and ginger beer to travellers on the post-cart. Like his brother Charles at Great Brak, he was teetotal, so water was the only option available to ginger beer. In 1877 in addition to selling *padkos* to travellers, he took over the operation of the post-cart route from Eersterivier, near Cape Town, to Humansdorp, via Blanco.

Henry Fancourt White, the "laird" of the village, began work on his dream house in 1859. The design, based on a Cotswold manor, was to be named "Blanco House", but barely a year later White, like many others at the time, had a financial set-back and work came to a halt. The house was never fully completed in his lifetime. He died in 1866.

In 1874 two colourful characters, Henri de Marillac and his brother-in-law, a retired Prussian army officer, Captain Max Jurisch, moved to Blanco. De Marillac, after building a double-storey factory and spending £16 000 to import machinery and skilled German and Swiss workmen, opened a shoe factory, while Jurisch opened a harness-works. In addition De Marillac bought Blanco House from White's widow. At much the same time a Mr J A Thwaites opened a tannery, and when De Marillac ran into financial difficulties, Robert Drummond took over the factory.

All of this hectic business activity came to naught. By 1893 a sub-editor of the *Oudtshoorn Courant*, the Reverend F J Ochse, reported that Blanco was almost a deserted village. This was due, he noted, because the main road had been diverted via George. "Only the large, beautiful oak trees seem to have outlasted the general decay." A new road to George cut through the orchards that James Murray and Richard Searle had both nurtured. Most of the fruit-trees that were left withered away, or were chopped down for firewood.

There were those families that stayed. Three of James Murray's daughters lived on in the old family home. There were even those who moved in: Ernest Montagu White, son of H F White and a successful businessman, diplomat and philanthropist, bought his father's old house in 1903, named it Fancourt and made a mansion of it. He and his wife Sarah lived in England, but visited Fancourt during the southern summer. Then in 1916 a tragedy occurred. Ernest White, his step-sister Elizabeth and a widowed friend sat down to a supper of mushrooms. Among them were some of a poisonous variety. All three died.

The years went by, together with a succession of owners. The rich man's mansion began to suffer neglect. It too was eventually locked up and began, like De Marillac's old factory, to crumble away.

* * *

In 1951 we drove from George to Oudtshoorn on the recently opened Outeniqua Pass. My father was very impressed, "The Chev just sailed up in top gear." Even my mother, who tended to be a nervous passenger and preferred to admire mountains from a stool in front of the canvas on her easel, approved of the pass. Although she did not say as much, my

209

father and I knew that this was the case because she did not have to hang on to the car's dashboard while going around corners.

It was said that the magnificence of the new pass was as a result of the work done during the Second World War by Italian prisoners of war. After all, everyone knew of the wonderful Italian roads and mountain passes. It is true that some Italian POWs did work on the pass, but none of them were skilled road-builders, just teachers and clerks, bakers and bus-drivers. No, the Outeniqua Pass was almost entirely a South African achievement, as were the Montagu and Cradock Kloof Passes before it, both visible from the one that took their place.

By 1951 the Montagu Pass was merely a scenic route. Blanco was entirely forgotten, there was no reason at all to drive through it. There was little enough to see there, anyway.

Then in 1960 a Johannesburg brain surgeon, Dr Roland Krynauw, bought Fancourt, added a new wing and started the long and costly job of restoring the old house to its former glory. In 1989 it was bought by the Pieterse family and turned into a boutique hotel. Today (2020) it is a part of the Fancourt Hotel and Golf Estate, and what was once the village of Blanco has become practically a suburb of the city of George. There are still some oak trees to be seen, but not many of them. Pines are common and Fancourt has bougainvillea, which is spectacular when in flower, along the street boundary. Its gardens too, reminiscent as might be expected of some English country estate, are colourful and typical of a bygone period. My mother, a dedicated colonial gardener, would have approved.

St Mark's Anglican Cathedral, George

George

The situation [of George] was selected by Lord Cale-
don, the late governor, and has, I think, been judicious-
ly chosen as a proper place for a town. A more pleas-
ant one I have not yet seen in Africa. It abounds with
wood, water and majestic scenery.

John Campbell. 1813.

The statistics indicate exactly what has happened to George since 1951 when my mother set out with her sketch pad to capture its charms:

George population: - 1950: 11 760 "all races".

2020: 157 391.

An increase of 1 238%!

In 1877 English author Anthony Trollope, agreeing with John Campbell, wrote that George is "the prettiest village in the world, at least the prettiest I have ever seen". It is no longer the prettiest village in the world. The citizens may wish

211

to lodge their claim to be the prettiest city, but sheer numbers bar them from entry in the village category. Inevitably too, those numbers have resulted in dramatic changes to the village so admired by Anthony Trollope.

Trollope was an interesting character. On the voyage out to South Africa he completed a novel he was writing and read Government Blue Books on the country he was about to visit. He came to South Africa, having earlier visited and written books about North America, Australia and the West Indies. He was a prolific writer and after a three month stay in South Africa, he completed, during the return voyage, the 800 page two-volume account of his travels. Inevitably perhaps, there were some errors – he referred, for example, to Port Elizabeth as "Fort Elizabeth" – but in general he painted an honest and attractive picture of the country as it was then, before the first Boer war of independence. He also noted something that seemed to escape many visitors to South Africa at the time: the country was inhabited by a large number of black people, and whites were in a minority.

Trollope is of course famous for his Barsetshire series of novels, concerned mainly with clerical intrigue in the cathedral town of Barchester. Had his stay in George been longer he might well have found enough material for another series of novels. While George only became a cathedral town in 1911, from the time of its founding in 1813 there were a number of unusual characters associated with the town, including clergymen,.

The district of George was the first new district to be proclaimed after the second British occupation in 1806. The town, at first known as George Town, was laid out by surveyor J H Voorman, and a young and energetic young landdrost, Adriaan van Kervel was appointed. One of his first tasks was to establish a route between George and the Langkloof. As you may remember, he built the Cradock Kloof Pass in record time, but it was not a success. He sent off a report to Governor Sir John Cradock, suggesting that he could do the job for a paltry 5 000 rix-dollars. Sir John was impressed. After a brief consultation with his senior staff, in January 1812 he gave Van Kervel the go-ahead. Work started the following month.

The Moravian clergyman, Christian Latrobe takes up the story:

> *12ᵗʰ April 1812. We intended to go by the new-made road across the mountains to George, but heard to our sorrow that the Landdrost, Mr van Kervel, had gone to Plettenberg Bay.*

The pass, 5½ miles (8.8 km) long and some 1 500 metres high had been completed in two months! There were soon complaints, some of which reached the Governor's ears. It often took wagons as much as three days to cross the Outeniquas. It might be shorter in distance than any other route, but it was not for the faint-hearted. Named in his honour the Cradock Kloof Pass, the Governor was belatedly having second thoughts about it and the new Landdrost of George.

Meanwhile Surveyor J H Voorman laid out a street plan for the town to be. It consisted of two parallel streets, York and Meade, with a cross street, Courtenay, which contained the main public buildings. Van Kervel set about planting trees on both sides of these streets, "not only for ornament, but for defending pedestrians from the searching rays of an almost vertical sun". Trees have been cut down over the years, but many are still offering their shade to passersby. Before now in mid-summer we have mentally thanked Van Kervel for his thoughtfulness.

At the top of the 60 metre wide York Street was the Drostdy flanked by the officials' dwellings, offices and gaol, with the Dutch Reformed Church at the head of Meade Street, in turn flanked by the parsonage and the doctor's house. The first erven were allocated free to six families of woodcutters living in the area, and by 1814, 77 residential plots had been taken.

Voorman was very probably also responsible for the design of the Drostdy. The contractor was Frederick Trench. In 1826 the building was destroyed by fire, but was rebuilt on the same foundations and to a similar plan for a private owner, Capt William Hollett. It later became the Victoria Hotel, but today is again a municipal property and houses the George Museum. Does it still have on show the black kid mourning gloves worn by Queen Victoria in 1889 at the funeral of German Emperor Frederick?

Cradock made two other important appointments: the first Dutch Reformed Church minister and the minister in charge of the London Missionary Society (LMS) mission at Hoogekraal, a few kilometres south of George. For the first position he chose the recently married Tobias Johannes Herold. Soon after his arrival in George and some years before the erection of "a moderate, simple building, fit for the size of the congregation which is to use it", Herold conducted the first *nachtmaal* service. He and his wife only moved into the "neat but modest parsonage" in July 1816, and it was in the following year that the first church building was consecrated.

The second appointee, Carl August Pacalt, was a German. After training in Berlin he was sent by the LMS to Mauritius, an island he never reached, ending up instead with Dr J T van der Kemp at Bethelsdorp, Port Elizabeth. Meanwhile Cradock received a recommendation that a missionary be sent to minister to the people of Dikkop, headman of the Khoekhoen Outeniqua group. Kerval was asked to choose a site for the mission and selected the farm Hoogekraal. Pacalt seemed an obvious choice for the job and agreed to the move. It was a happy choice, for Herold, from a relatively sophisticated background, and Pacalt, an older man but with a rather more humble upbringing, became great friends. Both ministers also enjoyed a constructive working relationship with Van Kervel.

After the Slagtersnek rebellion in 1815 Herold, due to the absence of the Uitenhage dominee, was instructed by Governor Lord Charles Somerset to attend the execution of five of the rebels. It became known as the execution where the condemned "died twice", for the rope broke and the men were revived and forced to wait until another suitable rope was found. Understandably, Herold was shattered by his experience of British justice. No doubt his friendship with Pacalt proved at this time to be a great consolation to him.

In 1823 Herold moved to Paarl, but he very obviously had a warm relationship with his parishioners, for both the village of Herold in the Langkloof and nearby Herolds Bay were named in his honour.

Pacalt arrived at Hoogekraal in 1813 and began work on a temporary church which during the week also served as a schoolroom, with Pacalt teaching. He meanwhile lived very simply in a two-roomed house containing a bare minimum of furniture or anything else, for he shared his few possessions with the community.

In 1819 Hoogekraal was visited by John Campbell, Inspector of LMS stations, who reported that Pacalt was "pious and active". A stone enclosure with "a six foot high wall" had been built to safeguard the cattle at night. In the garden he noted "peach, apricot and fig trees, potatoes, pumpkins, watermelons, cabbages, beans, pease, Indian corn . . ." the list goes on. His comments were entirely favourable.

Pacalt spent his days, preaching and praying, teaching children and adults, tending the vegetable garden, building the cattle-kraal and a smithy, and visiting the sick. In the five years of his mission, he so endeared himself to his parishioners, that on his death at the age of 45 in 1818, they chose to change the name of Hoogekraal to Pacaltsdorp. In his will he left £300 towards the erection of a church. The church stands today as a memorial to him, the only change in the intervening years being the replacement of the thatch roof with one of corrugated iron.

In 1822 the Rev William Anderson arrived in Pacaltsdorp. It was the start of an association between the people of the village and the Anderson family that lasted for more than a century. During that time the population grew from less than 400 to the present (2020) 16 400.

Taking the place of Tobias Herold in George, was another young man, 23 year-old Johann Stephan Simeon Ballott. He was the son of a clergyman and like his father was also a bibliophile. He struggled for 14 years to collect sufficient money to be able to replace the "moderate simple" church that Cradock had originally stipulated. The congregation was by now so vast, that in years to come 15 other parishes were formed from it. Eventually there was enough money and plans for the new church were drawn. There seems to be some confusion as to who was responsible for the design. The surveyor, J H Voorman sent plans of the Swellendam church for consideration, but was not responsible for the final design. Ballott himself may have come up with the design, but it seems more likely to have been by builder and architect Hermann Schutte, who was also responsible for the design and building of the Groote Kerk in Cape Town. Work on the church, supervised by Ballott, began in 1831, but was only completed in 1842. The octagonal tower atop the cruciform building collapsed in 1905, but was rebuilt to the original design.

Ballott was not only responsible for the mother church. He also founded a missionary community and attempted to establish a fishing harbour at the spot that now bears his name, Ballotts Bay. He believed strongly in the importance of education and built schools and established George's Public Library. His own library, to which in time was added his father's collection, amounted to 950 volumes. He died in 1868 and is buried in the grounds of the mother church. In 1945 the Ballott library was sold to the University of Cape Town.

Bishop Robert Gray and his wife Sophy also played a part in the town's development. The bishop first visited George in September 1848, barely six months after his arrival at the Cape. He had with him one of Sophy's plans, which was approved there and then by members of the local George, English-speaking community. Just over a year later his wife laid the foundation stone of the new church, to be called St Mark's. It was possible for the consecration to take place just 13 months later, in December 1850, thanks to the expertise and conscientious efforts of stonemasons Alexander Bern and the Lawrence brothers, Alexander and James. To have completed this stone building, complete with bell turret and hammer beam roof trusses, in so short a period was a remarkable achievement.

Unlike the majority of Sophy's country churches, there have been numerous additions to St Marks, all of which have been architecturally sound and in accordance with Sophy's original design. By 1860 the original church was already too small and further additions continued until 1934. Meanwhile, in 1910, it had been elevated to a cathedral. Its massive stone blocks somehow attach this very English church to its African surroundings, while the park-like setting enables it to be fully appreciated.

There was another appointment made in the town's early days, one which at the time must have been the subject of much gossip. In October 1816 Mrs J H du Toit was appointed the first postmaster of the new town. Apparently no man with suitable qualifications applied for the job. Reluctantly the authorities accepted the inevitable. For 12 years, during which time post office business increased phenomenally, and the office was twice increased in size, Mrs du Toit continued to give satisfactory and courteous service. By that time even the diehards were willing to concede that a woman was capable, in this instance at least, of doing a man's work.

Reginald Lawrence - superhero?

The birthplace of comic book superhero Peter Benjamin Parker, also known as Spider-Man, was apparently Forest Hills, New York. This was conveniently close to the centre of the New York garment industry, where his superhero outfit was created.

The birthplace in 1897 of Reginald Frederick "Lawrie" Lawrence, son of a magistrate and South Africa's spider man, was among the forested hills of George, Cape Colony. From an early age he showed an interest in nature and in creepy-crawlies of all kinds. He was to be found before long in the surrounding forests, finding hidden treasures under every second stone and beneath the bark of trees both indigenous and alien. Travelling away to Grahamstown for formal education at St Andrews College not only widened his horizons, but resulted in the discovery of different species and creatures.

His paternal grandfather, George Lawrence, arrived at the Cape more or less by chance. Dissatisfied with the allowance that his father gave him, he set off to join the Australian gold rush in 1851. The voyage to the Cape decided him against continuing his ship-board travels. He left the ship in Cape Town and shortly thereafter took holy orders. In due course he was appointed rector of Durbanville and married Mary Elizabeth Inglis, the daughter of a Paarl Anglican priest. It was George Lawrence who was responsible for the planting of the Bluegum Avenue from Bellville Station to Durbanville, once described as "the noblest avenue in Africa". So despite the gums being aliens, it seems that the Durbanville rector had an interest in nature that his grandson inherited.

The First World War, during which Reginald Lawrence commanded a Lewis gun section at Paschendaele, interrupted his education, but after his return to South Africa he enrolled at the University of Cape Town. Graduating with a BSc, he called on Dr Louis Péringuey of the South African Museum in Cape Town to ask for a job. Péringuey handed him a two volume French work by Eugene Simon, *Histoire Naturelle des Araignees.* "If you want a job young man, first impregnate yourself with this." Lawrence staggered home and found a French dictionary. In due course he got the job.

There followed years of travel in southern Africa. There was a memorable trip by donkey from Lourenço Marques (Maputo) to Inhambane and in the 1920s, annual visits to South West Africa (Namibia), to the Kunene, Kaokoveld and Etosha. These journeys entailed shooting for the pot and sleeping rough while catching, for the museum, anything that slithered, scuttled or flew. He felt that his French studies had been worth it, and he could not have wished for a better job.

In 1928 he was awarded a doctorate and became director of the Natal Museum in Pietermaritzburg and with his career path well and truly mapped out, he married Professor Ella

Pratt-Yule, founder of the Department of Psychology at the University of Natal.

Among the creatures that wakened Lawrence's special interest were the solifugae or solpugids, also known in this country as *Rooimanne, Baardskeerders* or Red Romans.

Now I must confess to what is I know a completely irrational fear of large, hairy spiders. With small spiders, even those of a dangerous variety such as Violin spiders – *Loxosceles* sp - I can cope, but show me a Baboon spider – *Harpactita* sp – with a body 50 mm across surrounded by eight furry legs, and as harmless as it may be, I reach for the nearest weapon or call for Caryl who picks it up in her hankey and takes it gently to the window before shaking it out.

My first meeting with a *Rooiman* took place in a shower cubicle in a Karoo farmhouse. Having no clothes on I felt defenceless when this large red arachnid which I took to be a spider, but which I later discovered was not, began racing around the floor of the cubicle at what seemed to be an extraordinary pace. By comparison with a Baboon spider's normally dainty steps, this creature appeared to be moving at close to the speed of light. No sooner was it seen in one corner than it appeared in another scuttling at breakneck speed past my bare feet.

At the time I did not realise that my shower companion was a nocturnal variety of the common *jagspinnekop* (Hunting spider) that dashes around amongst the Karoo *bossies* during the day. Despite the similarity in appearance, these creatures are not spiders. They have a body of three main parts, as opposed to the spider's two. Olive Schreiner's husband, Cron, wrote of the variety of hunting spider that he knew from near Cradock:

A most brilliant yellow, with a heavy black band down the back of the abdomen, while the legs are covered with long golden hair which in the male becomes a distinct mane and is iridescent. As it lies on the sand on a hot day, sparkling in the sunshine, it is a most exquisite creature.

The speed with which they move and the hairy legs of the diurnal variety, breaking its outline among the desert bushes, are of course simply means of protection, for other than great jaws, they have no other weaponry. Beautiful perhaps, but they are nevertheless most alarming creatures. Lawrence told of how an entire village of Ethiopians once fled from their homes when faced by an unexpected invasion of solpugids.

Lawrence's interest in these creatures resulted in 1954 in him being shown some sent to the British Museum by a collector in Arabia. One of these, sent in by a man named Philby, was new to science. Lawrence described it and in honour of the collector, named it *Biton philbyi.*

The collector was Harry St John "Jack" Philby, a keen arachnologist who had captured the creature during the period between the two World Wars. He was at one time a Colonial Office intelligence officer, but was dismissed from the service as the result of an "inappropriate" love affair. Perhaps with good reason he tended from then on to do his best to hamper the efforts of the British government in the Middle East. He converted to Islam, became known in Arabia as Sheikh Abdulla and was appointed personal adviser to King Ibn Saud, none of which stopped him collecting arachnological novelties and sending them to the British Museum. And not only arachnids, for he is also remembered by birders as the discoverer of Philby's partridge – *Alectoris philbyi* – and by reptile enthusiasts for a variety of the Middle Eastern lizard – *Uromastyx ornate philbyi.*

Best man at Philby's first marriage to Dora Johnston was his distant cousin, Bernard Law Montgomery, later to become a British Army Field-Marshal and to make a name for himself in North Africa and Europe during the Second World War.

Jack Philby and Dora had a son, Harold "Kim" Philby, and in time he too hit the headlines. He, like his father before him, became a British civil servant, and during the Second World War, was first secretary to the British Embassy in Washington, and a double agent. In 1963, while working as a journalist in Beirut, he was tipped off that the British authorities were on his trail. He disappeared and shortly thereafter was given political asylum in Russia. It was then announced that he had been involved with the espionage case of Guy Burgess, who was an old friend of his, and Donald MacLean. Philby himself had been a Soviet agent since the 1930s.

It seems that the Philby father and son were rather more dangerous, so far as the British establishment were concerned, than the average solpugid or Baboon spider.

In 1948 Reginald Lawrence left the Natal Museum to devote himself entirely to research for the Council for Scientific and Industrial Research. Once again he was able to range the country in search of scorpions, solpugids, spiders and centipedes, from the coastal forests to the banks of the Limpopo and beyond.

The Department of Agricultural Technical Services in 1964 published his *Conspectus of South African Spiders* in an edition limited to 500 copies. To the surprise of the department, but not to Lawrence, the *Conspectus* was soon sold out. Love spiders or hate them, there were considerably more than 500 people interested in them.

Then in 1975 he was presented with a *festschrift* – a collection of contributions from colleagues, former students and friends – honouring his achievements during fifty years of scientific research. He was indeed not only a spider man, but a definite superhero. He died at the age of 90 in 1987.

So should anyone happen to ask you where Spider-Man was born, be sure to answer, "In the forested hills of George." And tell them a little about this unsung, other than in arachnilogical circles, son of the southern Cape.

SAR 3669 at Knysna

10.

The Southern Cape Lake District

In 1905, Mr AF Stewart, in a report to the Cape Government Railways wrote:

"With its pleasant climate, fine scenery and good boating, fishing and shooting, the lake country [will] probably become a favourite holiday resort if opened up by a railway."

George to the Wilderness

The road to the east from George used to be one of the worst in South Africa. It is today, as a section of the N2, a different matter. Driving carefully, the only real danger is speed-traps. One accelerates slightly to pass an eighteen-wheeler that very sensibly is creeping down the hill at a snail's pace, and "flash" – you are captured on camera travelling a few kilometres an hour above the limit.

What would Andrew Geddes Bain have to say about the road to the Wilderness today? In 1856 he wrote:

This road has been worn down in the course of ages by "remming" [braking] at least two wheels of every wagon that descends it, into a deep channel, from six to eight feet high [1.8 to 2.4 metres], and so narrow that a man cannot pass between the banks each side of the wagon. . . It is quite a curiosity of its kind but there are many more such in this line regularly grooved out of the soft micaceous rock.

At the bottom was the dreaded Kaaimans Gat into which one plunged after sliding down the last 300 feet (91.4 metres) which were almost perpendicular. Surrounded as it was by tall, impenetrable bush, the Gat lay in thick shadow. Its black waters were one of the most frightful spots to behold. Having reached this far there was no turning back, yet if anything, according to early travellers, the terrors still to be faced were worse than those already endured.

The dreaded Gat lies downstream from the crossing of the Kaaimans, 1.6 km from Saasveld on the old road. When in 1869 Thomas Bain started work on the Seven Passes Road between George and Knysna, he built a causeway crossing the river. This, in 1893, was bridged with a tarred pine bridge which in turn was replaced by a stone bridge in 1903. From the old causeway it is possible to climb the amazingly steep old road and to see the deep grooves cut by the wagon wheels. According to Lichtenstein it required not only oxen, but in addition men heaving and straining to take an unladen wagon to the top of the hill. On reaching the top Lichtenstein admired the view which he earnestly recommended "to the notice of all future travellers in these parts".

My father, after the completion of the curved bridge on the N2 over the Kaaimans in 1951, used to delight in driving between George, the Wilderness and back. He had never before come across a curved bridge. In the family it became known as Grandpa's bridge.

My own favourite was the railway bridge over the mouth of the Kaaimans River. It was also a favourite of photographers, both amateur and professional, capturing the image of a great steam locomotive heading a line of coaches across the 13 arch bridge, with the incoming tide washing the bases of the supporting pillars. In the background the vast waters of the Indian Ocean.

Across the road from the Wilderness Station were the Wilderness and Fairy Knowe Hotels, the Touwsrivier and the meandering channels from the Lakes, Onder- and Bo-Langvlei and Rondevlei, the last of the lakes connected to the Wilderness system.

Beside the water in his retirement years lived *Die Groot Krokodil*, former State President PW Botha. What a suitable spot for a great crocodile to live! An elderly former National Party member told me, however, that the older generation referred to Botha not as a crocodile but as the "tea-boy". He came by the nickname, so I was told, because as the most junior member of the local party hierarchy in George during the 1940s, bringing in the tea was one of his functions. My informant remarked, "The name was not *entirely* derogatory."

In Dalene Matthee's book, *Toorbos*, she acknowledges the help she received from Botha when writing about the poor whites of the Knysna forests. It is as well to be reminded now and then that most politicians have both good and bad points, like any other human-being.

The derailment at Bo-Langvlei

To the east of the Wilderness and Touwsrivier estuary are three lakes linked to it: Onder-Langvlei, Bo-Langvlei and Rondevlei. A few hundred metres from the Duiwerivier siding, situated between Onder- and Bo-Langvlei, is a level-crossing. An incident occurred here about which I wished to discover more than the little I knew. The obvious source was the Snaddon family.

My friendship with Brian and Ann Snaddon spanned the greater part of a lifetime. At one stage they lived in the vicinity of the lakes. As a result I approached their children, now adults: Bruce, Chip, Jiggs and Kate. They came up trumps, producing not only their own memories, but their father's written record of:-

27ᵗʰ October 1972

The city of George in the Cape is linked to Knysna town in many ways. Not the least, but certainly the most beautiful (in terms of vistas and countryside traversed) is the railway line. This line, traversed solely by steam locomotives of the Class 24 variety pulling freight stock and one passenger day-coach, threads its way down sea cliffs, through tunnels, across rivers, past cow-rich meadows and pine forests and ending by the string of lakes in those parts. The tiny halts along the way have wonderful names: Victoria Bay, Ebb-and-Flow, Bleshoender, Ruigtevlei, Rheenendal. Apart from Wilderness Station, with its stationmaster, trimmed lawns and flower beds, the halts are lonely and austere, a name set in concrete and a small grey corrugated iron shed, with perhaps a livestock load-ramp. Not much else besides piles of timber awaiting transportation.

Ann and I, at a certain time, ran a school in the forests on a timber farm at Elandskraal on the road to Karatara, beneath the Outeniqua Mountains. No ordinary school to be sure: 11 children from three years of age up to 18.

Our library and texts were the incredible environment around us, the lost-in-the-past farmers who were our neighbours, our communal life, two cats, a rooster (Charley Claw) and three red hens. We also had the lakes and the seashore not far away. Shore studies, Marine Biology loomed big (we had a few books on that subject) but also that fascinating brand of study gave us the excellent excuse to do field trips. Rocky shore zonation (the intertidal zone) had everyone intent and scrambling, but it also included a bit of body-surfing and a picnic. So we decided to take the Knysna-George train one morning before dawn (at the lonely halt of Ruigtevlei), thence to Victoria Bay near George. We'd do our studies and take the same train (ex-George) in the afternoon on its way back to Knysna. Nothing could have been simpler, or more available.

At 6:45am the locomotive Class 24, No. 3669, and train steamed out of the sea-fog to load us up into the dank day-coach, the last of about 13 freight trucks. Much excitement – steam jets, the clunk of connecting rods on the drive wheels, breathy but assertive whistles from the engine – and so, as dawn broke we trailed through that unique landscape quite snug and yet agog.

By the time we pulled into Wilderness Station some kilometres down the line, the sun was up, the engine needed water and we needed a walk. We had all fallen in love with this train, so it was time to walk up the platform to meet Mr Harris, the engine driver, and his stoker, Mr Von Huysteen.

There must be something about steam locomotives and the men who drive them. A special pride and confidence in their machines, and an unspoken love of the unlikely whimsy of converting water and fire into portentous forward (and backward!) motion. It is a hot, dirty business fraught with danger and uncertainty. One cannot steer a train if there is trouble ahead, and though there are pneumatic brakes, and one can slam them on, the stopping distance has to do with speed and the massive weight behind the whole affair. In the face of these uncertainties these men affect a bluff nonchalance and certitude. They seem to be always polishing things – copper pipes, pressure gauges, tiny coal-dusted windows in the sides of the cab (steam loco drivers can't actually see forward, the bulk of the boiler obscures any such view). The stoker in blue shoulder-strapped overalls constantly feeds the inferno with coal from the tender, steel shovel scraping away, "pumping" in the fuel, even at rest! The pressure gauges must not fall. So into this crowded space Mr Harris admitted us all in small groups. He was both embarrassed and proud. *"Ja, jy sien hierdie blerrie ding . . ."* but it was clear that he felt good in himself and on the footplate, and Class 24 locomotive No 3669 was his love and pride.

So, onto Victoria Bay across the incredible elevated Kaaimans River Bridge, the tide waves laced in white beneath the clattering wheels. At the halt we climbed off to wave adieu to "our" train as it heaved off and up the incline towards George. We did at Victoria Bay what we'd gone there to do, but it was no secret that we couldn't wait for the return of Harris and 3669 at 2:30pm. Long before he and the train hove in sight on the return trip, we were up there waiting. And thus we, climbing aboard that day-coach, became part of an event minutes ahead of us.

After Wilderness Station, we entered a cutting – right-hand curve. We heard the locomotive give out its breathy warning shriek, and then suddenly there were three massive shocks of deceleration. Those of us facing forward skidded onto the floor; those facing aft on their seats simply sunk deeper into the green leather padded seats. Then silence. The last coach with its wheels on the rails was quite still in the cutting. Odd sounds of metal shifting, things flexing, and finding rest. Three girls in our coach from Knysna threw their skirts over their heads and wouldn't budge. The conductor got out and walked ahead to see what was up, he returned, clunking down the gravel next to the line, moments later; said we'd be on our way again "in five minutes". Got out the big First Aid box, with its straps, and disappeared along the way we had come: no doubt *a posteriori* reasoning. It was clearly time to take a look at what had befallen us. Everything was so silent, the odd cicada, water dripping onto the tracks from the toilet, the smell of iron-oxide and finely ground steel from the rails.

I walked up the track to gaze with growing disbelief on a monumental disaster. About 15 freight trucks were poised in different angles of chaos and repose. Their loads were spent and spilled in all directions. Some trucks arced up to the sky, others lay sullenly on their sides. As I clambered through this my heart sank at what could be the fate of Class 24 No 3669 and, above all, Mr Harris and his stoker. Moments later I got half the answer. No 3669 was off the tracks, lying in Bo-Langvlei shallows almost on its side. A single plume of steam was escaping into the air; coal tender at right angles to the engine, pointing heavenwards. There was no sign of human life. Except for the diminishing hiss of steam, a great silence relieved only by a fly-in of a couple of water birds who, settling on the water of the vlei, went about their dabbling and diving and preening.

There lay the great black hulk of 3669 half submerged. Where were Harris and Von Huysteen? Next half of the question, the chilled one, was now answered. On the lee side of 3669 emerged two drenched men. Coal dust on their heads, water weed draped all over them. Shocked and hurt, their hands raw and bleeding from grabbing onto steam-heated pipes in the cab as the engine keeled over into the Vlei.

My cry at these apparitions, "Thank God you are alive!"

Harris: "F--- the bastards."

Me: "What bastards?"

The stoker is bleeding from the head. Harris and I go back to what clearly was a level-crossing. Hunkering down we saw through the twisted steel chassis and stilled wheels the upside down form of a yellow, Cape Provincial Administration road-grader, so we crawled through to have a closer look at "the bastards".

Upside down, the grader was still making sounds of metal contracting. In the cab the driver was upside down with some half-eaten sandwiches stuck to the roof. He had a hole in his forehead but was breathing gently with his left leg wrapped around the rods and controls of the Caterpillar D8 grader. Behind the "baas", was one of the two black CPA employees who traditionally ride on the back of the machine. He was spread-eagled on the dirt road, eyes open to the sky, a dark red spreading stain behind his head. The other man we came across in a ditch, metres away. He had his chin in one hand and was gazing at the train chaos as if fascinated, the pupils of his eyes grandly dilated – concussed and not with us.

Then things began to happen in this Salvador Dali kind of scene. A black Mercedes Benz drew up on one side of the chaos. Behold – a Cape Town doctor. He quickly assessed the problem and sped off. Minutes later – about 30 – an ambulance arrived. We were left with our train prang and little else: frogs in a ditch and a few birds in the bush.

An empty stage however invites actors, and so they came, one by one. The news seemed to have spread.

Down the track skipped and hopped a retired ganger. As a railway man he probably waited every day for the train to roll by, with Harris in charge. To his horror (so he related it) the locomotive at the point of impact leapt into the air, bringing down the telephone lines before subsiding into the water. The ganger, seeing Harris alive, was over the moon.

Enough! – the stuff of friendship. How does a lowly ganger link with an engine driver? A few waves of the hands twice a day maybe, a subtle interdependency?

We had found a shady spot near the level-crossing to wait and see. A scraping sound on the rails beneath the trucks revealed a repair team of Posts and Telegraph men, wires in their mouths, brown overalls, and pliers in their hands. Then the editor of *Het Suidwestern,* the local newspaper, arrived. He took a cursory look at the shambles and then interviewed us in the shady ditch about our school and philosophies of education!

Arriving together in a flurry of dust came a Volkswagen and a blue Valiant: from the former a uniformed district nurse who gave me a scornful glare when I asked for an aspirin for one of our children. No aspirins from her! From the latter alighted the portentous Capt Johannes "Bosvark" Jakobs of the local drug squad. Men of his ilk were trained never to show surprise, but the scene before him took him somewhat aback. He reverted back to the usual SA Police displacement behaviour; clear the sinuses, flick aside the sports-coat to reveal the dull gleam of the service revolver, take out a crumpled Texan cigarette, tap it on the thumbnail and light up with one eye shut to avoid the acrid smoke. Normally, having got the cigarette going, they are instructed to walk around kicking wheels. This allows time for thoughts to gather, but clearly there were too many wheels for the Captain, who in any case was probably not in a thinking mode that day. After a searching question put to no one in particular, "Any drugs here?" he and the nurse disappeared.

The Wilderness Station-master then materialised: full uniform, silver braid on the cap and clipboard in hand. He showed not the slightest interest in our plight and need for onward transport. He seemed more concerned with serial numbers of trucks and dockets and how many baulks of timber were floating off into the Vlei. He did however suggest we walk on up the track to the next siding. After two hours of idleness and frustration, we took his advice. To wait for what?

At the siding, which was not far off, the final charade of the day was played out. Someone had assured us, now tired and hungry, that a Railway bus from Knysna would pick us up there, and that a steam-crane was on its way from George to get the line clear. Sure enough we could hear the steam-engine drawn crane huffing away towards the scene of the accident. Meanwhile coming past us in the opposite direction towards the accident scene, came four gangers going home at the end of a long day. They were on the rails on one of those quaint vehicles called a *skop-wa*. Two men perched up front, while two men faced backward kicking the right-of-way with well-hobbed boots. The wheels squeaked, the boots sent gravel backwards in rhythmic spurts, and thus they progressed to their well-earned rests. But lo and behold, the men at the front, not knowing about the derailment up ahead of them, saw the signs of a train coming their way: a totally unscheduled train on that quiet line. They were not to know, for the sun was in their eyes that between them and the train coming their way were mega-tonnes of mangled steel. But it was remarkable to note their evasive action to a perceived threat to their lives, their pockets and their pensions. Long steel bars were produced, the *skop-wa* was lifted up and turned around through 180° and with some pretty vigorous "skopping" squeaked off the way it had come. There were quite a few backward glances from the lads on board. No one wants to be run down by a steam engine, especially if you are a ganger not on first name terms with Mr Harris.

We finally got home after a memorable day. I still wonder about the *skop-wa* scenario. Why when they got their fright did they turn the thing around? Just change places *my manne* and keep those skops going.

All the injured recovered from their wounds, although I am not sure about the gangers. Class 24 Locomotive No 3669 was cut apart, transported to the Mossel Bay workshops, re-assembled and is today part of the Knysna Choo-choo team.

* * *

Bruce Snaddon, commenting on his father's account wrote:

For years after, when driving through the Garden Route, we would holler and shriek with delight when we spotted old 3669 puffing up an incline. The driver and passengers would have been amused at seeing a combi-load of crazies waving and shouting at them from the road. Many times we received a whistle from the driver.

* * *

The pupils of the Heronvale School had adventures unlike those of any other schoolchildren in the land!

Veld and Vlei

Travelling east from Rondvlei you reach the small town of Sedgefield and almost engulfing it, the expanse of Swartvlei. We at one stage made regular visits to Willow Point, on the banks of Swartvlei, home at the time to *Veld and Vlei*, an organisation started by Freddie Spencer Chapman.

Colonel F Spencer Chapman, DSO and Bar, was a British Army officer and very much an outdoors man. When during World War II Malaysia fell to the Japanese, he took to the jungle and against all odds managed to survive and evade capture for three years. He later wrote of his adventures in a book published in 1949, *The Jungle is Neutral.* He was already a published author, having written a climbing book, *Memoirs of a Mountaineer, Helvellyn to Himalaya* and another, *Lhasa, the Holy City,* which were an indication that when he took to the mountains, jungle, or anywhere else in the great outdoors, he was by no means a neophyte in the arts of self-sufficiency.

Spencer Chapman was a proponent of the educational philosophy of Kurt Hahn, founder of Gordonstoun School in Scotland. This was based on a respect for adolescents. Hahn believed that they responded well when given a chance to show leadership qualities and the opportunity to see the results of their own actions. For this reason his focus was on outdoor education and he stressed the importance of a concern for others, and a willingness to accept responsibility.

In 1956 Spencer Chapman was appointed headmaster of St Andrews College in Grahamstown, and at that school began to put these principles into practice. During the following year, together with Leslie Carter, headmaster of Woodridge Preparatory School at Van Stadens, he ran an Outward Bound training course at Woodridge where there were suitable camp-sites, a dam, the river for swimming and boating and the Van Stadens Mountains for climbing. Carter was already running a successful Scout group at the school, and fully supported Spencer Chapman's ideas. The camp would be a pilot scheme to help discover what did and what did not work, and to enable them to draw up plans for a future training programme.

By 1958 the Veld and Vlei Trust under the chairmanship of Sir John Killick, GCMG, former British ambassador to Moscow and thereafter NATO, was up and running. Possibly as a result of the Carters having a holiday house, Hangover Hall, at Sedgefield, arrangements were made to hold the first training camp at nearby Willow Point on the shores of Swartvlei. The organisation operated under the name Veld and Vlei, but was, as regarding its tenets, an offspring of the Outward Bound movement in Britain, also founded by Kurt Hahn. In due course another camp was established at Elgin in the Western Cape.

Overlooking the campsite and the seaside town of Sedgefield is an ancient and enormous bush-covered dune known as Cloud 9. In 1951, using a team of oxen, a steep dirt road was built from Willow Point to the top of the dune to enable a house to be built. Since then countless Veld and Vlei trainees and others have made the energy-sapping climb to the top from where there is a breath-taking view over Swartvlei and the surrounding countryside and seascape to Gerike Point. We made an early morning climb to the top a regular feature of our visits to Willow Point with Woodridge pupils. One of those early mornings was different from all the rest.

At the top Jumbo Williams, another outdoorsman of note settled the campers down:

I want you to sit here quietly for a minute or two and look, don't just glance, look at what is in front of you. Look at the sky and the water, and the birds and plants. Notice the colours of the clouds and of the water. Listen to the sounds and think what may be causing them. Notice the dew on the plants. Of what does it remind you? Are there any special smells? Don"t say a word to anyone. Just for a short while soak up all that is in front of, or surrounds you. When we are back in camp, make a note of your observations in your diaries.

For a moment there was complete silence, then an agonised voice uttered in a stage whisper:

Sir, I've got a problem!

Oh, for goodness sake, Sipho, why didn't you go before we left camp?

It's not that, Sir. There's a snake on my leg.

And there was too. Fortunately it was of a harmless variety, but that particular commune with nature certainly ended in an unexpected fashion and produced some unusual diary entries.

On the water

Next on the list of lakes after Swartvlei is Ruigtevlei, tucked away unseen in the forests to the north of the road, but Groenvlei, sometimes referred to as Lake Pleasant, is easy to spot as one drives along the N2, it being right next to the road.

Paravicini di Capelli and General Janssens were there in 1803 and Di Capelli recorded:

[It is] a lake of fresh water, rich in fish, separated from the sea by no more than a narrow high ridge; the banks are covered alternately with thick trees and

*reeds; thousands of wild duck, flamingoes, and other
waterfowl cover the lake.*

The fresh water so close to the sea is certainly unusual. It
is believed to come from springs beneath the surface.

Peaceful as the waters may appear, wild men have lived
in the area. At Buffelsvermaak, Janssens and Di Capelli were
met by the owner, Pieter Terblanche. They were interested to
discover that he made his living as a hunter in the Tsitsikamma forests with a smooth-bore, front-loader and were, no
doubt, entertained by his tales of kills and derring-do.

Little did the children of the Heronvale School know when
they set out to emulate the adventures of Tom Sawyer and
Huckleberry Finn on the waters of the Goukamma River, that
the descendants of the pioneers of the area were as quick as
their forebears to grab hold of a firearm.

In preparation for the expedition rafts were built on which
tents were set up. The geography and history of the area were
studied, and a budget drawn up using the school "currency"
of "furs" and "blakes" in place of rands and cents.

Keen to ensure complete authenticity Bruce and Chip Snaddon made themselves corncob pipes and filled them with a
mixture of Fox tobacco, purloined from their father, and oak
leaves.

A map was consulted, one of the very best, Pete Slingsby's
Garden Route map. Packed in its water-repellant cover it was
carefully stowed away on one of the rafts.

Come the great day they set off with the rafts down the
dirt road to the N2, near Ruigtevlei siding, before heading
eastwards to where the N2 crossed the Goukamma River.
Here, with some difficulty, for the bank was steep and the
rafts heavy, they took to the water.

As the crow flies they had to cover only about 5.5 km
to the river's mouth, but the Goukamma flows down to the
sea in great loops and ox-bows and despite the accuracy of
Slingsby's map, they found that at water level they were quite
disorientated. They had also started much later than originally planned, and daylight was fading fast.

The largest raft, named *Jabula 1*, had six 44-gallon drums for floatation and carried Brian and Ann Snaddon, and their two daughters, Kate and Jiggs.

Kate: One of the lasting memories of that trip was the little tent built on the raft we were on. We felt so safe. In my mind the trip lasted for weeks, but I'm sure it was just days.

Jiggs: My memories are mostly about always feeling safe and protected by Mum and Dad, despite some crazy escapades. It was only a bit later in my life that I realised that my parents didn't evaluate risk quite the way I may have done. As for my siblings, they seemed to roll with things a whole lot better than I did.

The boys, Bruce and Chip, shared their raft with Cathy Goodwin, who in years to come was to be crowned Miss South Africa.

Bruce: Chip and I in our pre-teen years were besotted with Cathy and gave her pride of place in the tent!

They had hoped to be much further down the river when darkness set in and they had to make their way to the river-bank and camp for the night on private land.

Bruce: That night I went sleep-walking and my foot got stuck in a tin of instant coffee. I woke the next morning with coagulated Ricoffy in my sleeping bag. It may have been about breakfast time that a small boy approached us with a message from the farmer, "Jy moet dadelik pad gee!" We packed speedily and took to the water again.

At lunch time, still sailing past private land, they headed once again for the bank and went ashore. A number of curious cows came down to investigate the intruders. No sooner were they all on dry land than shots rang out. Kate remembered taking cover with her mother "in a bathtub", which Bruce remembers as a drinking-trough.

We didn't hang around to see where the shots came from, but leapt onto our not so speedy getaway craft and did some hasty paddling.

Not long afterwards they reached the safety of public land. In the distance they could hear the breakers at the mouth of the river.

Bruce: Not all the farmers were hostile. I remember one lot asking us as we drifted past, whether the water was drinkable in the middle where we were. Although, come to think of it, they may have been the same ones that took potshots at us!

Heronvale School no longer exists, more is the pity, but prospective rafters should keep a lookout for descendants of former Tsitsikamma hunters!

Millwood c 1870

11.

From George to Knysna via the Passes

To avoid the difficulties of the Lake District, Thomas Bain decided on an inland route.

The road to Pampoenskraal (Saasveld)

We crawl out of George. The traffic is nose to tail for George is no longer the quiet country town we once knew. We are surrounded by shopping centres, houses, and buildings of indeterminate use and origin. Traffic lights and direction signs are scattered along what was once a quiet country road. A police car with flashing blue lights hurries past.

Then the reason for our slow progress appears. A trailer has lost its load. The road is covered with polystyrene which is rapidly turning into a blizzard of small white particles. The driver of the lorry stands on the pavement scratching his head, while his assistant scurries in and out of the traffic retrieving pieces of polystyrene. The police car has pulled up ahead of the lorry and a policeman begins to direct the traffic. A large, black plastic sheet is draped shroud-like over what remains of the load.

Shortly after negotiating the first hazard of the journey we turn off left on to Madiba Drive and after a kilometre or two start the long descent into the valley of the Swartrivier, once a descent dreaded by wagoners, but now a pleasant drive through densely wooded country. Climbing the opposite bank of the river we come to the entrance to Saasveld on a farm once known as Pampoenskraal.

The farm Pampoenskraal, once owned by Barend Stander, an affable man known for his hospitality, was host to many of the botanical collectors of his day. François le Vaillant visited Pampoenskraal towards the end of the 18th century and was much taken by what he saw there.

> *The sumptuous grottoes of your wealthy financiers, magnificent villas of English nabobs; what are your purling streams, your cascades, your artificial mounts, zig-zag walks, bridges, statues, or all those objects which satiate the senses and fatigue the eye? What compared to the simple unaffected beauties of Pampoen Kraal?*

The Swedish natural historians, Carl Thunberg and Anders Sparrman also enjoyed its hospitality and sylvan setting, as did the Germans, Johann Franz Drège, Christian Friedrich Ecklon and Karl Ludwig Zeyher.

In the 1850s Pampoenskraal, by that time the property of William Bidulph, was subdivided and put on the market. A portion was bought by the Baroness Gesina van Rheede van Oudtshoorn. She named her property *Saasveld*, after her ancestral castle in Overijssel in the Netherlands. By the 1930s, when the Department of Forestry was looking around for a new home for its trainee foresters, the property was still known as Saasveld despite having had two or three owners since the Baroness.

The South African College School (SACS) in Cape Town started a course for forest rangers in 1902, but it was soon felt that there was a need for men with a more comprehensive knowledge of silviculture, and in 1906 the prospective forest rangers were moved to the new South African Forestry School at Tokai under the direction of Joseph Storr Lister, Conservator of Forests.

Lister, born in Uitenhage in 1852, after education at the Diocesan College (Bishops) in Cape Town, served in the Indian Forest Service before being appointed, in 1875, as Superintendent of Plantations at the Cape. He rose through the forestry ranks and also made a name for himself by reclamation work on the Cape Flats and at Driftsands, west of Port Elizabeth. He retired after 38 years dedicated service to the State. Like some other civil servants of that era he seemed to spend a great deal of time on the move. He married Georgina, the daughter of another peripatetic civil servant, pass-builder Thomas Bain, and I have at times wondered how the two, Joseph and Georgina, managed to meet one another.

In 1932 the Forestry School moved from Tokai in Cape Town to Saasveld and in 2005 became the George campus of the Nelson Mandela University in Port Elizabeth.

Over the years Saasveld has turned out not only countless eminent foresters, but also nature conservationists, ecologists and botanists. Of the latter there can be few to equal Jan Vlok.

It was in 1982 that Jan made headlines in connection with his rediscovery of *Acrolophia ustulata*, or the Black Orchid. This acrolophia had last been seen in 1904, when in 1980 a young Jan Vlok set his sights on re-finding the rare – so it was believed at the time – member of the family. For two years he tramped the forest of the southern Cape without success, and then one day while carrying out a routine survey of the Ruitersbos area near Mossel Bay he came across it. He could hardly, he says, believe his eyes.

As soon as he could, with no cell-phones in 1982, he hurried back to contact Professor A V Hall, head of the endangered species project at the CSIR in Pretoria, who was clearly sceptical. Jan explained how he had made a detailed study of the plant and that he had been looking for it for two years. The professor, impressed by the young man's obvious sincerity, then told him that he should be especially pleased as he, the professor, had spent 20 years searching unsuccessfully for *Acrolophia ustulata.*

Today the Black Orchid, although regarded as no great rarity, is classified as "vulnerable", for it is highly sensitive to fire intensity and has been totally lost from some sites due to very hot fires, usually due to the presence of alien vegetation. The total population is estimated at roughly 1 000 mature plants. It flowers only during the first two years after fires and is still seldom recorded.

Very often nowadays there is not just one pair of Vlok eyes on the lookout for rarities, but two pairs, for Jan has been joined by Dr Anne Lise Schutte-Vlok. In 2010 their book, *Plants of the Klein Karoo* was published, a second edition coming out in 2015, giving 1 450 of the almost 3 200 species found in the area. It is not only a field guide, but also covers the ecology of the area, contains a treasure trove of photographs and gives reasons as to why plants favour certain localities.

One of the delights of the book, and of being in their company, is their ability to explain in simple terms apparently complex relationships between plants and the environment. This in turn gives one an idea as to where one should look to find a particular species. A case in point was *Fockea capensis* (=*crispa*) which we found, admittedly far from the leafy glades of Pampoenskraal, in the Klein Karoo, and in the company of Johan and Anne Lise.

First let us establish that in the Red List of South African plants the status of *Fockea capensis* is given as of "least concern". While it is restricted to the Klein Karoo it is found growing in large numbers on the rocky slopes of the mountains, and there is no immediate likelihood of it becoming extinct.

Towards the end of the 18th century Baron Nicholas von Jacquin of the Schönbrunn Gardens near Vienna sent two staff-gardeners, Franz Boos and Georg Scholl to the Cape to collect bulbs, plants and seeds. They were in fact more interested in horticulture than botany, but returned with some 300 cases of plant material. Amongst these was a plant with a "tuberous mass", actually a caudex, a combination of root and stem, 30 cm long and with a diameter of 15 cm. No one had seen anything like it before. It was named after a German physician, Gustav Waldemar Focke who after working in the botanical gardens of the University of Vienna, went on to become a plant physiologist and was a founder of the science of micropaleontology and microbiology. The plant was given a place of honour in the Royal collection of the Austrian Emperor Joseph II. No further specimens were found and it was believed to be the sole survivor of an extinct species; the rarest plant in the world.

We were together with Jan and Anne Lise in the Anysberg on the northern boundary of the Ladismith district of the Klein Karoo when I mentioned my interest in the "rarest plant in the world". Jan of course knew all about the plant and had frequently come across it. He explained briefly and in simple terms the physiology of the plant and pointed out how this gave clues as to where one might find it. Shortly afterwards, while driving along he pointed out a spot that fitted the bill, and there, sure enough, within less than ten minutes we found *Fockea capensis*.

In 1905 there was held in Vienna an International Botanical Congress. The western world's leading botanists gazed in awe at the rarest plant in the world. Back in South Africa Dr H W R Marloth, professor of chemistry at the Victoria College (later Stellenbosch University), read the proceedings of the Congress with interest. Within a year he tracked down a plant in the Sandrivier Mountains near Prince Albert. To be doubly sure he waited until he saw it in bloom before sending a specimen to Schönbrunn. Later hundreds of plants were found near Ladismith, and it was discovered that local women made a jam from the plant.

All this came as a shock to the staff at the Schönbrunn, though I can find no mention of how, in 1906, Emperor Franz Joseph I of Austria reacted to the news.

In December 2010 Jan Vlok, a Botanical Society member since the age of 18, was awarded the Marloth Medal by the Society. He was honoured for

Botanist Jan Vlok and his wife Dr Anne Lise Schutte-Vlok

the way in which he had broadcast botanical knowledge to civil society in simple language by means of popular articles in newspapers, radio, television, personal presentations and publications such as *Plants of the Klein Karoo* in which he and Anne Lise had not only shared their "unparalleled knowledge of the Cape flora, but also their insight into intra-species variations and causative factors". But all this was simply because Jan believes that knowledge is of little value if not shared. One of his aims is to bridge the gap between scientific papers and the everyday world. In doing so Jan has not only received personal recognition, but has put the name of Saasveld firmly on the map.

Bain and De Smidt

A Select Committee was set up in 1861 to investigate why it was considered easier for goods sent from George to Knysna, to first go to Mossel Bay and from there by sea to Knysna, rather than by the shorter and more direct land route. It was decided that the main problems were Kaaimans Gat, followed almost immediately by the Trek-aan-Touw, considered by Andrew Geddes Bain as "something worse than Kaaimans Gat".

Before building a road could begin a route had to be found through an almost impenetrable wilderness of trees and a number of deep gorges. Thomas Bain and his relative by marriage Adam de Smidt were allotted the task. Bureaucracy being what it is, even after the survey was complete it took years before a start was made on the road.

De Smidt and Thomas Bain were not only fellow road-makers working on the George-Knysna road, but brothers-in-law, for Bain was married to Johanna de Smidt, Adam's sister. This was not enough to stop a difference of opinion between the two men as to the route the road should follow. This, together with possible political connections, developed into a bitter quarrel which resulted in Bain and De Smidt never talking to one another again.

Saasveld was just one portion of Pampoenskraal, another was later acquired by Adam de Smidt. He named it Woodifield after an inspector of the Public Works Department, Mr Matthew Woodifield. Strangely the former inspector is also commemorated in the Eastern Cape where he worked on the Zuurberg Pass above Addo. Carved into a large, bare rockface is the inscription, "Woodifield Krantz 1855".

De Smidt became an esteemed Member of the Legislative Assembly at the Cape after he retired, and a familiar figure in nearby George. An invitation to Woodifield was regarded locally as an accolade.

The way forward

We cross the Kaaimans and Silver Rivers and climb towards Ginnesville. Here there is a road, Whites Road, down to the Wilderness and the N2. Like the Whites Road (now John Kani Road) in Port Elizabeth it was named after a member of the White family, but in this case after Montagu White, the wealthy son of the road-builder Henry Fancourt White of Blanco.

Near Ginnesville was Barbier's Kraal, of which Lichtenstein writes that it was so named because, "the colonist who undertook to cut this footpath through the woods, made a vow not to be shaved till the work was accomplished; and although he had many slaves to assist him in the task, his beard enjoyed a four weeks' respite". It is a good story and has been repeated ever since, but I do wonder whether or not the path-cutter was not perhaps Dominique Michiel Barbier of Strasbourg, who arrived at the Cape prior to 1785, or even one of his descendants.

Next river crossing is that of the Touw, the once dreaded Trek-aan-Touw of the early travellers. A team of Khoekhoe with *toue* – ropes - pulling on one side of the wagon or the other, were necessary to keep it upright as it negotiated the steps – so they are described – that had to be negotiated going up or down. Today there is a gradual descent through a thickly wooded valley before crossing a lattice-work iron bridge. Once at the top again a tarred road leads down to the Wilderness, but we carried on to Woodville Forest Station. This was the point reached by Bain in 1871 and where construction work came to a halt for the best part of a decade. In the mean time Bain was transferred to construct the Tradouw Pass.

Before 1812, when Adriaan van Kerwel, the George landdrost, constructed the Cradock Kloof Pass, there were many who followed this route to the Duiwelskop Pass into the Langkloof. At Woodville it is possible, with a permit obtained from the forestry office, to follow in their wagon tracks. A drive from Woodville takes one through the forest to Bergplaas and Kleinplaat where one leaves the car. From here one walks along the Outeniqua Trail. The trail continues to climb the mountains until one is looking down on the Langkloof, having missed the highest point, Duiwelskop, 1 000 metres above sea-level. In 1835 Sir Harry Smith, travelling on the original pass, actually reached the top. He was an impetuous man of action. When war broke out on the frontier in 1835 he rode from Cape Town to Grahamstown, a distance of 950 km which he covered in six days, setting a riding record which to my knowledge still stands.

No one is completely certain as to when and by whom the Duiwelskop route was built. It was never really a road despite being used by wagons, but the evidence seems to point to a date prior to 1785, and by local farmers. The names Jacobus van Beelen and Stephanus Terblanche have been suggested.

Back at Woodville, once again we find the busy Chief Inspector of Public Works, Mr Murrell Robinson. From the Forestry Station he suggested that the road should go via Hoogekraal, Karatara, Barrington, Homtini and down what is today the Phantom Pass.

Governor Sir Henry Barkly favoured a different route via Ruigtevlei and bypassing Barrington. Local landowner Henry Barrington supported Robinson's suggestion for obvious reasons. He believed that the Governor's route was motivated simply by spite, as Barrington had opposed in parliament proposals made by the Governor.

Henry Barington was the twelfth child of the 5th Viscount Barrington, prebendary of Durham and rector of Sedgefield (England). Henry, educated at Oxford, became a diplomat, but after an unhappy love affair, resigned and sailed for the Cape where he bought the Portland estate from Thomas Duthie. He was a progressive farmer and experimented with silkworms, cider-apples and bees. He also erected one of the first sawmills. He was described as being of superior intellect and was strong and fearless, but also arrogant and tyrannical. In the devastating 1869 fire he lost everything, but continued to farm his land.

By the time Bain returned in July 1880 he was faced with at least three possible routes, those of Robinson, Sir Henry Barkly and Adam de Smidt, who favoured a route closer to the foot of the mountains. In Bain's absence gold had been discovered in the area which further complicated matters, and a start had been made on the Ruigtevlei road. No sooner was Bain back in charge than the road crew was recalled to Woodville and work continued on the Robinson (and Bain) route.

With the master *padmaker* supervising work the road continued due east crossing the Dieprivier and on to the Hoogekraal valley, then across the plateau to Karatara Forest Station and on to Portland, where Barrington farmed.

At Homtini the rate of progress slowed, for here another major pass was required through the heavily wooded valley. But not for long - the pass was officially opened in 1882, although it was not officially handed over to the Divisional Council until 1887. The crossing of the river was by causeway until 1899, when the red-painted iron bridge was completed.

Despite Henry Barrington recording in his 1881 diary that he had consented to the new pass being named after him, nothing came of this. It seems that the name Barrington did not go down well with Cape Town officials.

Gold fever - Millwood

In the mid-1870s, James Hooper while collecting grit for his father's ostriches in a tributary of the Karatara River near Ruigtevlei discovered what he thought to be gold. On his next visit to Knysna, Hooper took his find to hotelkeeper, confectioner and apothecary William Groom who confirmed that it was gold and offered him £2-10-0 for the 17 dwt (dwt = pennyweight) of precious metal. (After leaving Knysna, Groom went on to become a photographer in Cape Town. He was obviously a man of many parts.)

Hooper then approached civil and mining engineer Charles Osborne who at the time was working on a road near the Lakes. Osborne confirmed Groom's identification and together with Hooper began prospecting. In due course he exhibited a nugget to the House of Assembly in Cape Town and was made a grant of £100, a considerable sum at the time, to investigate further.

At this point Osborne was transferred to Port Nolloth and later Natal. It was left to Hooper to soldier on. He came across numerous traces of gold from the Karatara to the Dieprivier. By this time the gold-find was no secret and numbers of others with more enthusiasm than ability were taking up the search.

After Thomas Bain's return to the area in 1880, he was appointed Gold Commissioner, with John Barrington, eldest son of the Honourable Henry Barrington as Assistant Commissioner.

In 1886 Charles Osborne resigned from government service and returned to Karatara, and in March requested that the Millwood area be opened for pegging. Osborne teamed up once again with Hooper, but having worked for some time without success, Hooper returned to the farm, while Osborne moved to the Homtini and began working up the river towards Thesen's Mill. He came across a gully with which he was reasonably impressed and took his finds to Bain. Together they worked on a report in which they stressed that the alluvial gold found was such that the area would never be a poor man's diggings, but that they believed it should be thrown open so that the general public could "practice sluicing". The results of this would provide a better idea of what was available. It was the start of the Millwood gold rush, Millwood being named after the presence of Thesen's Mill. The first gold sold was from the house of Mr Frank Franzsen, the miller at Thesen's Mill.

In next to no time there were a thousand diggers. Seventy-five wood and iron houses were erected on the 135 stands laid out by Government Surveyor W Newdigate. There were six hotels, three boarding houses, a hospital with two wards and a doctor, Edward Garroway, a Methodist church, a mineral water factory, three weekly newspapers, 25 shops, seven butchers and four bakers. A post office was opened with weekly deliveries to and from Cape Town, a police-station and a Standard Bank agency.

Before long it was not only alluvial gold that was found. By June 1887 14 reefs were registered and there were 24 tunnels. Gold was definitely to be found, but finding it in payable quantities was another matter, and there was news of gold in the Transvaal. Before long the diggers began to leave.

By 1892 the population had dropped to 110. The following year there were only 74. Before very long all that remained of the miners were the approximately hundred graves in the cemetery. Among the graves were those of Amelia Graham, aged 34, who died in 1891 and left three minor children and a husband; James Clingen, aged seven, who died in 1891 as a result of a snake-bite, and John Lichter who, when he died in 1887, was just five months old.

Today there are foundations, odd pieces of machinery and tunnels. All the dreams of riches beyond belief faded away at the break of day. Perhaps even the level-headed Bain had his dreams, but as might be expected, nowhere among the official reports will you find any mention of them. The real treasure of Millwood has remained: the indigenous forest, the ferns and the bulbs, the waters of Jubilee Creek, the birds and all the creatures of the forest both great and small that have returned.

* * *

Along the road to Millwood you will find a picnic spot at Krisjan-se-Nek. In 2008 a memorial was erected here to Dalene Mathee, writer of books about the Knysna Forest and its creatures and people. This was one of the writer's favourite spots, and after her death in 2005 her ashes were scattered here. It is said that it was here that she was inspired to write the first of her four books on the forest, *Kringe in 'n Bos.* It is indeed a magical spot and well worth a break in one's journey. Dalene crops up again later in this record of a journey.

Phantom, the last of the passes

From Rheenendal there is a tar road which continues down to the N2, but shortly after leaving Rheenendal there is a turn-off to the Phantom Pass and one is back on dirt following the road that Bain built.

It was in 1860 that Bain first visited the Knysna area. Since at least 1832 travellers had crossed the river at a drift in the upper reaches of the estuary. This was situated near the turn off to Charlesford, the upper portion of Westford, Robert Sutherland's farm. The crossing was only possible at low tide, as attested to by numerous travellers including the doughty Bishop Robert Gray, and local landowner Thomas Duthie. Even at low tide the water reached a horse's belly and wagons often ran into difficulties.

Bain solved the problem by building a causeway using large stones too heavy to be moved by the ordinary flood-waters of the river. This raised platform provided a safer, although perhaps just as bumpy a crossing as the earlier one.

Work on the Phantom Pass began in 1862 and was completed by the 22 convicts in only two months, which seems to indicate that there were no particular problems to overcome. It is possible that Bain made use of an existing track leading to the Zuurvlakte Crown Forest.

There are several theories as to how the pass acquired its name. They range from the historical to the entomological, from the Honourable Henry Barrington and the Italian silk workers of Gouna, to the lifecycle of *Leto venus*, the Ghost (or Phantom) Moth. I personally favour the latter perhaps because it is less fanciful than the first.

The female Phantom Moth lays her eggs in soft earth near the roots of the Keurboom - *Virgilia divaricate* - before flying off to die. After hatching from the eggs the larvae drill through the bark of the tree extracting their food from the sawdust, which is also used to "cap" and thus seal off the tunnel. When mature they break out of the tunnel and once out, unfurl their wings, before taking off on a nuptial flight. As this takes place more or less simultaneously throughout the forest, there are certain nights of the year when the glades are filled by these spotted-winged phantoms.

In 1882 Bain was back again after working on the Hom-tini Pass to work on the Phantom Pass, and seven years later returned once again to renovate or possibly realign the pass, which was said to be in a terrible condition.

Thereafter, apart from routine maintenance, work cen-tred around the crossing of the Knysna River. A wooden bridge was constructed by local contractor John Littlejohn in 1895, but by 1915, when it was replaced by a steel bridge, the wooden bridge had been rickety and unreliable for ten years.

The steel bridge did not last for long, either. The year after it was completed it was washed away.

For seven years the people of Knysna were ferried across the river or took their chances and waded at low tide. Finally a second steel bridge was built. Fifty years later, in 1973, it was closed to traffic and everyone made use of the present con-crete bridge on the N2.

What about the women?

It was a busy day and now we cannot find the GPS. We last remember seeing it at Jubilee Creek while pin-pointing the position of ferns on a data sheet. What chance of finding it in the forest? The chances are next to nil. Still, even with the light fading fast there's nothing for it but to climb into the Isuzu and make the long trek back. And on the way back, a miracle: there it is lying in the road! No one has driven over it and it is still working. It was probably left on the roof of the bakkie. We turn about and in a more cheerful frame of mind head back towards Knysna.

It is out of season and tonight there are only two caravans in the park. We may choose whichever site suits us best. Find-ing a relatively level one, for we cannot adjust the level of the Isuzu as one can with a caravan, we settle down for the night.

The spaghetti bolognaise only needs to be heated and we can have supper.

Now for the second mishap of the day; we cannot find the matches to light the gas burner. There is nothing for it; we will have to ask one of the caravaners if they can let us have a box of matches.

It is a balmy evening and Ben and Sheila are sitting un-der the awning outside their caravan looking out into a black velvet night sky adorned with a veil of stars. In the light of the lamp on the camp table moths are intent on their circular suicide flights. It is difficult to be sure, but not one of them appears to be a Phantom Moth.

Sheila has on a flowery blouse and Ben a more sober checked shirt; both are wearing shorts and slops. We explain our predicament and Sheila is up at once and produces a box of matches while Ben finds two more folding chairs.

"Have a beer?"

Sheila ducks back into the caravan and some minutes later comes out carrying a plate of snacks.

Ben is balding, tanned and has an incipient boep. To judge by his large, capable, scarred hands his work did not take place in an office. He has recently retired after thirty-odd years on the mines.

Sheila is a cheerful brunette and also worked on the mine as a secretary. "Nowadays they call them 'personal assistants', but I was just a secretary". They are from Boksburg and have been caravanning for years; "mainly Durbs, LM and the Kruger". This is their first visit to the southern Cape. "Well, you know what it's like with kids." Indeed, we do. "It's lovely here. We never realised just how lovely the Cape is. There is so much to see in this country, and we've only just begun, haven't we dear? My dream is to crisscross the country, to go wherever we can in South Africa." Ben nods his head, "Ja, that's Sheila's dream."

Later, back at the Isuzu, eating hot spaghetti bolognaise, we comment on the kindness and warmth of the couple from Boksburg.

Next morning we are up early. The door of their caravan is shut and the chairs folded and lying beneath the van. No sign of life. We drive off.

Should you ever read this, Ben and Sheila, thank you for the matches, snacks and the beer. Thank you too for your company on a warm, starlit night beside the Knysna Lagoon. Travel well in search of South Africa!

* * *

First owner of the farm Uitzicht, so far as we know, was Solomon Terblans, who at an early date "sold" the southern section of the farm, which included the Western Head at Knysna, to Hendrik Barnard for an ox-wagon and a span of oxen.

George Rex of Melkhoutkraal, on the opposite side of the river, bought the entire Uitzicht farm from Terblans and Barnard in 1830. In the same year Lieutenant Thomas Henry Duthie of the 72nd Highlanders spent a fortnight at Melkhoutkraal, where he admired Rex's new acquisition and not only admired, but fell in love with Rex's daughter, Caroline.

In 1833 Duthie and Caroline were married in Cape Town and left for Britain where Duthie resigned his commission and studied Natural History and Botany at Edinburgh University. This he felt was a suitable preparation for farming in the southern Cape.

On their return, Duthie bought the former Terblans lands from his father-in-law and set about establishing a village, Belvidere. Ajardine, a Malay builder began work on Belvidere manor house, while Duthie, together with another local resident, William Newdigate, rode to Cape Town. There they discussed with the newly arrived Bishop Robert Gray, the possibility of a church in the new village. Gray later visited Belvidere and a site for the church was chosen, with the Bishop promising to produce a plan for a church capable of seating a hundred, "but capable of enlargement".

There were probably very few living at the Cape at the time that were aware that the Bishop's wife, Sophy, was a self-taught architect and an expert on ecclesiastical architecture.

Sophia (Sophy) Myddleton had no particular theological background when she married Robert Gray, but she drew and painted in water-colours, that typically English medium, scenic views and architectural details. Married to Robert she began to take an intense interest in "correct", usually Norman or Gothic-style, churches.

In 1847 Sophy encouraged her husband to accept nomination for the Bishopric of Cape Town. Preparing for the

253

journey she spent a great deal of time sketching fonts, hammer-beam roofs, windows, arches and other features and in studying architectural drawings, for one of Robert's tasks would be to establish English churches throughout the Colony. They set out in 1847 aboard the *Persia* and arrived in Cape Town on the 24th of February the following year.

Their first task was to set up home at Protea, formerly Boschheuvel, in Claremont, a 120 hectare estate. From the start Sophy took charge of the property, later to be known as Bishops Court, and ran it as a viable entity, complete with vegetable garden, orchards, and poultry, with cows to provide fresh milk; all the while playing an active part in church affairs; raising money for the diocese, acting as the bishop's adviser, consultant and amanuensis, planning their travels and supporting and influencing his policies.

Duthie of Belvidere had in mind a place of worship for family, friends and servants. Sophy took from among the plans the Grays had brought from England the drawings for a Norman style chapel with typically thick stone walls, rounded arches and windows. With the approval of Duthie and Newdigate, she then produced the working drawings for what was to become the Holy Trinity Church, Belvidere.

At Belvidere a building committee was formed. Henry Barrington provided stinkwood and yellowwood and funds were collected. Thomas Duthie's brother in England, the Reverend A H Duthie took charge of fund raising overseas and organised the casting of a bell. (This, when it eventually arrived in the Knysna lagoon, was accidentally dropped overboard and had to be brought up from beneath the fortunately shallow waters.) A source of suitable sandstone was discovered just five kilometres away, and with the arrival of the Scottish stonemasons, Alexander Bern, Alexander Lawrence and his brother James, quarrying began and the foundations were laid out. Three thousand Welsh slates were sent out aboard the *Apame* and unloaded at Belvidere. The "Monster Stone", from which the complete pulpit for the new church was carved, was quarried.

* * *

It was while delving into the diaries and other records of the early travellers at the Cape that I first became interested in Sophy Gray. At a time when women seldom undertook lengthy journeys into the hinterland, Sophy was an exception. Everywhere that her husband Robert went, with the exception of his nine month tour of his diocese in 1850 and his visit to Tristan da Cunha, Sophy went too. In full Victorian dress she climbed the Outeniquas and riding side-saddle was soaked to the skin coming down. Yet she also raised four daughters and a son. Her daughter Louisa, married a clergyman, the Reverend Edward Glover, the first warden of Zonnebloem College in Cape Town. He was later, as archdeacon of George, responsible for the maintenance of one of his mother-in-law's churches.

Reading played an important part in Sophy and Robert's lives, particularly books on architecture and on ecclesiology; her husband's particular interest. Besides being a self-trained draughtsman and architect, Sophy took a keen interest in practically everything and everyone she came across in her new homeland. Clergy who visited and stayed with the Grays spoke highly of Sophy as a hostess yet understandably, considering all her responsibilities, she had little or no time for a social life.

During a period of roughly 30 years, she was involved with the building of about 40 church buildings. Her work might be regarded as an attempt to Anglicise an African land, but a century and a half later her churches have become a part of our heritage, buildings cherished by their congregants and accepted by other communities as a part of the tapestry of their lives.

* * *

We stand outside the little church in its peaceful setting by "the lake", as Robert Gray referred to the lagoon, which to be strictly correct is an estuary. Around the corner are oak trees and the graves of Thomas Duthie's descendants. It is said that the Holy Trinity, Belvidere, is probably the best known of Sophy's churches, and definitely the most visited, which is not surprising for it is an architectural gem and a memorial to a remarkable woman.

Inside the church, in the form of a stained glass window, another remarkable woman is commemorated, Augusta Vera Duthie, the last of the Duthies to live in the Belvidere manor house.

Augusta was born at Belvidere in 1881 and from a very early age took an intense interest in her natural surroundings. After school she attended UCT and was capped MA in 1910. This was followed in 1929 with a DSc from UNISA. She then spent a year at Cambridge before going on to Australia for a further year.

At the age of 20 she became the first South African trained botanist to be appointed a lecturer in botany at what was to become Stellenbosch University, and as a senior lecturer served as Head of Department for 18 years. During this time she developed a botanical library, a museum, herbarium, botanical garden and facilities for morphological research.

She did a good deal of original research, publishing papers on the Orchids, Eriospermums and others, described several new plants, and discovered and described five varieties of Urginea. She took a particular interest in the flora of the Cape Flats.

She was considered to be an excellent lecturer and encouraged her students to develop a love of nature. One of her former students, Professor Gert Nel, became head of the University botany department in her stead in 1921.

She retired to Belvidere in 1939 where she ran the family farm. There she lived with a companion, the former village school-teacher, Miss Annie Armstrong.

Before her retirement in 1926, aged 62, Miss Armstrong taught the Duthie children and others, in the "schoolroom" on the ground floor of the manor house. At Miss Armstrong's school, despite what anyone else might have to say about it, there was no colour bar. A former pupil said of his old teacher after her death in 1952, that she played an integral part in the life of the whole community, and that her life and service to man could not be separated.

Miss Armstrong's former pupil, Augusta Duthie, lived on until 1963. She, like her old teacher, lived a busy and useful life increasing the sum of human knowledge, and introducing young people to the wonders of the natural world around them.

Knysna forest railway locomotive and crew. (Ch 12)

Irma von Below
(Ch 15)

Robberg Peninsula, looking out over
Nelson Bay. (Ch 13)

Right: A
Fairmile
Motor
Gun Boat
(MGB) at
speed.
(Ch 12)

Clarkson church
& bell (Ch 15)

A A S le Fleur and
supporters at Kok-
stad
(Ch 13)

Cullinan dia-
mond. (Ch 13)

Belvidere
(Ch11)

1931 Chevrolet Independence Sedan

12.

Knysna and the forests

A walk around town

We cross the White Bridge, the present bridge on the N2 over the Knysna River, and turn sharp right towards the town of the same name. The roadside has stalls selling everything from cheese to carved, elongated, wooden giraffes. Africa's indigenous trees are leaving her shores for Europe, the Americas, the Middle East, Asia and Australasia as representations of Africa's wildlife: giraffes, elephants, hippos and rhinos.

First stop in town is at the House of Classic and Sports Cars at 70 Main Street. No, we have no intention of buying a replacement for the Isuzu, I simply enjoy seeing again some of the cars I knew as a teenager, and today we are particularly lucky. There stands a 1931 Chevrolet four-door sedan with a dark blue body with black mudguards, white sidewall tyres, and a grey interior. The marked price is R380 000, which is a bit more than the £15 my friend David Starker's father paid for a second hand model in 1953.

Mr Starker came across the car at an auction. He thought that it might keep us out of mischief during the school holidays. The engine and transmission were working, but not much else. Neither David nor I were old enough for driving licences, but under the circumstances that did not make much difference. We were delighted.

The 22 year-old vehicle had spent its working life at Swakopmund (in present-day Namibia) and salt roads and seaspray had marred the finish and damaged the wiring. Few things relying on an electrical earth connection were operating. In addition the mechanical brakes were non-existent. David and I began work on the car, and his father was quite right, it took us the best part of the holidays to have it (almost) roadworthy. .

We never managed to adjust the brakes to our satisfaction. They stopped the car and the handbrake held, but there was always one wheel that tended to lock unless one braked very gently. Finally, everything else was working, even the klaxon under the front left headlamp. There was one exception; the tail-light standing on the top of a stalk on the back right mudguard.

The holiday was almost over and term was due to start. It was time to celebrate. Our friend Winnie was a licenced driver and could drive us to the cinema.

There was just the question of the tail-light, and we would be out at night. We eventually sorted that out by borrowing the extension lead for Mrs Starker's vacuum-cleaner, and made a direct connection from battery to tail-light. Problem solved, and with Winnie at the wheel, off we went.

A few kilometres down the road we were stopped by a traffic-policeman. We could hardly believe it. What could possibly be wrong?

"You've got no tail-light."

"No, no", we protested, "there must be some mistake. The tail-light is definitely working."

"Get out and come and have a look."

We got out and he was quite right. The wiring had come undone.

"What else on this old rust-bucket isn't working?"

At this he put his booted foot on the tail-light on its long, slender, rusted stalk, and it broke off from the mudguard. This brought about a sudden change in his attitude.

"Jislaaik! Man I'm sorry about that. Look, we forget about the light. Seriously though man, it's blerry dangerous driving around without a blerry rear-light. Go and park the car somewhere and get your friends to pick you up."

After he had left we continued to the cinema with David sitting on the back seat holding the re-wired light up to the rear window. It worked like a charm.

* * *

I do not know what make of car the famous playwright and former journalist George Bernard Shaw was driving from George to Knysna in February 1932. Perhaps it was a 1931 Chev, but somehow I tend to think that it was more likely to be a Ford. Whatever the make, he trod on the clutch when he should, according to what he told the police, have pressed down on the accelerator. The car left the road and his wife Charlotte (née Payne-Townsend) was injured. This resulted in a month-long stay in Knysna while his wife and the car were set to rights. Shaw was not too despondent: "For sunshine, scenery, bathing and motoring the place (Knysna) is unbeatable." Not one to let an opportunity slip by, Shaw began writing a book, which he called a novella, incorporating his experiences in South Africa.

262

When white South Africans first heard that Shaw was coming to the country, there were mixed reactions. He was, of course, a world-famous playwright, but his atheism offended many, and his liberal views on the colour question caused much alarm and condemnation. The *Cape Argus* summed it up:

> *No doubt our politics and our native policy will strike him as astonishingly funny. But... our respectful interest in Mr Shaw may lead him to deal lightly with our very obvious short-comings.*

While in Cape Town he made the first broadcast to be relayed all over the Union of South Africa, an indication of how important a visitor he was considered to be, but there was no denying that he was also potentially dangerous.

Now in Knysna, between outings to The Heads to go swimming, and visits to Charlotte, he settled down to write *A Black Girl in Search of God.* The tale is an allegory of an African girl recently converted to Christianity who goes out, armed with a *kierie*, to find and speak to God. She is an emerging feminist, a naïve but superior person supposed by popular prejudice to be inferior both by her sex and her race. There are many people that she meets during the course of her search. All give inane answers to her searching questions. The *kierie* is used to knock sense into them. She eventually settles down with a coarse, red-headed Irishman and rears a "charmingly coffee-coloured" family before, after the children have grown up and left home, continuing her search.

The book outraged religious believers. Shaw's belief that miscegenation was a cure for the country's ills probably infuriated South Africans of all colours, but very definitely the whites. In Britain it was taken as a bad joke, and in Nazi Germany as "blasphemy". All of which was very pleasing to Shaw who set out to provoke just such a reaction in the first place.

Despite the car accident he considered the visit to South Africa to have been a great success. The country, and Knysna especially, was not only "unbeatable" for bathing and scenic beauty, but had inspired a rewarding piece of work.

Next stop along the way is at the traffic lights at the inter-section of Main and Long Streets. In years gone by the dou-ble-storey building on our left housed Melvilles Ltd, General Dealers. Both travellers and those residents who did not live within walking distance of a corner café, tended, particularly with a weekend approaching, to stop at Melvilles to stock up with milk and bread. For years it was not only the retail, but also the social, centre of Knysna.

The original building was enlarged in 1922 to designs drawn up by architects Simpson & Bridgman, a firm that de-signed a number of buildings in the town. Travelling with a father-in-law who was an architect one often picked up in-teresting tidbits about the urban environment and the men responsible; men, because in those days there seemed to be very few women involved.

In 1912 the building was bought by Thesens and remained in their keeping until the 1970s when the company was ac-quired by Barlows Ltd. This was at much the same time as the spread of supermarkets across the country was reaching the last of the *platteland dorps*. There is much to be said in favour of supermarkets, but I for one regret the passing of the gen-eral dealers of 50 years ago or more.

Turning right into Long Street we drive down towards the old jetty, but stop at the corner with Union Street. There on the left is another double storey building, Thesen House, with a definite resemblance to the old Melvilles in Main Street. This is not surprising as it too was designed by Simpson and Bridgman. Originally there were corner turrets, but these disappeared in a 1926 fire. The pointed gables that replaced them increase the similarity to the Main Street building. The offices of the Thesen Steamship Company were housed here, together with the Thesens' wholesale business. It was no chance decision that resulted in the location of the building in close proximity to the jetty, the focal point of Knysna Harbour.

* * *

The year 1868 was one of economic depression in Stavanger, Norway, and the trading company of Mathias and Arnt Thesen, faced with a ledger full of bad debt, was forced to close its doors. They bought a ship, the *Albatros*, loaded it with stores and timber and in July 1869 sailed off to find a home in New Zealand. East of the Cape of Good Hope they were storm-battered and were forced to return to Cape Town. While making the necessary repairs they were approached with an offer to take cargo along the Cape south coast. Ultimately this resulted in their arrival in Knysna in 1870. There they continued their shipping business with the *Albatros*, but later expanded into trading and timber.

In the years to come the Thesens became merchant princes of Knysna. What helped was the establishment by Charles Wilhelm Thesen, son of Arnt Thesen, of a limited liability company, Thesens of Knysna.

C W Thesen went on to represent George in the Cape Legislative Council, became Mayor of Knysna, was Chairman of the Knysna Divisional Council, and was a founder member of the Knysna Yacht Club.

His first marriage was to Bessie Harison, the daughter of Christopher Harison, former officer in the Black Watch, friend and collaborator with Thomas Bain in planning the road route from Knysna to Humansdorp. Harison, based at Witelsbos, was also Conservator of Forests. His daughter Bessie is remembered by the lych gate to the old St George's Church in Main Street. The church was designed by Sophy Gray of course.

Which brings us to author Hjalmar Thesen, born in 1925, brought up in Knysna and educated at St Andrew's in Grahamstown. He finished school in 1943 in the midst of the Second World War. As might be expected from someone with his maritime connections, he joined the South African Navy.

All the time, bubbling away in the background, so to speak, were his experiences in this very special part of the Cape coast. The result was a salmagundi of natural treasures and human history spiced with his gifts as a raconteur. First helping from the pot in 1969, was a novel, *The Castle of Giants*. More novels followed, while in the *Eastern Province Her-*

ald there appeared a fortnightly column, a collection of which was published in 1974 entitled *Country Days: Chronicles of Knysna & the Southern Cape.*

You will already have come across a soupçon to whet your appetite in these pages; his remarks regarding karri beer.

* * *

St George's Street in Knysna runs to the west and roughly parallel to Long Street.. On the left, looking down the street, was Geo. Parkes & Sons in a building designed by Simpson and Bridgman, which now (2020) houses the Woodmill Lane shopping complex. On the right was Templeman's saw-mill.

The year 1904 saw the formation of the South Western Railway Co., Ltd (SWRC), the principal shareholders being Messrs Parkes, Templeman and Thesen. In the same year C W Thesen laid a proposal before the Legislative Assembly that a railway be built from Knyna to a point at Yzernek in the forests. This led to the passing of Act No 16 of 1904 authorising the SWRC, under certain conditions, to go ahead with the project. One condition being that the line be of a 24 inch gauge so that at some future date it might link up with the Port Elizabeth to Avontuur line.

No time was lost and a Swedish engineer, Carl Westveldt, was engaged to oversee the work. By 1907 the 35 km line was complete at a cost of £49 858, which was pleasing to all, as the estimate had been £71 609. Apart from the terminus at Diepwalle, in the Yzernek area, and at Knysna, there were three stations: 1. Bracken Hill, the site of the Thesens mill; 2. Parkes Station; 3. Templemans. With the railway providing inexpensive and easy transport, a contract was drawn up with the Cape Government Railway to supply 120 000 sleepers (7 500 tons) annually. The Yellowwood giants were to come crashing down.

To operate the line there were three German-made Orenstein and Köppell locomotives, and a driver, Mr Tom Kennett. As there were to be only three trains a week, a minimum of staff was employed: besides the driver a fireman and guard. No station was manned as there was insufficient work to keep a stationmaster busy. In 1930 a British-built locomotive was added to the shunt of steam-engines.

The line was obliged by the Act to carry passengers, but initially passenger accommodation consisted of a "home-made caboose". This made little difference to the woodcutters who were the most frequent passengers. However, from 1926 tourists began to use the train during the summer season and a coach was provided for those unable to face conditions the woodcutters took for granted.

* * *

A champion of the woodcutters was the novelist Dalene Matthee, whom we first met in Uniondale. She was an accomplished pianist before ever taking up writing, starting with children's stories to supplement the family income. She judged whether or not a story was successful by reading it to her young daughters at bedtime. If one or other of them started picking the blanket, she knew there was more work to be done on the story.

The family moved to Hartenbos in 1978 and while there went on a three-day back-packing trip which took them to the former Millwood goldfields and to Krisjan-se-Nek, situated off the Passes Road between George and Knysna. This had a profound effect on Dalene and was to result, in 1984, in the publication of the first of her four "forest" novels, *Kringe in 'n Bos*, later translated into English as *Circles in a Forest*. Not only into English: the forest novels have been translated into 17 different languages and she has become one of the most widely read of Afrikaans authors. The other three forest novels are: *Fiela se Kind* (1985), *Moerbeibos* (1987) and *Toorbos* (2003). In addition the first two books have been turned into the films: *Circles in a Forest* and *Fiela's Child*.

Circles in a Forest tells the story of woodcutter Saul Barnard who is considered a traitor and banished from his home, and of his fight to save the vanishing forests. It is the story too of the heartless exploitation of the less privileged, and of the woodcutters in particular, and a vivid portrayal of the forest and of its life, both plant and animal, with a heartfelt plea for their preservation.

All of the forest novels contain a wealth of historic detail concerning the local community. Dalene found a source of this information at the local museum housed in Millwood House, one of the original wood and iron houses erected at the Millwood. When the gold ran out, Millwood House, like so many of the other buildings, was taken down and transported in sections to Knysna. The Museum is one of the few that remain.

* * *

We are back in Queen Street and shortly before we reach the Town Hall lying straight ahead, there on the left is Millwood House. Strangely enough this house, with its low-pitched corrugated iron roof complete with 19th century finial and its wooden verandah, in which Dalene Matthee, the former Dalena Scott, spent so much time, was home while at Millwood to a Scott family. Now, once again it was sheltering a Scott within its walls. She emerged from her research with the material which was to be added to her own experiences in the forests to produce four of the most memorable books to tell the Knysna story.

Messing about in boats

It was not only the restoration of a 1931 Chevrolet that kept David Starker occupied during school holidays, but also boat building. For months the partially completed hull of a sailing-dinghy was to be seen beside the stone cottage in his parents' back garden. The cottage served David as both bedroom and workshop and also as a convenient getaway for two teenage boys, anxious to be able to do what they wanted to do away from adult eyes.

With the Chev now roadworthy and licensed we could concentrate on the dinghy. In the cottage the glue bubbled away in a double-boiler on a Primus stove, while we were hunched over the framework of the dinghy with hand-drills or screwdrivers. Fiberglass and powered hand tools were only just beginning to enter our lives. It was somewhat similar to what happened in 1826, when boat-building started beside the Knysna River; hand tools were then also the order of the day.

* * *

After initial enthusiasm the authorities at the Cape lost interest in the port of Knysna, and in 1826 the pilot scheme was abolished. With no one to guide craft through the Heads, ship-owners were loath to make use of the port. Those that did were faced with an increase in insurance charges. There was an immediate decrease in the number of ships visiting the port. George Rex decided that the only way out was to build a vessel of his own, and went into partnership with a Mr William Robertson of Cape Town. Before the year was out the keel had been laid on the Rex farm, Westford near the ford across the river.

On-site supervision of the work was undertaken by Captain James Smith under the watchful eye of another old salt, Captain D Watt, who was later to take command of the new vessel on its maiden voyage.

It was perhaps fortunate that there had been several wrecks in the estuary, and Rex was able to make use of the remains of the *Emu*, the very first to have sailed safely through the Heads in 1817, only to strike a submerged rock, known ever since as the Emu Rock. Then there were also the *Adolphus*, when crossing the bar in 1819, and the *Harmony*, which was wrecked while leaving port earlier in 1826. To some it might appear that there were an inordinate number of wrecks in the waters off Knysna.

Lieutenant Cowper Rose, an engineering officer in the British Army, visited Rex at his home at Melkhoutkraal in 1828 and was taken to see the activity at Westford. He reported that Mr Rex was building a boat to "coast" between his residence and Cape Town, and that its name was to be *Brittania*.

269

"I begged hard to have it called the *Knysna* as the first (vessel) which had been built from its forests or launched upon its waters." His wish was granted.

In 1829 Rose wrote a mildly controversial book, *Four Years in Southern Africa,* about his experiences at the Cape. Then, 30 years later and by then with the rank of Colonel, he, more or less at his own request, returned to the country as Commanding Engineer at the Cape. This was largely to give him the opportunity to revisit the scenes of his youth. At the time he was expecting within a year to be raised to the rank of Major-General, an expectation that was never to be.

During this second visit to the Cape, Rose in 1859 set out aboard the SS *Waldesian* to visit his old haunts along the southern coast. Disembarking in Algoa Bay he was drowned whilst attempting, through dangerous surf, to come ashore in a whale-boat. He was buried from St Mary's in Port Elizabeth. For many years his was an unmarked grave in St Mary's cemetery, but in 1966 a simple marker was placed on the grave.

The *Waldesian* did not last that much longer: in October 1862 it was wrecked on the Bulldog Reef at Struispunt near Cape Agulhas while on a voyage from Durban to Cape Town. It struck at night in a light, south-easterly breeze.

During the whole of the 19th century there were five times more shipwrecks along the Cape coast than during the 20th century and this despite the fact that there was far more maritime activity in the latter century. In addition there was much loss of life, such as that of Cowper Rose, not attributable to wrecks. Travelling by sea was a risky business, and the number of wrecks at Knysna was not in any way extraordinary.

In 1831 the *Knysna* was launched and on the 26th of July, skippered by Captain Watt, it set out on its maiden voyage. Unfortunately the captain took ill and had to be put ashore at Mossel Bay, but the *Knysna* reached Cape Town safely, together with a load of timber and one passenger. From then on she sailed under the command of a Scot, Captain John Findlay, calling regularly at Mossel Bay, Plettenberg Bay, Algoa Bay and Cape Town, with occasional voyages to St Helena and Mauritius.

The *Knysna* is remembered particularly because of the Government charter in 1836 that took her to investigate the possibilities of the Buffalo River as a port, still under the command of John Findlay. Also on board were John Rex, son of George Rex, and John Bailie, regarded as the founder of East London. From then on the little vessel was a regular visitor to the Buffalo.

Then on the 3rd of April 1839, George Rex died and in the terms of his will the *Knysna* was sold. It eventually sailed for England and in November 1844, while on a voyage from Westport to Bristol, went aground. All the men were saved, but it was reported that the first ship built at Knysna had "gone to pieces".

Over the years other boats were built at Knysna: in 1855 the schooner *Rover*, and in 1867 another named *Annie Benn*, together with various small boats.

Then, with the coming of the Second World War a number of different types of boats were built for the armed forces. In 1942 the production of 112 foot (34 metre) Fairmile motor torpedo boats and submarine chasers began, using largely imported timber. In all, ten of these vessels went down the slipway before the end of the war. Thereafter it was back to leisure craft and fishing boats, some of the latter being very large purse seiners.

In April 1966 there was a brief but disastrous fire at Thesens Boatyard. When it reopened in June the following year the hull of an historic yacht was well on the way to completion, the fifty foot (15 metres) racing yacht *Voortrekker* designed by Dutch naval architect Ricus van de Stadt. Built specifically for the Plymouth to Newport race, she was skippered by Bruce Dalling, and finished second, only 128 km behind the winner. The sloop-rigged *Voortrekker* was then acquired by the South African Navy and with "Biltong Berty" Reed at the helm, took part in the first three Cape-to-Rio races.

To mark the centenary of Thesens in 1970 another yacht was built for entry in the Cape-to-Rio race in 1971. It was to be named *Albatros II* after the original *Albatros* that brought the Thesen family from Stavanger in Norway to Knysna. Designed once again by Van de Stadt, the sloop-rigged vessel was to be skippered by John Goodwin.

Albatros II was launched on the 14th of November 1970 at a gathering of Thesen descendants, sixty of them, and over a thousand other guests. A Kruger rand lay beneath the main mast from which at the top flapped the red flag with a white star of the Thesen Shipping Line. Tied for'ard was a posy of everlastings and Erica. Also evident was John Goodwin's flag with a dove with a sprig of laurel in its beak, embroidered by John's wife, Laurel Zahn. It was a great occasion and the fact that *Albatros II* failed, when officially launched by Mrs Hildur Stent, a Thesen great-granddaughter, to slide down into the water, the tide being too low, did not in any way detract from proceedings. At the next high water the yacht glided down in as stately a manner as might be expected.

On the 21st of January 1971 the race started from Granger Bay in Cape Town and *Albatros II* went on to become the first yacht to cross the line and also to win on corrected time. There was general celebration throughout South Africa. Knysna went wild. The nine trophies won were brought home and proudly displayed in the window of Melville's, in the Main Street.

Skipper John Goodwin was born in Essex in 1930 and was brought up on the Isle of Wight. At the age of eight, together with his family, he made his first transatlantic crossing, in his businessman-father's yacht, to the Potomac River. There his father bought a farm and the family settled down for a while. When the time came for John to go to a secondary school they once again crossed the Atlantic and John went to Kurt Hahn's Gordonstoun.

In 1952 the family moved once again, this time to Cape Town, where his father again went into business and John took to producing high quality woodwork; a Goodwin-family tradition. When the time came for his mother, father and brother to move on yet again, back to the United Kingdom, John decided to stay. With the Group Areas Act in force and "non-white" families being moved from their homes, he became one of the first to buy cottages, restore them and rent them out. Some were at Waterloo Green, in Wynberg, Cape Town, and it was here that I had my only contact with him.

With his interest in wood, he now went into the timber business and bought plantations in the Knysna area. He also married the noted portrait painter, and daughter of the Conservator of Forests, Laurel Zahn.

In 1956, while in Britain, they bought their first yacht, *Speedwell of Hong Kong,* and sailed to Bermuda before returning to Cape Town by way of Tristan da Cunha. In 1963 *Speedwell of Hong Kong* was sold. For nine months John skippered *Stormvogel* and went on to take the helm of *Jacaranda,* which he sailed to a fourth place in one leg of the Round-the-World race in 1974.

Back in Knysna he began work on a 15-ton ketch designed by Arthur Rose. John worked almost single-handed on the moulded macori hull and teak deck. Down below it was fitted out with Knysna stinkwood and yellowwood. Named *Speedwell of Good Hope*, the yacht was launched in 1980. Hjalmar Thesen, the author, presented the Goodmans with a copy of *The Captain is Cook*, a nautical recipe book he had recently reviewed for the *Eastern Province Herald.*

There on the lagoon *Speedwell of Good Hope* lay for a while, "sleeping in her own reflection" as the late Keith Sutton of the *Herald* wrote, and to whom I owe a debt for much of the above information on Goodwin. Sutton also mentioned how modest a man he was, making his achievements sound "quite run-of-the–mill", which was my own reaction on meeting Goodwin in Cape Town years before.

Speedwell of Good Hope did not rest for long on the lagoon. Within days she had sailed for the West Indies, North America, Europe, the Adriatic and the Greek islands. Thereafter it was to be Panama and Canada, possibly followed by the Pacific.

Speedwell, wrote Sutton, was "the remarkable work of a remarkable man".

* * *

Eventually the last screw went in and the last seam was caulked. David and I took the dinghy with no name out to Hartebeestpoort Dam and, finding a spot where we were unlikely to have any onlookers, we carefully lowered her into the water. To our delight she floated level and true and did not appear to leak. We set up the mast and rigging, put down the centre-board and raised the sail. In the very lightest of breezes we headed off from the shore.

Later, having tied her up at a friend's jetty we stood back and admired our handiwork. We were as proud of ourselves as if she were *Speedwell of Good Hope* and about to sail through the Knysna Heads for Bermuda.

* * *

Stuart Kay and Robert Brand, May 2000

Forest

Looking out from the offices of the Department of Water Affairs and Forestry at the Denmar Centre, as we were some twenty years ago, one has a good view of the passing traffic in Main Street, Knysna. Out of season the traffic is reasonable, but during the summer holidays we sometimes wish that the once proposed Knysna N2 by-pass had been accepted and built. No doubt Johan Baard, heading the Department in the area, has an opposing view. After all, his job is to protect the forests.

We are at the office to collect permits and to seek his help in locating certain plants. Leading our small group is a sallow-skinned, dark-haired American botanist of South African origin, Robert Brand. Like Thunberg, Masson and all the other 18th and 19th centuries European travellers, Robert is here to collect plants, but not for the gardens at Uppsala or at Kew, but for the New York Botanical Gardens (NYBG). Today, perhaps subconsciously hoping to make a good impression, Robert has on his chocolate-brown, soft-felt fedora, but in the field he more usually wears a dark green baseball cap emblazoned with the NYBG logo. His long-sleeved khaki shirt has sleeves rolled-up to just below the elbow. The outfit is completed with khaki slacks and brown boots.

Robert, with his big black beard, reminds one somewhat of James Backhouse, the 19th century English Quaker, nurseryman and plant-collector. Like Backhouse he is generous, a gentleman and softly spoken, despite having a gravel-voice reminiscent of the jazz-trumpeter, the late Louis Armstrong. And just as Backhouse had a driver and *voorloper* for his ox-wagon, so Robert has young Stuart Kay to drive his Landrover, help with the collecting chores and cook the evening meal. Stuart, with fuzz on his cheeks, has no need to impress anybody. He has on a green NYBG T-shirt, white rugby shorts and slip-slops.

Caryl and I, like Stuart, are *handlangers*, although Robert is kind enough to introduce us as his colleagues.

275

Baard goes out of his way to be of help, showing us on a map the possible locations of the plants in which Robert is interested, describing the easiest routes to take and naming those people who may be of help to us in the forest. Robert makes notes on the squared pages of his collector's notebook. Finally all is settled and we go to the door together with Johan. He gives us a wave and wishes us well as we head for the Landrover.

While the Landrover is not as big as Backhouse's ox-wagon, it is packed from the roof-rack down with collecting gear, tools, botanical presses, maps, sample-bags, supplies, a water container, refrigerator, our personal belongings and camping gear. Everything is in its place, rather like a yacht's galley.

Stuart takes the steering-wheel; Robert sits in the front passenger's seat surrounded by maps, botanical lists and field-guides, while Caryl and I are squeezed into the back seat. The Landrover edges out into the traffic and we are on our way.

* * *

The Dutch India Company established the first woodcutters' post at Swartrivier, near present-day George in 1776. Two years later Governor Joachim van Plettenburg was in the area and noting the destruction already evident in the forests, was quick to blame the woodcutters. Only a few years later the flamboyant Frenchman, François le Vaillant joined the chorus aimed at what he called the "degenerate hewers of timber".

The first person to speak up in the woodcutters' defence was the Englishman, John Barrow. His remarks deserve some attention, for he was not generally complimentary about the rural Dutch that he met on his travels. He described the woodcutters as "the only class of people, in the whole colony, that deserve the name of being industrious. To fell the large trees . . . and then drag them out, is a work of labour and toil; and their profits are so trifling . . ."

As Dalene Matthee points out in her novels, the woodcutters were poor, they were underpaid and exploited, were kept in debt forever with the issue of vouchers for buying goods in advance, but they were not decadent numbskulls. They were religious and hard-working and took a great pride in their work. Using only hand-axes and saws they were capable of producing sleepers, planks, billets and even wagon-wheel spokes – six spokes in exchange for a bottle of "Cape smoke" - brandy - as accurately as those turned out by machinery in the sawmills.

We once watched a woodsman making a two metre long pelmet. Finding that no quarter inch (6.35 mm) plywood was available for the face of the pelmet, he without hesitation took a plank of the required length and with a handsaw cut a 6 mm wide piece by hand as accurately as any power-saw.

It is true that they were uneducated in the accepted sense of the word. There were no schools for children to attend, nor any other facilities provided, but they knew the forest like the backs of their hands, knew its creatures and its plants.

The opening paragraph of Dalene Matthee's *Toorbos* gives an indication of this. Karoliena, daughter of a woodcutter is walking along the Oudebrandpad when she suddenly realises that there is an elephant nearby, not that the elephant has made any noise whatsoever. Karoliena hears instead the *sis en gorrel* – the hiss and gurgle – of the Knysna lourie sitting high in the branches overhead, and interprets the call correctly as a warning to the elephant of her presence.

When entering the forest one is at first overwhelmed by the trees that completely dominate the ecosystem. There are the monarchs of the high forest: yellowwoods – *Podocarpus falcatus* – of 45 m or more, and stinkwood – *Ocotea bullata* – and so many others. It is the trees that provide the bulk of biomass, but if one looks carefully one finds that one is surrounded by herbs, bracket fungi, mosses, ferns and epiphytes that far outnumber the trees in both abundance and diversity.

The woodcutters knew them all and which might be used and where in the forest they might be found. The *bitterbessie* or Christmas berry – *Chironia baccifera* - with its delicate pink flowers and shiny red fruits in season, was used for the treatment of boils, acne and haemorrhoids, or as a blood pu-

277

rifier. However anyone administering *bitterbessie* treatment
in the form of a tincture or infusion had to know precisely what they were doing. The berries are potentially toxic.
Woodcutters may have missed out on the three-Rs, but they
were certainly not uneducated.

* * *

Having found the plants we set up our collecting point in a
glade that once was home to a forest giant, felled by man, or
as there is no sign of a stump, by a winter storm.

Robert opens up the back of the Landrover and takes out
a press, data sheets, tags, and collection bags. Every specimen must be tagged before mounting and go into the press
together with its data sheet. Five specimens of each plant are
collected, to be divided amongst the NYBG, the University of
the Free State which has organised the expedition in South
Africa, the sponsor (a pharmaceutical concern) and Eastern
and Western Cape herbaria.

The aim of the expedition is to collect as many as possible
of the more than 1500 different genera in the Cape Floristic
Region.

The collection bags are for plant material which will be
subjected to chemical analysis. These too require data sheets
and tags and have to be stored in such a way that the material
dries out and does not rot.

Robert has his time cut out filling in the sheets and tags,
and doing the pressings. Stuart, after helping collect material,
begins to process it before putting it in bags. Caryl and I select
specimens with as many features as possible to aid identification: leaves flowers, stems, fruit, roots, bulbs and so on. This
done, Robert and Caryl squat down to study the guides and
produce a possible species name.

It is a time consuming occupation and I usually find that
I am the one designated to produce the lunch, a task which I
happily perform as it allows me to keep an eye on the forest
around me and to think my own thoughts.

* * *

In September 1867 Queen Victoria's second son, Prince Alfred, Duke of Edinburgh, visited Knysna and was taken on an elephant hunt in the Knysna forests. The Prince spent the first night of his stay at the St George's Tavern on the corner of Main and Queen Streets. The Tavern was run by Master Mariner Captain Thomas Horn who was delighted when the Prince granted him the privilege of changing the name of his hostelry to "The Royal Hotel". Since the Prince was there, the hotel, still known as The Royal Hotel, has increased greatly in size.

Accompanying the Prince were Sir Philip Wodehouse, Governor of the Cape, Sir Walter Currie of Grahamstown, a superb horseman who could ride with or without boots or saddle, but "could not move without adjectives", and Major-General John Jarvis Bissett, who was a descendant of William the Conqueror. Very suitable companions for a royal hunt.

The hunt, so far as the organisers were concerned, was a great success. The Prince returned to England with two elephant heads and the skin of one. It is possible that there are today members of the Royal Family who would rather forget the hunt and the Prince's participation.

He also, as you may remember, returned home with a walking stick carved by Thomas Bain. I wonder whether there is anyone who remembers what happened to it.

It was in the same year as the hunt that Christopher Harison and Thomas Bain were appointed by Parliament to investigate the plight of the forests. Harison believed that to control the cutting of timber it was necessary to find an alternative source of income for the woodcutters. He surmised that if there were a road through the forests they might be willing to become small-scale farmers. He and Bain began the hunt for a route through from Knysna to Humansdorp.

Then in 1869 there came the Great Fire. Not until 2017 was there to be another of quite the same size and destructiveness. But as a result of the fire the government strengthened control over the forests and Harison, from being a part-time Conservator at Witelsbosch, moved to Knysna as the first full-time Conservator of Forests. The fire also made the task facing Bain and Harison of finding a route to Humansdorp that much easier. The road was eventually built, but failed to produce the results for which Harison had hoped.

Although some attempts at scientific management of the forests had been made since at least 1867, the appointment of Count Medéric de Vasselot de Regné, a graduate of the famous Nancy School of Forestry, as the first Superintendent of Woods and Forests in 1880, saw the first really determined efforts to manage this valuable asset. The woodcutters, however, remained a problem.

In 1913 all the woodcutters were required to register, and thereafter no new names were added to the list. Finally, in 1939, with the passing of the Woodcutters Annuities Bill, the remaining woodcutters were pensioned off.

The woodcutters, cut off in their forest home, lived off a diet of sweet potatoes, bread and black coffee. Every so often this was supplemented by the flesh of bush-pigs and buck snared in the forest. And also in the forest there were bees' nests and honey-filled combs with which to vary their diet. Their critics pointed fingers at these sweet-toothed woodsmen for chopping down trees simply to get at the golden nectar that livened up their food and was used to brew karrie.

At our collection site all that is on offer for lunch are brown bread sandwiches with cheese and tomato, followed by fruit. Eaten in a forest glade we are happy enough and there are no complaints. After lunch and a ten minute rest, we move on to the next site.

Declining denizens of the forest

In the issue of the *Graaff-Renet Herald* dated the 9th of May, 1837 there appeared the following short snippet of news:

> G W B Wehmeyer's two younger brothers of the farm *"Dingley Dell"*, together with some young men from the Langkloof, went out elephant hunting and with the 35th shot, brought down an elephant, the tusks up-

wards of 5 ft in length, which together weighed 105 lbs. Had it not been for rain, they would have shot more.

* * *

It happened on the main road near Harkerville in 1950. My father was the first to see it.

Elephant!

Where, Dad? Where?

Straight ahead. There. On the road.

And there it was, apparently in no hurry, ambling across the road. For a moment it was there. Then like an apparition it was gone. Gone into the forest. Its huge grey bulk swallowed by the vegetation. We waited for some time beside the road, but neither the original animal nor any others appeared. Eventually my father started the engine and we drove on.

That's something to remember for the rest of one's days!

Later my school friends were not that impressed. What was one elephant on the road near Knysna compared with the dozens that they saw in the Kruger? But my father was right: I still remember that remarkable presence on an early summer's morning in my youth.

Nothing like the, at times, frightening and potentially dangerous situations in which Hjalmar Thesen found himself while stalking the elephants with Nick Carter. (See *Stalking the Knysna Elephant* in *Country Days*.) Nor was I young enough to be more impressed by a magical frog than a forest elephant. (*Through the Eyes of Children*.) No, the huge majestic presence has remained with me for the equivalent of a Biblical lifespan.

As the years have passed so the chances of seeing one have lessened. When in 1920 there were only an estimated twenty elephants left of herds that once numbered many hundreds, a permit was granted to Major PJ Pretorius to shoot one for scientific purposes. During the hunt an additional four were killed.

In 1970 there were reckoned to be five Knysna elephants left in the forest. By 2019 the number had dropped to a solitary female.

It is not only the elephants that have disappeared; also trees and even views. With one of the finest views in the world, Knysna allowed developers to dot the Eastern Head with suburban houses. Thanks to the late Professor JLB Smith and subsequently to his son, the Western Head has up to now escaped the same fate. More recently there has been rampant development, both authorised and informal, to the east of the town.

During the 19th and 20th centuries the forests were only just saved from being stripped bare by woodcutters working for a pittance and at the behest of timber merchants and the government. Alien vegetation along the fringes of the forest, which is what most people see, smothers a lot of what remains. (Although the authorities have fought, and continue to fight, an apparently never-ending battle to eradicate these pests.)

* * *

The last buffalo was killed near Blaauwkrantz in the 1880s.

Thank goodness the gold at Millwood ran out, or there would be another Witwatersrand beside the Knysna lagoon.

That despite all this Knysna with its forests, mountains and lagoon still has an appeal is undeniable, but its guardians have an increasingly difficult and arduous task to perform to ensure that what little remains is not trashed, burnt to a cinder, swamped by aliens or lost to global warming. We are all faced, to a greater or a lesser degree and wherever we may be, with similar problems, but for those living along the Garden Route it is indeed a daunting duty.

* * *

Despite the long ago elephant encounter near Harkerville on the N2, Caryl and I chose to rather take the longer, dustier road less travelled to Plettenburg Bay. This meant back-track-

ing for roughly two kilometres from the centre of town towards the bridge over the Knysna lagoon. At the Soutrivier
(Salt River) one turns sharp right up the Salt River road to
follow for a time the eastern bank of that river. One passes
through pastures bordered by trees and neat farmhouses before swinging up into the hills, leaving the traffic of the N2 far
behind.

After passing the Simola Golf Estate, we take the turn-
off to Gouna and shortly thereafter stop for lunch beside the
road. Just a single car drives by, the occupants turning their
heads to see these *vreemdelinge* in the forest. We give a wave,
but the car's dust prevents us from noting any response there
might be. Then, on our way again along the gravel switchback,
we head down through dense undergrowth before facing an
equally steep climb, through what once was elephant country. Slowly winding through the trees we eventually reach a
plateau and Gouna forest station.

Here in 1881 a group of Italian silkworm-farmers in the
care of an Italian speaking Englishman, William Christie, were
settled, but one is almost tempted to use the word "dumped",
by the colonial authorities. Outside of the archives very little was recorded concerning this apparently hare-brained
scheme to set up a silk industry in the Knysna forests. Thanks
to the meticulous research work done by the late Dalene Matthee for her 1987 historical novel, *Moerbeibos* (*Mulberry Forest*), we now know considerably more about the incident.

For some time Henry Barrington, of Portland, was keen on
the idea of silk production. The Great Fire of 1869 destroyed
not only his farm but also his dream of becoming a silk-pro-
ducer. Although he had once talked of bringing Italians to the
Cape, he was no longer in a position to contemplate such a
venture.

Meanwhile however, the British Colonial Office, on behalf
of the Cape Government, was looking into the possibility of
bringing a group of Italian farmers skilled in the art of silk
production to the Cape, and specifically to Knysna. Working
through the British consulate in Turin a group of families was
identified as interested. Eventually they were taken to En-

gland, and left Plymouth on the 26th of April 1881, bound for the Cape on board the *Anglian*. Arriving in Cape Town they trans-shipped to the *Natal*, the *Anglian* being too large to enter the Knysna lagoon. They stayed for some weeks beside the lagoon before undertaking the last stage of their journey to Crown Land at Gouna, where each family was granted 20 acres (8.1 ha) of land and the use of 180 acres (72.9 ha) of commonage for grazing.

But there were no mulberry trees and the soil and conditions were quite unsuitable for their propagation. The eleven families were expected to live in tents through a cold, wet winter while building their houses and establishing not only the industry, but vegetable gardens. They received rations for six months and thereafter were expected to be self-sufficient and capable of paying back any money forwarded to them. The scheme was a complete failure and the fact that any survived the winter close to a miracle.

Like the elephants the Italians eventually disappeared from Gouna, but as a result of their arrival in 1881 there are today South Africans, many of whom are Roman Catholics, who are of various skin colours and home-languages, and with surnames such as Fardini or Cruci. To meet an Afrikaans-speaking Sciocatti (formerly Cuicatti) in the Knysna area who cannot understand Italian is not an impossibility, but there are not that many around.

Up on the plateau, *die platrand* at Gauna, where the elephants once roamed and where at the sight of an elephant woodcutters and forest-rangers ran for the trees and Italians were scared out of their wits, there is little that remains of the small settlement. Even the road and street names have little or no apparent connection with the Italians: Church and Denne Streets, Anandalay and Commonage Roads.

Across through the forests we travelled to Diepwalle, once the terminus of the South Western Railway. Here, according to some, was the centre of elephant activity in years gone by.

It was in 1925 that an article about the forest elephants written by J F V Phillips of the Forest Research Station,

Diepwalle, caused concern amongst conservationists. In the article which appeared in the November 1925 issue of the *South African Journal of Science,* Phillips stated that in 1880, despite hunting, elephants ranged from west of George to Witelsbosch in the east, but that their range had contracted and most were now restricted to the Diepwalle area. He added that they avoided for considerable periods areas where they had been molested or their fellows killed.

Regarding their habits he noted that elephants were quite capable of making their way through thick undergrowth, but preferred well-defined paths and ridges, always crossing valleys and rivers by the easiest route. He believed that at the most there were just 12 elephants left in the Knysna forests.

The Great Fire of 1869 had scarcely affected their numbers. It failed to penetrate the main forests, laying waste the outskirts, rivers and valleys. The elephants found sanctuary in the depths of the forest.

Woodcutting and the Millwood gold-rush had put pressure on the forest, which in turn influenced elephant numbers. It was also possible that their forest diet had played a part in reducing numbers, but without doubt hunting was the main cause of the decrease in population. A secret ivory trade still flourished with the tusks being smuggled out on loaded timber wagons, or even on ships calling at Knysna. Hunters were paid half-a-crown a tusk (the equivalent value in 2020 being about R2.63). Most of the ivory was sent to the Transvaal.

In 1968 an elephant calf was killed by a falling tree. This ultimately led to the Wildlife Society organising an elephant survey under Nick Carter, a professional game warden. From February 1969 until January 1970, Carter together with trackers Aapie Stroebel and his son, Anthony, descendants of the P Stroebel who played a prominent role in the Royal Hunt in 1867, undertook this survey.

In his report Carter noted that there were three old bulls, two young bulls, four cows, one youngster aged about five, and a calf: eleven in all. While he was convinced that poaching had occurred, he felt that more of a threat was posed by the indiscriminate shooting by irate smallholders after elephant raids of their vegetable gardens. He suggested a fenced reserve, but the experts, for a variety of reasons, felt otherwise. The Forestry Department undertook responsibility for the elephants, but in the years to come little was heard from them.

Carter also commented that far from being dangerous, he had never come across as "civilised" a group of elephants, adding the rider that this applied to their normal activities. If there was any question of serious tracking, it was a different matter altogether, for which Hjalmar Thesen could vouch!

By 1980 there was reckoned to be just one old bull, a cow and a calf left, and the two main factors for population loss were given as harassment by small-holders and the elephants' restricted habitat.

In 1994 three orphaned elephant cows, aged seven to nine years were translocated from the Kruger National Park in an attempt to boost numbers. Within three months the youngest cow died of stress-related pneumonia and the experiment was abandoned.

DNA testing of dung in 2006 indicated a possible five cows in the forest with perhaps some bulls and calves, but by 2019 it was reported that camera traps set up for 15 months over a large area had secured images of only a solitary female. Going . . . going . . .

* * *

Since 1950 I have treasured my brief glimpse of an elephant crossing the road near Harkerville.

The old rectory, Plettenberg Bay

13.

Plettenberg Bay

Strawberries and Joseph Conrad

So far as Jean was concerned the interview was not going well.

"Do you type?" asked Mr Groombridge - soon to become Harry.

"Er, no."

"What about shorthand?"

"No, not at all."

The next question came as a complete surprise.

"How about lunch, then?"

287

It was the first surprise of many. At the Italian restaurant it was followed by another. Mr Groombridge was clearly a regular patron and was greeted by beaming faces.

"*Buongiorno,* Admiral Byng!" the waiter exclaimed, showing them to a table for two. "Will this table do, Admiral?" Just who was this man with whom she was having lunch?

The meal ended with the greatest surprise of all.

"Will you marry me, Jean? And before you answer let me warn you that if you should say, 'No', I will continue to ask you until such time as you say, 'Yes'."

In time she got to know more about Harry Groombridge. His father was a staid farmer from Sidcup, near Dartford to the south-east of London: staid, but not too staid, for he ran off with a floozy, leaving Harry's Cockney mother in the lurch. She promptly divorced him. Harry reckoned that he had inherited his mother's sense of humour. Perhaps it was from his father that he acquired his love of gardening.

During the war he joined the RAF as a member of 129 Squadron. Other than for a short period flying Mustangs, the squadron flew Spitfires of various marks throughout the war. They provided escorts for bombers, were later involved with the D-Day landings and finally with the V1 flying-bomb campaign. Harry played what he described as an "undistinguished" role in affairs. While he may not have picked up any gongs, like his friend the fighter-ace and later Air Vice-Marshall "Johnny" Johnson – DSO and two bars, DFC and bar – Harry must surely have been the life and soul of any party.

When Jean at last answered, "Yes," they moved, after visiting the registry office, to his "castle" at Sidcup, where the well-tended garden's most prominent feature was a large mausoleum. But that, of course, followed their honeymoon in Greece where Harry was attending a conference.

"I'd like you to meet my wife," said Harry.

"Good heavens," said the other delegate, "I didn"t know you were married, Harry."

"Oh yes, indeed, we"ve now been married for three days."

There followed a period with Ethiopian Airways, where Harry ended up as General Manager, but life was by no means seemly. An incident in Saudi Arabia resulted in Harry's disenchantment with the Arab rulers.

During an earlier spell in Kenya, his vegetable garden, together with the visits thereto by the local population, raised suspicions among the colonial authorities that far from being a greengrocer, he was a Mau Mau sympathiser.

When the communists took over Ethiopian Airways, the Groombridges decided that the time had come to make a move. They arrived in South Africa together with a genuine horse-drawn Gypsy caravan that they parked on some land at Harkerville. It was here that Harry set himself up as a strawberry farmer. Jean made the scarecrows to keep the birds off the plants, but they were forced to erect an electric fence to keep the baboons out. One in particular became such a regular visitor that they named him Fred.

On one occasion during the strawberry season in 1973 Harry had to go off on business. Despite Harry's misgivings, Jean insisted that she and 18 month-old Justin would be perfectly safe. Waking in the caravan after a good night's sleep she became aware of some unusual noises and looked out the window. There, just beyond the strawberry patch was a large elephant. She did not have a gun or any other form of deterrent. While she worried about what to do the elephant took care of the problem itself by turning and disappearing into the forest.

When Harry returned he was disappointed to have missed seeing the elephant. However the elephant appeared again the next day. The Groombridges eventually decided that there were both a cow and a bull together with a calf that never ventured forth from the forest. Jean remembers them as beautiful creatures that were never ever a problem. "We eventually just took them for granted, as I am sure they did us."

I wondered to myself whether or not one of these elephants was the one we saw crossing the road near Harkerville in 1950.

It was during this period that the Groombridges came to meet their near neighbours, Jules and Helen Mudge.

Jean:

The first time we met them they were on the roof of their cottage. Harry looked up and saw Helen and fell for her instantly. I could tell at once. He always had an eye for a pretty girl. We were friends with the Mudges from that moment on. Harry was a straight-forward sort of man. He called a spade a spade. He was always great fun and full of surprises, but never unpleasant surprises. He adored Helen Mudge.

Helen Mudge takes up the story:

Harry was a very colourful character. Always up to mischief. When the municipality advertised for an electrical engineer or something of the sort, he applied, listing tongue-in-cheek, his qualifications. He ended up with "For seven consecutive years I have successfully connected the Christmas-tree lights."

Plett was full of real characters in those days. Jean is herself the granddaughter of an Archbishop of Canterbury. Nowadays the nearest we get to a character is a Johannesburg corporate retiree.

Jean made the scarecrows for their strawberry-patch. She made one of them a likeness of Harold Wilson, the British Prime Minister. It was at the time of UDI when Wilson sold the white Rhodesians down the river. A Rhodesian tourist stopped to buy some strawberries. Seeing the Wilson scarecrow he took out a revolver and blasted it to smithereens.

Harry and Jean were those sort of people. Not only did they do unusual things, but unusual things happened to them.

I first heard of Harry Groombridge in the Port Elizabeth office of the late Keith Sutton, columnist of the *Eastern Province Herald.* On his desk, amid a pile of books, papers and photographs was a chunk of iron acting as a paper-weight. Sutton noted my interest and told me that he had received it through the post. A Harry Groombridge, an antique dealer from Plettenberg Bay, had sent it to him. When feeling the weight of the parcel the thought crossed his mind that it might be a letter-bomb. (1984 was a year for letter-bombs.) He eventually decided that he was an unlikely target for an incendiary device and opened the parcel only to find the piece of metal together with a letter from Groombridge.

The explanation given in the letter told of how Groombridge, while visiting his brother Alan in Hobart, Tasmania, heard of the remains of a ship on the east shore of the Derwent estuary near East Risdon. Borrowing his brother's wellies, Harry went in search of the remains, sloshing through the mud and water until he found the iron ribs and rusted plating of the vessel. He removed a section of reinforcing plate to which the shrouds of the standing rigging were once bolted. Keith Sutton's paper-weight was a small section of this plate.

Harry Groombridge's find were the remains of the barque *Otago.* Built in Glasgow in 1869, it came to Australia in 1872 and from then on was based at Port Adelaide.

In 1887, in Bangkok, a 30 year-old Pole, Józef Teodor Konrad Korzeniowski became captain of the *Otago* for a period of 15 months. Then, after a maritime career of 19 years in all, he returned to Europe, took out British citizenship, became a writer and changed his name to Joseph Conrad. Many of the stories he told were set at sea, and all were in English, a language he only came to know in his twenties. Today the books are regarded as literary classics and forerunners of the modern novel.

The official record of Conrad's period of command aboard *Otago* is prosaic. Let us rather, as I am sure Harry Groombridge did, consider the account given by Conrad in his book, *The Shadowline.* He referred to this ordinary small cargo carrier as "an Arab steed" and wrote of how the former captain, from whom he took over, had "cabin fever", locked himself in his cabin, played the fiddle and refused to go on duty, before finally throwing himself overboard. While under Conrad's command the crew went down with fever one after the other. It was then discovered that the dead captain had sold the quinine from the medicine chest. In general that first voyage under the new captain was a nightmare.

The days of sailing ships were numbered, and in 1905 the *Otago* sailed to Hobart where the Arab steed was used to store coal. In 1931 it was sold to a Captain Dodge for £1. He stripped it and sold what he could. The ship's bell went to south-eastern Australia, the wheel to Britain. Today you will find the companionway in the Hobart Maritime Museum. Then, of course, there is part of a reinforcing plate that went to Plettenberg Bay.

Seeing that small piece of rusted iron on Keith Sutton's desk struck a chord with me. Caryl and I have a number of mementoes of places we have visited: river pebbles, dried pieces of plant material, snail shells and fragments of bone, a chunk of copper and others. We do not carve our names into trees nor ancient monuments, and so far as our collection is concerned, draw the line at archeological or historic sites, but shards of Victorian pottery from a farm rubbish dump are fair game. Seeing that lump of metal convinced me that Harry Groombridge and I would find much in common. Alas, I never did meet him.

Castaways camping on Millionaires' Mile, Plettenberg Bay

Another calm, starry evening and this time we were lucky enough to be on private land overlooking the beach, with the Robberg peninsula just to the south-east of us. Fortunately we still had the box of matches that Sheila gave us in Knysna, so we were entirely self-sufficient. After supper we turned down the *klap* and lay in our sleeping-bags in the back of the bakkie, looking out at the stars over the ocean and with the gentle murmur, mutter and slosh of the breaking swells on Robberg Beach to send us to sleep.

We woke to a windless morning, with the sun emerging like a coral tree blossom from the ocean. Red sky in the morning, a shepherd's warning, but these old adages are not always true, and it turned into another sunny day with sufficient wind to ruffle the sea's surface and nothing much more. From where we were we had a good view across to Robberg and down into the water surrounding it. For years one could see from there the remains of the *Athina* in her watery grave, but it is now little more than a dirty smudge on the sandy bottom.

It was on the 1st of August 1967 that the Greek MFV *Athina*, after hitting Whale Rock and holing the engine-room, sank off Robberg together with its cargo of 1 000 tons of fish in refrigerated holds.

While fishing in the Indian Ocean the *Athina* was caught by surprise by the Egyptian closure of the Suez Canal on the 5th of June 1967. Captain John Katsiaris was left with no alternative but to return home by way of the Cape. Being unfamiliar with the coast he set a course too close to the shore, which resulted in the loss of the vessel.

Navigators' knowledge of the Cape coast during the first half of the 17th century was far sketchier than that of John Katsiaris, but had little to do with the loss of the Portuguese East-Indiaman *São Gonçalo* in July 1630.

The *São Gonçalo* left Goa in the company of two other ships on the 4th of March 1630 on a homeward voyage with a cargo of spices, rice and Chinese porcelain. She was under the command of Captain Fernão Lobo de Meneses, an elderly man in ill-health. In mid-ocean the ship sprung a leak and the captain ordered a change of course towards the Cape coast where hopefully repairs would be undertaken. The ship cast anchor off Robberg Beach and for seven weeks they battled unsuccessfully to stem the leak and to clear the pumps which were blocked.

A man was lowered into the hold to clear the blockage. When he failed to respond to calls from on deck, a second man was lowered into the hold, and then a third. It was only after a fourth man, seeing the lifeless bodies of his fellows in the hold, signalled desperately to be pulled out, that it was realised that the others had been asphyxiated.

The position on board the *São Gonçalo* was worsened by the conduct of "disorderly officers", which caused dissension amongst the rank and file. Eventually about 100 men decided to go ashore, leaving 133 on board where work on the pumps and the leak continued.

Early in August the ship was struck by gale force south-easterly winds and thunderous seas and was driven ashore. All those on board lost their lives, the ship broke up and much of the wreckage was washed ashore. One can appreciate the feelings of those on the land watching the break-up of their ship and the death of their compatriots.

Those on shore now made use of the timber to build wooden huts and to start work on the construction of two pinnaces in which to sail to safety, a task that was to last for a further eight months.

Captain De Meneses now gave the crew permission to choose a new leader, but this led to further dissension. The man chosen, Roque Borges, was one night attacked by rival Simon de Fignérdo. Borges was seriously wounded, but during the course of the struggle, "having lost all patience", managed to stab his rival to death. With the death of Fignérdo the men apparently settled down to a more disciplined and harmonious existence. To add to their shelters they also built a small church and when bees took up residence beside the altar, but did not sting the communicants, they took this as a propitious sign. It is recorded that the sermons, there were five priests among the castaways, helped build up their courage and "restrain them from vice".

They planted pumpkins, melons, cucumbers, onions and coriander, all of which grew well. In addition there was plenty of rice from the wreck and they caught fish off Robberg. Rescuing iron from the wreckage, they used it to barter with local people for cows and sheep. Communication with the inhabitants was difficult and sign language was resorted to as the Portuguese were unable to understand the "curious noises" the local people made "with their tongues and their mouths".

The Portuguese also took an interest in their natural surroundings. A list of birds compiled by Friar Francisco dos Santos included turtle-doves, and somewhat surprisingly, turkeys and geese. Elephants and buffaloes were noted but apparently did not bother them, and also deer (antelopes) and wolves (hyenas). The numerous large trees made an impression, as did the huge variety of sweet-smelling flowers, wild onions, mint and lavender.

While preparing for their departure, a wooden cross was inscribed with an account of their trials. The cross was erected on a nearby hill, but no trace of it has ever been found. However in 1858 Edgar Layard, curator of the South African Museum in Cape Town was taken to see a sandstone block on which were inscribed words thought to be in Portuguese.

With the completion of the pinnaces it was decided that one boat would sail westwards in the hope of reaching Portugal, while the other would sail for India. The second vessel reached Moçambique safely and the survivors opted to wait there until rescued by a Portuguese ship.

The first pinnace made little progress but was fortunate to meet up with the homeward bound *Santa Ignacio Loyola* which took them aboard. During the course of the voyage the unfortunate Captain De Meneses died and his body was committed to the deep.

All went well until they reached the mouth of the Tagus River where, in sight of home, the *Santa Ignacio Loyola* foundered on the bar with the loss of all hands.

However, that is not quite the end of the story. In November 1979 work began on the holiday home, *Klein Deel*, of Mr Johann and Mrs Ingrid Jerling, Johann being a descendant of an early Plettenberg Bay resident of the same name.

Levelling of the ground and the digging of foundations took place on a piece of ground adjoining the Robberg peninsula. Workmen had no sooner started digging than they began to uncover pottery, coins, nails, medals, musket balls and other bric-a-brac. Most people would probably have bulldozed the site and let the china fragments join the rest of the rubble. The Jerlings, thank goodness, decided to collect all that they could find. Experts Caro Woodward (porcelain); Professor Eric Axelson (historian) and Jalmar Rudner, an archaeologist of the National Monuments Council were called in to study the Jerlings' finds. After studying the artefacts the conclusion reached was that more than three centuries later, the campsite of the castaways from the *São Gonçalo* had been discovered. The pottery was of the late Ming period and an expert was able to date it as having been made between the years 1623 and 1635. The *São Gonçalo*, you will remember, was wrecked in 1630.

In 1984, 17 of the finds, including restored Ming porcelain, were put on display in a portion of the new library extension in Plettenberg Bay. They formed the central feature of a display "Gifts from the Sea" which included sea shells and photographs.

The remains of the *São Gonçalo* have never been found. They probably lie buried beneath the sand off Robberg.

* * *

We finished our breakfast and packed the Isuzu which was parked within metres of the survivors' campsite. If perhaps we grubbed beneath our feet we might in turn find a square-headed Portuguese nail or some other reminder of the wreck, but we refrained from doing so lest we damage our host's grass.

Beachyhead Road, Plettenberg Bay, beside which we spent the night, was reckoned in 2017, according to a *Fin24* list of South Africa's most expensive streets, to be the most expensive suburban street in the country outside Cape Town. Properties sold for an average of R42 000/m^2, so it is understandable that the locals refer to it as "Millionaire's Mile".

296

We were discussing this one day some years ago with a long-time Plettenberg Bay resident and old friend, Gladys Snaddon, since deceased, with whom we used to stay on occasion. She told us the story of her brother, who in the early 1930s went from university to work for De Beers. He dearly wanted to buy a modest property in Plettenberg Bay, but did not have the deposit and could find no one to lend him the money. Greatly daring, he one day approached his boss, Sir Ernest Oppenheimer, who heard him out. The great man then gave her brother the following advice:

> *Holiday homes are like yachts. They require constant upkeep and cost a lot to maintain. In addition one can seldom if ever sell them profitably. This applies particularly to houses on the Cape south coast, which few people choose as a holiday destination. I feel that you should look for some other investment that will result in capital growth. Should you do so, do not hesitate to approach me.*

It took a little time, but in due course her brother, by that time a senior De Beers executive, ignored Sir Ernest's advice and bought a Plettenberg Bay property.

Of history, archeology, a bed and a curate

In the middle of the 19th century an obscure Hereford clergyman in his thirties, the Rev Kilvert, kept a diary. He was only 39 years old when he died in 1879 and by now would be entirely forgotten had not his diary been discovered in 1937 by South African poet William Plomer. Today, thanks to Plomer, Kilvert's descriptions of his life and environment in graphic and humorous detail make fascinating reading. He had a low opinion of some of his countrymen:

> *Of all noxious animals . . . the most noxious is a tourist.*
> *And of all tourists the most vulgar, ill-bred, offensive and loathsome is the British tourist.*

The 19th century French novelist, Gustave Flaubert, suffered from epilepsy and as a result seldom travelled. He made an exception during the writing of *Salambô,* a story set in the ancient city of Carthage. In order to acquire background material he travelled to Tunis via Alexandria, and while in that city of the Nile delta visited tourist sites, one of which was Pompey's Pillar. There he was enraged to see that this ancient monument had been defaced. A tourist named Thompson had taken the trouble to carve his name on the stone:

> *You cannot see the Pillar without seeing the name of Thompson. This cretin has become part of the monument and perpetuates himself along with it. All imbeciles are more or less Thompsons from Sunderland.*

I sometimes wonder whether or not the Rev Kilvert ever met Thompson of Sunderland; probably not, for there are plenty of Thompson's ilk around. We have our fair share of them in South Africa.

* * *

In 1778 the Dutch Governor Joachim van Plettenberg visited Plettenberg Bay, known at the time by a variety of names – Angra dos Alagons, Formosa, St Catherine's Bay, Keurboom Rivier Baay, Piesangs Rivier Baay - and set the matter to rights in his eyes by naming the bay after himself and erecting a stone proclaiming the fact.

Perhaps the French are particularly sensitive to this sort of behaviour: two years later François le Vaillant came across this stone announcing the new name and commented:

> *I examined this wretched monument, which had nothing but an inscription in verse to render it still more contemptible.*

Not long after that, in 1803, another Dutchman, Governor Janssens, visited Plettenberg Bay and found the stone lying on its side. By 1936, although other vandals had made their mark on the memorial, it was considered sufficiently venerable to be declared a National Monument. Finally, in 1964, tired of removing the names of those seeking perpetuity and repairing damage caused by memento-seekers, the authorities removed the stone to Cape Town and the comparative safety of the Cultural History Museum. A replica was erected and placed behind a stout metalwork barricade. This has discouraged but not entirely eliminated the efforts of our own Thompsons, be they from Sannieshof, Sasolburg or Saxonwold, to express their political views or to perpetuate their names.

In 1786 the Dutch East India Company (DEIC) sent the Cape Harbour Master, François Duminy, to investigate the possibility of a harbour being established at Plettenberg Bay. The report was favourable, with the result that a woodcutter's post was established under a former Prussian soldier, Johann Frederick Meeding. A free burgher, Jan Jacob Jerling, a name you may remember in connection with the wreck of the *São Gonçalo,* was commissioned to build a woodshed. In due course Duminy was back again in his ship the *Meermin* to take aboard the first load of timber from Plettenberg Bay to the Cape.

But, as Sir John Barrow pointed out after the British took possession of the Cape, Plettenberg Bay as a harbour had its limitations. It is entirely open to south-easterly winds, as was apparent in the case of the *São Gonçalo* wreck. The British chose instead to develop Knysna as a harbour.

At the foot of the eminence upon which Van Plettenberg dictated that his stone should be placed, lie the remains of Jerling's wood store. The stonework has stood up well to more than two centuries of wind and rain, and of seepage from above, but the roof and the wooden doors and windows have all disappeared.

Not far off was the home of Meeding, the Postholder for 26 years. When he died in 1813 he was buried a hundred metres or so from the Lookout parking area. Then a block of flats was built in the vicinity, the grave was in the way and the only memorial to the founding father of Plettenberg Bay was pushed aside and obliterated by a front-end loader. One finds Thompsons even, some say especially, amongst property developers.

Not far from the wood store were the Company store-house and barracks, for in the 18th century the DEIC was very aware of the possibility of a foreign power attempting an occupation of the area. Travellers John Barrow, in 1797, and Heinrich Lichtenstein, in 1803, mentioned the barracks, but the likelihood of an invasion gradually faded and the soldiers were removed. For many years a whaler, John Sinclair, had the house and then, in 1869 Bishop Robert Gray, whom we have so often met in these pages, bought the house and from that time it has been known as the Rectory. When a new rectory was built in 1939, the original building became the Old Rectory.

In 1913 the occupant was a young priest, the Reverend William Gratton Sharples, usually known as John. He was, it seems, a shy young man, but with a keen interest in archeology, as we will discover later. One day he received two visitors, Pauline Smith with her Aunt Jean. The writer Pauline Smith you may remember from the farm Molenrivier and subsequently at Mossel Bay, where she and her father missed the boat. Now Pauline and her chaperone were to spend a night at the rectory.

Pauline wrote a detailed description of the building:

The roof, which ought to have been thatch, was red iron; the windows all small-paned (15 panes) but casement, not sash, which is uncommon out here. The walls three feet deep. The house very lonely: the kitchen in a gable to the front; everything terribly dilapidated and poverty-stricken looking.

After mentioning the layout of the house she describes the room she and her aunt shared:

Our room nice and large: a window in the gable to the sea, a second in the long wall on to the old Batavian barracks and the monument above it to Governor Von Plettenberg . . . Our room has several sets of shelves, a washstand, very old but nice and big; a plain deal table as a dressing-table, and a wooden home-made bed-frame. Mr Sharples seemed rather afraid

*we might not find things comfortable, but the room
looked so nice and simple and clean that I quite fell in
love with it.*

It was the bed that was going to cause the problem. Sharples did mention how he, after the bishop's recent visit, had returned the mattress borrowed for the prelate. But it was not only the missing mattress that was the problem, the design was faulty: ropes connected the head- to the foot-board.

*(Aunt Jean) got on the bed to see what it would be like,
and the bed promptly shut up like a concertina, the
ropes sinking down and dragging up the footboard
(not exactly like a footboard after all) and shutting
A.J. up in the middle. When with some difficulty and
terror, she got up with a "Mercy", the footboard fell
down with a clank. She tried it several times and each
time the same thing happened, and the thought that
if we slept in that bed at all it would be on our heads
with our heels high above us, made us both very hys-
terical.*

* * *

Sharples was interested in archeology and was no sooner installed in the rectory than he was to be seen scrambling around Robberg investigating the caves.

Robberg is an unusual feature jutting out into the ocean along an extended stretch of coastline, from Cape St Francis to Mossel Bay, that has over countless centuries become submerged. Initially irregular, the shore has been gradually smoothed out by waves and current into wide, curved bays, and the cliffs cut back during a series of depressions and up-lifts.

Plettenberg Bay however, has at one end, the Robberg peninsula, covered with a relatively youthful and soft sedimentary formation composed of sandstone, conglomerates and breccias. That this has resisted the waves and currents that eroded the coastline elsewhere may be attributed to the fact that they are perched on top of folded Table Mountain quartzite. It is this resistant basement rock that has for the time being checked the onslaught of the ocean.

Nonetheless there is evidence on the peninsula of severe wind and wave action. There are several hollows and five deep caves. The Nelson Bay Cave has an entrance that is 20 m across and is some 30 m deep. Ventifacts, stones shaped by extreme wind action, are to be found in this cave and some of the others. At first glance they often resemble stone tools with a sharp edge that in their case has been sharpened by exceptionally strong winds.

The caves provided early man with ideal sites for temporary homes, and it did not take more recent humans long to discover signs of their occupation. It was evident everywhere: stone tools, shell middens, bone needles, pottery, drilled tortoise shells, ostrich egg-shell beads and skeletons. The South African Museum in Cape Town ended up with a collection of perhaps as many as 50 skeletons.

One of the earliest collectors of stone tools was the road engineer, Thomas Bain. Noting the need for a scientific approach he carefully catalogued his collection before sending it to the Colonial and Indian Exhibition in London in 1886. Sharples, the resident clergyman in 1913, was soon to follow suit and in his turn become fascinated by these ancient artefacts, sending his to the Museum in Cape Town.

It was in the same year that Pauline Smith and Aunt Jean stayed the night in the Rectory that Dr Louis Peringuey of the South African Museum in Cape Town called on the Reverend Sharples. Unfortunately there is no record as to whether or not he spent a night in "the bed", but almost certainly Sharples accompanied him to Robberg where they spent time investigating caves, especially Guanogat and Hoffman's Cave (also known as East Guanogat). If not already addicted to archeology, this proved a turning point in Sharples' life, for from now on he excavated under the indirect guidance, by post, of Peringuey.

The year 1917 was, so far as Sharples was concerned, a particularly successful one. He excavated several skeletons, as well as bone points, pottery, both indigenous and either European or Asian, wood with "paint" – probably red ochre – a drilled tortoise shell, a notched bone shaft, an ostrich egg-shell necklace and four large patella shells. He had a special interest in painted gravestones, and during the time he worked on Robberg found 18 of these memorials of early mankind.

In the years to come Sharples rose in the hierarchy of the Anglican Church to become Canon of St Marks, George, while in connection with his other interests he became a member of the Royal Society of South Africa. He never lost his interest in archeology, together with anthropology and geology, and in later years worked at stone-age sites in the Oudtshoorn, Beaufort West and Knysna districts.

Sharples died in 1954. Since then a number of excavations along the Cape south-east coast have resulted in a multitude of exciting new finds, including those described earlier at Pinnacle Point. Evidence has emerged that points to the occupation of the area by some of the very earliest examples of modern man, *Homo sapiens.* How thrilled Sharples would have been to know that his excavations were a small step taken along the way to the present discoveries.

The first scientifically controlled excavation of a Robberg cave occurred just ten years after Sharples' death. Between 1964 and 1971 the Archeology Department of the University of Cape Town (UCT) together with the universities of Chicago and Louvain (Belgium) concentrated on the Nelson Bay Cave. Archeologists leading the excavation were Prof RR Inskeep of UCT, Dr Richard Klein of Chicago and Dr Hilary Deacon and his wife Janette of the Albany Museum in Grahamstown. Among the findings and conclusions reached as a result of the dig were:

1. Humans had sheltered in the cave for 70 000 years.
2. The cave was apparently unoccupied from about 50 000 to 20 000 years ago. .
3. Signs of both pottery manufacture and sheep-herding dated to 1900 BP.

4. Stone tools made from large quartzite flakes were found in the 12 000 to 9 000 year-old layer.

5. In the 9 000 to 5 000 year-old levels numbers of small convex scrapers, crescents and other minute tools were found.

6. The bones of an 11 year-old child were radiocarbon-dated 2 700 BP, at the time the first accurately dated human skeleton to be recovered from South Africa.

The archeologists regretted the fact that so many of the sites on Robberg had been damaged by amateurs delving for souvenirs. The South African Thompsons, like those found world-wide, had been hard at work for many years.

Rondebos farm

We turned off the road and drove down the grass-covered *middelmannetjie* driveway of Rondebos, heading for the Nut-hut, a wooden-walled, asbestos-roofed house. Living here at the time of our visit was Mrs Gladys Snaddon née Brown, known to her grandchildren and us, as Gaga and to her friends as Glad, or Glad-Snad. She and her husband Robert moved to Plettenberg Bay after his retirement from the Johannesburg corporate world, and here she lived on alone after his death, but for her two assistants, Mannetjies, who had a drinking problem –"If only I could control his inordinate fondness for his *dop*" – and one-armed Freek, who despite his missing limb coped with Glad's garden, the chickens and geese.

The farm actually belonged to Glad's brother Ted, Uncle Ted to the rest of us, and in the high-flying world of diamonds, for he headed the Industrial Diamond Division of De Beers, as E T S Brown. In the 1970s Uncle Ted together with the firm of a former American football player from Detroit, Frank L Christensen, was selling diamond-tipped drill bits to more than 50% of the world's oil-well drillers. No wonder he was able to keep on the farm for holiday use an elderly gas-guzzler of note, a dusty pink Buick Roadmaster. There was also a

Landrover, in which the younger generation learned to drive and go down to Robberg beach for early morning swims.

The diamond connection in the Brown family went back a long way. Gladys was born in Kimberley, the diamond city, during the siege by Boer forces in 1900. This was convenient for her grandchildren who, by using the easily remembered year, were able to tell Gaga's age. It was said that the wine-coloured birthmark just visible under her chin that she so hated as a young girl, but wore with pride in old age, was as a result of the stress her mother suffered during the siege.

With the Anglo-Boer War over, the family returned temporarily, because of her father's ill-health, to Britain before returning to Thomas Cullinan's Premier Diamond Mine near Pretoria. There they lived in a large tent believed to be British Army surplus. Lined with scarlet material and with her mother's blue brocade curtains hanging, an attempt was made to keep it free of flies by packing fresh Bluegum branches into four-gallon paraffin tins. Gladys's parents' double bed stood on a thick layer of sand.

The children loved their new camping existence; their mother was less enthusiastic about roughing it. Gladys remembered her mother crying and being comforted by their father.

Then, one morning, the 26th of January 1905, there was great excitement. "Pater" came running down the koppie from the mine, calling to his wife to round up the children and bring them to the shaft. Off Gladys went in her starched pinafore together with her two brothers. They found everyone at the mine assembled, the miners, rugged sun-burnt men wearing thin shirts and pants, heavy boots and wide-brimmed felt hats, and the more formally attired mine manager, Mr Donald McCardy.

The assembled company standing under a zinc roof supported by rough-hewn poles, were now addressed by McCardy. What he had to say meant little or nothing to Gladys. A large diamond of great worth had been found by miner Fred Wells. Then she found her father urging her forward towards the table where Mr McCardy stood. The manager placed a small diamond in her left hand and a very large one in her right. Her father helped support her right arm. Only later did she realise that she had played a small but central role in the first public viewing of the world's largest gemstone-quality diamond, the 3 106 carat Cullinan Diamond.

Thomas Cullinan, owner of the mine, sold the stone to the Transvaal Government for a nominal £150 000, and in 1907 it was presented to King Edward VII on his birthday, the 9th November. Cut by Joseph Asscher of Amsterdam, the largest cut stone, the 530 carat Cullinan I (or Star of Africa I) was mounted in the Royal Sceptre, with the next largest, Cullinan II being mounted in the Imperial State Crown. The next two stones, Cullinan III and IV, were given to Queen Mary as a brooch, which she was fond of wearing. As a result the Royal Family refers to them still as "Granny's chips".

The Crown Jewels are on display in the Tower of London. In later life Gladys visited the Tower to see them and to be reminded "of a very hot day in the Transvaal, when the Cullinan Diamond was put in my hand to hold, a little freckled-faced maid of five".

* * *

Less than 20 years after the end of the Anglo-Boer War, young South African men, both black and white, volunteered to go to war again. They fought in South West Africa, East Africa and Europe. In 1916 at the Battle of Delville Wood, many gave their lives for the British Empire. Lance Corporal Frederick Charles Lee took part in the fighting and was the only surviving NCO in C Company, 3rd South African Infantry Regiment. Of the 4 000 strong South African Brigade, barely 300 survived. On the 21st of July 1916, Lee wrote a letter home:

My darling mother,

It is with a very sorrowful heart that I sit down to write you these few lines. We are a couple of miles behind the firing line now, having just come out of the Wood (Delville). After five days of absolute awfulness poor Angus Brown, my pal, died of wounds after about three hours awful suffering. He had both feet blown off by a shell on the 18th July.

I wish you to let Mrs and Mr Brown know this. I saw him a little after he was hit. He was quite conscious and showed real grit . . . I gave him a drink of water, and the only complaint he made at that time was, "My God, Fred, the pain is awful."

Frederick goes on to describe how he had to go back to the front line and when next he called at the dressing station, Angus was dead.

I had no idea he was going to die, he seemed so very cheerful.

I"ve had a good cry. I couldn"t help it.

And so Mr and Mrs Brown and family came to learn of the death of their son, Harold Angus Brown, 1896-1916, a private in the South African Brigade.

Less than a year later Frederick Lee, by that time a 2nd lieutenant, was himself to die of wounds near Arras.

Thomas Brown, father of Angus, died shortly after the end of the First World War, his end hastened, so it was said, by a broken heart. On Gladys's dressing-table at Rondebos was a framed photograph of her brother Angus.

* * *

Elsewhere I have recorded my first meeting with the Snaddon family, the former Gladys Brown, her husband Robert Snaddon, and the three boys, Robin, Mike and Brian, with whom I was of an age[7].

As adults Brian and I met up again and carried on from where we had left off as teenagers. In the interim Brian had married Ann Donald and before too long there were two sons, Bruce and Chip, and two daughters, Jiggs and Kate.

Holidays were often spent at Rondebos. Chip remembers visits to his grandmother on the farm, and how it seemed that they had no sooner arrived than Gaga hurried off to feed the

7   See *Toasted Marshmallows & Obies.*

"Snaddon Eating Team" with their favourite bowls of chicken broth, "soep" she called it, together with great hunks of brown bread.

The main ingredient of the soup came from the flock of fowls, "ground-scratching chooks" that Gladys kept despite the constant battle fought with a "dynasty of spotted gennets", referred to by Gladys and one-armed Freek as *die Muishonde*.

There was also a gaggle of grey geese, called to their daily feed of mielie pips with a rousing cry of "Gozgazgeeze! Gozgazgeeze!" at which they began an ever-quickening waddle down a long grassy patch behind the Nut-hut with a cacophony of honks and hisses until, picking up speed, their wings began to beat and the whole flock became airborne for a few seconds before crashing down amongst the scattered mielies. And some of the geese also made an appearance on the table. Slaughtered, plucked and roasted, a goose was always the main dish at the Christmas lunch shared by the Brown and Snaddon families on Rondebos.

Less popular with Bruce and Chip was the daily dose of malt and cod-liver oil, "guaranteed to banish the winter snuffles" according to the manufacturers. Snuffles were a tribulation the boys were willing accept if it meant avoiding a daily spoonful of the "viscous, black, tarry mixture" on which they gagged.

Bruce remembered that his Grandmother had many good friends in the area. They stood together in troubled times such as the summer fire-season. They went on painting trips together and there was much "sharing of garden slips and tips", but Gladys also took an interest in the community at large, and a feature of life at Rondebos was the packing of Kupugani food parcels for the elderly and indigent living in the nearby township of Kranshoek. Gladys was a Kupugani volunteer, working for the organisation that in the 1960s was established to combat malnutrition in South Africa. Before the monthly trip to Kranshoek all available hands were enrolled to pack brown paper parcels. The grandchildren not only packed parcels, but often accompanied their grandmother to Kranshoek to help with distribution. There, among others, they were introduced by their Gaga to Oupa Gert Gahl.

Jiggs Snaddon remembered Oupa Gahl, with his wrinkled brown face, as "the oldest person I had ever seen". Bruce recalled visiting him in his tiny house:

> He had a way of telling a story with his eyes and hands and plenty of pauses for dramatic effect. We would sit at his feet entranced by his old blue eyes, full of mischief and liveliness. He had verve and energy and warmth about him.

It was he who told them tales of his people, the Griqua people, and of their trek in search of freedom.

* * *

Gaga did not live to witness the devastating fire that in June 2017 swept through the south-eastern Cape coastal districts, including Knysna and Plettenberg Bay. Her Nut-hut was spared by the flames, but Thatch, the younger Snaddons accommodation when on the farm, and also the Brown's home, were burnt to the ground. The latter was rebuilt and the vegetation is slowly recovering. Memories of how it once was remain:

> I loved the concrete stoep (of Thatch) overlooking the valley, buchu fynbos and the distant sound of the sea.
>
> The tiny yellow sit-in bath and the horrid outside loo. My loo phobias started there! Didn't you find a night-adder there, Bruce?
>
> Yes, at my birthday party I went to the loo and there was a night-adder. I rushed out without my pants. Dad came and blasted away with a shotgun. Missed the snake but perforated the plumbing. My mates thought it was the best party entertainment ever!
>
> Those huge and heart-filling hugs from Gaga when we arrived, and at our departure at the end of the hols tear-shedding and Gaga's waving figure dwindling among the trees and protea bushes of her indigenous garden. Good times!

The Griquas of Kranshoek

Living north of the Orange (Gariep) River during the first half of the 19th century were the Basters, a mixed group of Dutch-speaking people of various origins but very largely the offspring of whites and Khoekhoen. Their leader, write the historians, was the remarkable Adam Kok, a freed slave who had worked as a cook, which may well have been the origin of his surname; a cook who became a leader of men.

According to Oupa Gahl at Kranshoek, Kok was a freed slave from the East, who arrived at the Cape as a ship's cook. On arrival he fell on his knees and kissed the ground. He swore that this land, the first in which he would experience freedom, would become his homeland.

Today there are various Griqua groups, but all have in common a special regard for their forefathers and a belief that they are the children of God who has led them, as their own Adam prayed, through the valley of the shadow of death.

As the century progressed, so the Basters came under pressure from northern raiders led by Klaas Afrikaner, and from the south by covetous white farmers in search of grazing land.

Under the not entirely incorrect impression that the missionaries were representatives and agents of the Cape authorities, the Basters appealed to them for help against the threats to their sovereignty.

In 1813 they were visited by John Campbell of the London Missionary Society (LMS) who indicated to them that the name "Baster" was highly unsuitable and that they should from then on be known as Griquas, and that their main settlement would no longer be Klaarwater, but be called Griquatown (Griekwastad).

While under the leadership of Dr John Philip, the LMS in the 1820s developed an ambitious plan for the Griquas to form a bulwark on the northern frontier of the Cape, protecting the tribes from the incursions of the white farmers while at the same time protecting the Colony from attack by tribes from the north. But the balance of power in the Transgariep shifted; white farmers moved into what was considered to be Griqua territory while the Sotho and Tswana peoples came to outnumber the Griquas.

Internal bickering led to a large group moving from the Griquatown area to what became in 1826 Philoppolis in the present-day Free State, and named after their mentor, John Philip.

With the death of Philip in 1851 the Griquas lost their champion and the LMS no longer had the influence that it once enjoyed. Determined to keep their independence, in 1861 some 2 000 Griquas, under the leadership of Adam Kok III, abandoned Philippolis and set out on a trek which lasted two years and was to be as momentous as that of the Dutch trekkers. To this day the Griqua people are reminded of this trek, just as the Afrikaner *volk* were once reminded of their ancestors' Great Trek. While crossing the Drakensberg, the Griquas were at times forced to use gunpowder to clear rocks and enable their wagons to pass. They finally set up a laager at Mount Currie in Nomansland (Griqualand East), and after some years spent living in a laager, founded Kokstad.

In 1867 few paid much attention to the birth of a future leader, Andrew Abraham Stockenstrom le Fleur. At the age of 12 he had a remarkable experience. After three days out in the veld looking for donkeys near Manyane Mountain in the Matatiele district, he was about to give up when he heard his name called three times:

> *Andrew! Andrew! Andrew! It is the Lord your God. Go forth and gather together the people of Adam Kok, so that they may become my people, and I their God.*

> Struck dumb he stood transfixed as the voice continued, *The donkeys that you seek are behind the koppie. Let this be a sign to you that it is the Lord your God.*

The young boy went home with the donkeys and told his father what had happened. It was the start of a life-long mission.

Meanwhile a British Resident, Joseph Orpen, was placed in the territory to keep an eye on the Griquas. Ignoring their needs or wishes, Orpen openly lobbied for the annexation of their territory by the Cape government, which eventually led to the annexation of East Griqualand in 1874.

In the following year Adam Kok III died and the mantle of leadership fell not on his younger brother, Adam "Muis" Kok, but on his widow, Magriet Kok, who played a prominent role during the Griqua rebellion against Cape rule in 1878. The bloodline of the Kok dynasty passed to the Le Fleurs, when Le Fleur married Rachel Susanna Kok, daughter of Adam Muis Kok, in 1896.

Le Fleur now set about re-establishing the Griqua captaincy, which alarmed the Cape government. After a brief and inconclusive skirmish between those supporting Le Fleur and government forces, Le Fleur was arrested and charged with treason. In May 1898 he was found guilty and sentenced to 14 years hard labour at the Breakwater Prison in Cape Town.

A religious man rather than a political leader, Le Fleur saw this as his "time in the wilderness", a means chosen by God to strengthen his resolve. In January 1903, during his incarceration, he prophesied to his fellow convicts that he would soon be released, giving not only the day but the time of his release; Friday the 3rd of April 1903 at three o'clock in the afternoon. In addition he stated that their unpopular prison-overseer would salute him.

On the day he foretold, he was unexpectedly set free and at 3 pm was escorted from the prison by two high-ranking warders. They passed the unpopular overseer, who saluted the trio as they went by.

To try and rid themselves of this thorn in their flesh the Cape government now offered Le Fleur, on behalf of the colonial authorities in Rhodesia, a senior government post in that colony at a salary of £1 000 per annum. Le Fleur turned down the offer, preferring to remain with his people. It was from this time that he became known to the Griquas as the *Kneg* – the servant of God.

In his efforts to uplift his people, Le Fleur did his utmost to encourage agriculture, and attempted to persuade the government of the day to release Crown Land "to enable us to pull our people out of the gutter". This led in 1917 to a second trek, this time by train, to Touwsrivier to establish a small-scale agricultural scheme, which failed due to a lack of government support and an absence of infrastructure. Many distressed Griqua families straggled back to Kokstad.

In 1928 a more successful trek was organised, this time to Kranshoek, a place where "the grass was green and their children and cattle could grow fat". This was the trek in which Oupa Gahl of Kranshoek was involved. They left Kokstad in donkey-carts, wagons and on horseback. The fame of Le Fleur had spread and they were joined along the way by others from Trompsburg and Philippolis, Campbell and Louisvale, Kat River and Maclear. Le Fleur, the Kneg led daily prayers, and told them of God's message, that he, Le Fleur, was to guide the people and to build a new nation. They were three months on the road before arriving at Plettenberg Bay, and this time they stayed, hiring and later, in 1957, buying 244 hectares of land at Kranshoek.

Le Fleur was convinced that the salvation of the people lay in agriculture, which would provide jobs besides feeding the people. In 1934 in a letter to Jan Smuts and J B M Hertzog, joint leaders of the ruling United Party he wrote:

> *I give you good advice, give the black man, the brown man, the Griekwa and the poor whites land so that they can earn a living from it and by so doing their children can be kept out of the streets. Should you not take my advice you will not be able to keep ahead of the need to build jails.*

Andrew Abraham Stockenstrom le Fleur died on the 11th of June 1941, in a house not far from the site of his grave. In the two decades before his death he made several further prophecies, some of which have since come about:

- His grandson, Andrew Abraham Stockenstrom le Fleur would head the Griqua nation, which he did in 1951.

- A railway line would be built from Sishen to Saldanha across a Griqua farm, Ratelgat. The line was built in 1976.

- The Griquas would acquire the farm Jakkalsgat on the Piesang River near Plettenberg Bay. A A S le Fleur II received the title deeds in November 2001. It is now one of the most productive dairy farms in the area.

- The Griquas would be represented in Geneva. Today a Griqua representative participates in the annual meetings of the United Nations Working Group on Indigenous Populations.

Today there are Griquas to be found living throughout South Africa, but along the Cape south-east coast there are, beside that at Kranshoek, Griqua communities at Blue Lilies Bush, The Crags, Covie, Kurland and formerly at the mouth of the Salt River.

* * *

If on leaving Rondebos Farm one heads towards Robberg and the centre of town, there, not far from the west end of the Robberg peninsula is a road to the right. Not far along it is a white-painted grave with a small gravestone. On the stone is inscribed:

Ter nagedagtenis van ons
Volksleier en godsman Kaptein
Andrew Abraham Stockenström
Le Fleur, stigter van die
Griekwa Volkshervormingsbeweging.
Gebore 2 Julie 1867-1941.

Visiting it bare-headed, we nevertheless metaphorically raised our hats to a remarkable man who sought not only to take his people to a Promised Land, but also to make them worthy citizens of that homeland. Le Fleur stressed what the Reverend Campbell had said so many years before: they were not second class citizens, not Basters, but a proud, independent people. They were Griquas and must act accordingly.

Every year at New Year, Griquas from all over South Africa gather at the grave to celebrate the Kneg, the servant of God who was sent to take them to Kranshoek.

Keurbooms ferry

14.

Wittedrif, Keurbooms, Salt River, Nature's Valley

The way to a golfer's heart

A pale pink and grey sky in the east changes gradually to orange as a dull red ball rises slowly from the sea: it looks like another good day in the Garden of Eden, with the millionaires' mansions, RDP[8] matchboxes and holiday homes still hidden by the early morning mist. Perhaps the Khoekhoen shepherds and the survivors of the *São Gonçalo* witnessed mornings like this looking out over the Bay. We will be well on our way by the time the town of today emerges from beneath the haze.

Traffic on the N2 is light at that hour of the morning and passing Goose Valley Golf Estate we wonder just how many such estates there must be on the Cape south-east coast.

---

8. RDP matchboxes = Government subsidised houses.

When was it that South Africans became so obsessed with golf? From the 1940s on, Bobby Locke and later Gary Player drew our attention to the game, but what about the 1965 winner of the Natal Open, Sewsunker "Papwa" Sewgolum? His win that year, beating Gary Player in the final, certainly focused attention not only on golf, but also on our politics, for the little Indian was forced to stand outside the Durban Country Club in the rain to accept his trophy. Later, of course, the apartheid government banned him from playing golf or even entering a golf course as a spectator. He died in poverty at the age of 48. Too bad that he was unable to live longer and spend his retirement years living on a swish golf estate.

No, the "Sewgolum affair", while drawing attention to the game, could not have aroused such interest that there is now, announces Caryl, who has been busy on her tablet consulting Uncle Google, with 19 courses along the coast from Mossel Bay to St Francis Bay. (In Bobby Locke's day there were just three.) No, there has to be another reason. What could it be?

Reaching the Bitou River brings an end to this speculation, but no answer to the question.

* * *

At the Bitou River there is a turn-off to Wittedrif and a road that eventually takes one to the Prince Alfred Pass; a delightful drive through the foothills of the Outeniquas.

If you are lucky, as we were one day, there will be a *Vroue Landbou Vereeniging* gathering at Wittedrif, and you will be able to admire *naald- en breiwerk* (needlework and knitting), *lapwerk en blomme rangskikking* (patchwork and flower arranging), and not only admire, but also taste *melktert en Hertzoggies* (milk-tart and jam-filled cookies), and besides the normal braai delights of *karbonaadjies en boerwors* (mutton chops and farmer's sausage) also *slaphakskeentjies en skilpadjies* ("weak little heels" = cooked onion salad - and "little tortoises" - portions of liver in "vests" of fat), and that is a mere foretaste of all the delights available.

My mother, an English rose if ever there was one, looked askance at South African meat dishes. *Braaied boerewors* and a *kop-en-pootjies* stew were not for her, but confectioneries were a different matter entirely. I still associate Christmas with *mebos*, a sweetmeat of salted and sugared dried apricots, which she prepared, if my memory serves, according to a recipe by Hildagonda Duckitt, South Africa's Mrs Beeton. And at about the same time of the year my mother would produce *perskesmeer*, a thin layer of sun-dried, sugared, pounded peaches. Along the Garden Route the fruit for these delights comes from the orchards of the Langkloof, just over the Tsitsikamma Mountains.

For her ladies' tea-parties my mother put on the table, in addition to her English cake and scones, *oblietjies,* thin wafers with cinnamon and rolled like a brandy snap. As a child I accepted this offering for the sweet-toothed as a matter of course and only in my late teens did I realise just how typically South African they were.

In the pantry were shelves with ranks of Ball jars filled with preserved peaches, pears and apricots, ripe and unripe fig jam. My father's annual announcement that the figs were ready saw the "copper", a large brass bowl, come down from the top shelf of the pantry and preparations made for jam-making on the slow-combustion stove, a process that seemed to take days. I was unsure, and still am, as to why the electric stove was not used for jam-making, but I have come to accept that it was one of those culinary mysteries that my mother chose to keep to herself.

My introduction to South African meat dishes began during my very early teens. I had been helping a friend's parents move some furniture and was sitting on the open back of their *bakkie,* something of which my mother would not have approved, when my friend announced that they were going to have a *braai* that night, and that his mum and dad had said I could join them if I liked. And so for the first time I discovered the delights of *boerewors* and *sosaties* – sausage and kabobs - grilled on the coals.

Here along the Cape south coast it is as likely to be a fish such as a Yellowtail wrapped in aluminium foil that one finds on the coals, and we have already mentioned one of the local staples, Tsitsitsikamma burgers; a chunk of grilled fish in a sliced *aspatat,* sweet-potato baked in the coals.

Should this seem a little crude, what about our friend Mike's black mussel potjie, with cleaned and de-bearded mussels in white wine, with finely chopped parsley, onion and tomato and a sprinkle of lemon juice? To be really decadent add some cream to the mix. The irony of this meal was that Mike, who had both collected and prepared the mussels, and acclaimed it to the assembled company did not join the feast, preferring to dine on grilled English sausages. Perhaps his Western Cape upbringing had something to do with his strange behaviour.

Then there is also *smoorvis,* which is served with onion and potatoes and sometimes tomato. Basically *smoorvis* is what one buys at a fish and chips shop; fish braised, stewed or fried in boiling oil, but prepared by a good Cape cook it nonetheless has a flavour all its own.

One of my favourites is certainly *ingelegde vis*, fried and curried kabeljou or any other firm fish preserved with vinegar and bottled with onions and mango chutney. Traditionally, among many of the Cape's inhabitants, it is served at Easter together with hot-cross buns or bread.

The Wittedrif exhibition and sale of work by farmers' wives took place a long time ago and is probably an annual event. However, up and down the coast there are plenty of farm stalls and farmers' markets, the one at Sedgefield being known country-wide. There is really no excuse for remaining ignorant regarding the delights that are still produced in country kitchens. Why not start with something simple, such as home-baked brown bread with ghokum (or gaukum) jam? The fruit with which the jam is made is the "sour fig" of a sprawling ground-cover, *Carpobrotus edulis,* and by asking for it on your bread you not only have a delicious snack, but establish at once that you are a knowledgeable food lover.

Then instead of opting for the usual Spaghetti Bolognese, insist on *Tamatiebredie* – Stewed mutton with tomatoes, not tomato paste or sauce. Oh, and a tip, a little good sherry both added to the stew during the making and sipped while eating, brings out the flavour wonderfully.

Are you travelling further east along the coast? Now is the time to tuck into a bowl of *umngqusho,* otherwise known as samp and beans, traditional soul food of the majority of the residents of the Cape. Should you insist on meat with your meals, flavour with a little animal fat. .

There, now you are on the way to making some gastronomic discoveries that will bring pleasure to the rest of your days; even after you are no longer able to swing a golf-club!

Tsitsikamma Road

In the initial stages Captain Christopher Harison had almost as much to do with the planning of the "Tsitsikamma Road" as Thomas Bain. Harison was a former British Army officer (Black Watch) who had served on the eastern frontier before resigning his commission to take up farming. Not being successful in this venture he joined the forestry service and rose to become, in 1874, Conservator of the George, Knysna and Humansdorp forests.

Harison, while stationed at Witelsbos in the Tsisikamma, dreamed of a road to open up this wilderness area. Among his responsibilities were the woodcutters whose only source of income came from the trees that they felled. He envisaged woodcutters, living in villages and cultivating plots to generate additional income. This would benefit not only the woodcutters, but would also reduce pressure on the indigenous forests that he was tasked to preserve. All that was needed was a road to provide a means of taking their surplus produce to market.

In Knysna Harison met Thomas Bain and shared his dream. Bain was enthusiastic and believed that the sale of Crown land for the villages would help defray the cost of the road. The road together with the villages would not only help protect the trees, but also its wildlife. Unschooled woodcutters would learn new skills that would help them develop self-supporting communities. This was the plan and ulti-mately Harison's humanitarian scheme was to prove at least partially successful.

In 1868 Harison and Bain explored the area, looking for a suitable route, before submitting a joint report to parliament. Bain made light of the difficulties: "The road in general will not be difficult to construct." No mention was made of the rivers to be crossed or the forest giants to be felled and their stumps removed, although he did admit that a good deal of blasting would have to be done.

The wheels of officialdom in the 19th century turned as slowly as in the 21st century and a decade went by before work actually began. In Bain's report to Parliament on the work done during the period 1878 to 1879, he noted that he had established a convict station at the Groot River (Groot-rivier), where today the Nature's Valley Rest Camp is to be found. The station was essential because the construction of the "Road" required the labour of some 350 convicts. Later there were also convict stations at Bloukrans and Storms River.

During the 12 months on which he reported, Bain had also worked on three other passes, two roads and a canal, while "inspecting", which entailed putting up milestones and doing further finishing touches to 26 other roads. Bain usu-ally travelled from job to job in a horse-drawn Cape cart, and only occasionally by train. He was a busy man.

Two years after the first ground was broken, the pass through the Grootrivier was complete and the road-build-ers, under the supervision of Bob Bromley, who was later to become Bain's son-in-law, were starting the descent into the gorge of the Bloukrans. By the end of 1883 the road through the Blourans was complete. Only the Storms River Pass re-mained, but heavy rains disrupted work and Bromley was kept busy repairing wash-aways. Finally the road through this last gorge was finished and by the end of 1885 the Tsitsikam-ma Road joined up at Kareedouw with the road through the Langkloof from Humansdorp.

Bain's name "Tsitsikamma Road" was soon forgotten, for this magnificent scenic route soon came to be known as the Garden Route, and discounting the forests, it was indeed a garden of fynbos, ericas and restios, everlastings and watsonias, brilliant red George lilies and blue agapanthus in summer, flame-red aloes in winter, strelizias, crassulas, haemanthus, nodding passerinas and blue lobelias.

Then, in the second half of the 20th century, came the bridges: the first, in 1956, over the Storms River, was designed by Italian civil engineer, Ricardo Morandi. The single span bridge was constructed in two parts; semi-circular supports being lowered from opposite sides to meet in the middle. Nothing like it had been attempted in this country before, and it received a great deal of publicity. There were stories about the site-engineer being in a more than anxious state lest the two halves not meet. Prof Morandi back in Italy first saw the bridge only after its completion, but was said to be "calm". His faith in the South African engineer was confirmed when the two halves were barely millimeters out.

A bridge over the Bloukrans was next, but this required the building of two other bridges, one over the Bobbejaans River and another over the Groot. This time design was by local engineers and construction by Murray & Roberts and Concor, South African firms.

These three bridges have also received well-deserved praise. Thomas Bain and any other 19th century *padmaker* would be astounded and full of admiration for the engineers. For those in a hurry they are a godsend. This applies not only to the drivers of 18-wheelers, but also to the drivers of ordinary cars. They no longer approach blind corners on the Grootrivier Pass wondering whether or not they are going to find one of these massive horse-and-trailers attempting to take the bend and heading towards them on the wrong side of the road.

The bridges are a great improvement, but the N2 toll road that now crosses them can no longer be referred to as a part of the Garden Route. For safety sake the verges of the unofficially reinstated Tsitsikamma Road are mowed regularly and your chances of seeing a patch of watsonias while travelling at 120 km/h are slim. Should you wish to enjoy the "garden" you will have to use the old R102, Thomas Bain's road, and the only pass that remains open is the Grootrivier: this despite promises made in 1983 that the passes would remain open.

It now takes less than a day to drive from Cape Town to Port Elizabeth. There are no longer innumerable drifts and the "more than 150 gates" that Chatty Knight and Joy Hofmeyr had to open and close in 1925. But there are still some of us alive that regret that there is now no chance of seeing an elephant cross the road near Harkerville, or stopping to admire a kilometre or more of watsonias in bloom near Bloukrans.

Crossing the Keurbooms

East of Plettenberg Bay lay the forests, gorges and rivers of the Tsitsikamma; an insuperable barrier in the 18th century. All the early European travellers were forced to either turn back or find a route over the mountains and into the Langkloof. The first obstacle to progress was the Keurbooms River. The river was crossed on occasion, for its waters were not normally that deep nor fast flowing; the banks not especially steep. However the only means of transport across was a rowing boat. A rider, having seated himself in the boat, held on to his horse's reins and hoped that the animal would follow across without capsizing the boat in the process. .

Then in 1860 local landowner William Henry Newdigate sent his own men to construct a pontoon. A heavy chain from a wrecked ship was used to keep it in place and enable the ferryman to pull it across the river. It was now possible for both rider and horse to cross the water dry shod.

Soon after the completion of the pontoon, a post office was established beside the river and a Mr C Mussman was appointed postmaster, serving a large but sparsely populated area to the east of the Keurbooms. Business was obviously not brisk, for two years after his appointment he offered to serve without payment. Then not long after, in 1869, his position was abolished. Despite this, the delivery of the little post that there was apparently continued. Much of it, no doubt was directed to the Newdigate family.

William Henry Newdigate arrived at the Cape in 1845 together with his younger brother, George, who later returned to England. Within days they were met by the Honourable Henry Barrington of Portland, near Knysna. He very naturally insisted that the Knysna area was where they should look for a suitable property to farm.

The Newdigates, following his advice, first bought farms beside the Piesang River at Plettenberg Bay, but later also acquired land at The Crags, to the east of the Keurbooms River. This property W H Newdigate named Forest Hall and set out to establish a Cape country estate similar to that of an English country gentleman.

Much of the income of the estate was to come from timber cut in the indigenous forests, but the distance from Plettenberg Bay and the lack of any well-maintained road was to prove a severe financial handicap. His friends also complained about the isolation of his estate and the difficulties they experienced visiting him, but nevertheless agreed on the magnificence of the setting. Here he built, with local materials and labour, Forest Hall, the equivalent of an English manor house, and set himself up as the local "squire".

At two o'clock in the afternoon of the 9th of February, 1869 the house at Forest Hall was so filled with smoke that the lamps were lit. The Great Fire of the Tsitsikamma, which was also to wreak havoc in the Humansdorp district, surrounded a house that held not only the Newdigate family, but also servants and neighbours. There was some distance between the house and the fringes of the forest and William, head of the family, opted to stay put rather than to flee the flames. An unexpected change in wind direction saved the house and possibly the lives of those within it, but large areas of woodland, pasture and crops were devastated. Although the Newdigates did not realise it at the time, the Great Fire marked the beginning of the end of a way of life that was unsustainable.

To the roadmakers at least, the fire was a blessing. It enabled them. at last and with comparative ease, to find a route through to Humansdorp from Plettenberg Bay. But from envisaging a road to actually building it takes time and it was only in the early 1880s that Thomas Bain actually started work on the long awaited road. At the Keurbooms a new 19 metre pont was built to replace the old Newdigate one. Fittingly, Mrs Caroline Newdigate (née Duthie of Belividere) was called on to perform the opening ceremony. She broke a bottle of champagne across a handrail, and the first crossing of the river was made.

The new pontoon also marked the arrival of the Stanley family beside the river. George Edward Stanley, previously a teacher at the Wittedrif School, was engaged to operate the new pontoon. He continued there, together with his wife and eventually 13 children, until his death. Not only did he see to the pontoon but he, and later one or two of his sons, hired out boats, rowed parties wishing to picnic beside the river or to explore it, and also acted as gillies.

Many travellers were surprised by the ferryman's cultured English tones and quaint, pedantic manner of speech. This also rubbed off on his Dutch-speaking wife, Johanna Acker of Mossel Bay, and several of their 11 sons and two daughters.

Pauline Smith and her Aunt Jane, on their way to stay with the Reverend Sharples (see chapter 13) crossed the Keurbooms and met Mrs and Mr Stanley. Pauline described them thus:

> *A faded little old woman in a brown skirt, blueprint blouse, and untrimmed straw hat. The old man was very small, his features all strongly marked and clear, but so small. His nose a little beak, and his chin coming towards it. Small blue eyes. But his voice and accent most astonishing of all.*

After the death of their parents, three of the Stanley boys, Eddie, Poley and Osmond, continued to live by the river and scratch out a living. They must have been there when my parents and I first crossed the Keurbooms, but I do not remember them. Much later Caryl and I and the children camped beside the river on what was once Stanley land, but no member of the Stanley family appeared to question in upper crust accents our presence there. The nearest thing to the small ferryman that we came across was a friendly, bright-eyed vervet monkey.

With the ferry now in operation, the post office started to plan an extension of the postal service eastwards. Their first move in this regard was to establish an office at Forest Hall in 1881. The squire, Caroline's husband, in addition to his other duties, added those of postmaster, a position he held until his death in November 1884. His heir, Francis, known as Frank, was a surveyor and seldom at home, so the job of running the estate, and acting as postmaster, became the responsibility of the youngest son, Arthur, aged just 21.

The financial state of the family gradually went from bad to worse. In July 1899 the saw-milling machinery was sold off, but the family hung on at Forest Hall until after the death of Caroline Newdigate, aged almost 90, in 1922. Only then did Arthur and his three unmarried sisters move out of Forest Hall to build at Longridge Farm, nearer the main road.

Today Forest Hall, as "inconveniently distant" as ever, is a popular wedding venue, and perhaps the distance from the main road is just a part of its appeal.

The Keurbooms was eventually bridged in 1927, but the bridge lasted only four years. Once again travellers had to make use of a ferry. Concrete bridges over both the Bitou and Keurbooms Rivers were completed in 1947, and in 1956 it became possible for the first time to travel the entire distance along the coast from Cape Town to Port Elizabeth on tar and over bridges.

Salt River

Travelling from the Keurbooms River along the R102, and just before the road drops down from the plateau and into the gorge of the Grootrivier, there is an overgrown track leading off to the right. This was once the road to a settlement located above the mouth of the Salt River. Eight Griqua families lived in this isolated spot, the men working as fishermen and/or independent woodcutters.

Many years ago, but after the Griquas had moved on, we bumped down this track together with the Snaddon family. We parked the cars where once the houses stood, and from there both adults and children helped carry camping essentials. The youngest two, for reassurance, went hand-in-hand down the hill, one carrying a kettle, the other a braai-grid. The loads were dumped beside the river and the younger members of the party stripped off and took to the water. The adults sorted through the pile of clothes, camping gear and provisions to establish order. In the river mud a strenuous but light-hearted mud-fight took place.

Brian and Ann gathered together the makings of lunch while Caryl and I collected large rocks for a fireplace and secured some firewood. The party of desert-island castaways, for that is what we resembled, now made their way down the Salt River to the mouth. There we came across a large wooden, double-ended fishing boat, no doubt of Thesen of Knysna manufacture, pulled up well above the high water-mark.

We sat in the shade of the nearby trees and ate our lunch. With hunger-pangs quelled we lay back on the sand and some of the youngest fell asleep, lulled by the noise of the nearby breakers. The older children walked down to investigate the shoreline of the estuary.

Later, Brian told us the story of the fishing-boat; a story that began, he explained, a long time ago and beside another river, the Gariep, or Orange, where the fishermen, or their forefathers, lived before making the long trek by way of Griqualand East, to here beside the waters of the Salt River and

Indian Ocean. A story told to the Snaddon children by Oupa Gahl of Kranshoek. But for now Brian focused on the fishing boat and the tale of a disaster.

Here, beside the river and the sea, the small Griqua community made a comfortable living from felling trees, hunting or trapping bush-pigs and bushbuck, and catching fish. Unlike some of the woodcutters, they received cash for the timber they cut, and were not continually in debt to the sawmills. They caught sufficient fish not only for themselves, but to provide extra income in the form of dried fish.

Traditionally, as mentioned concerning the fishermen of Jeffreys Bay, they were non-swimmers. As you may remember a swimmer was regarded as a liability among a crew, for he might, when most needed, decide to save his own life, leaving his fellows in the lurch. This was to prove the downfall of the Griquas at Salt River.

Making for shore one day a giant comber smashed into the boat, which turned turtle, throwing the crew into the wild water and blown spume. Only one man survived. It signalled the end of the little community. Widows and orphans moved out and sought work on nearby farms. Soon all that remained was a Thesen fishing-boat and the foundations of the houses where we had parked the cars. (Now even the boat has gone.)

That evening we sat around the fire playing games and telling stories, but many of these stories seemed to revolve around fishermen and disasters at sea, so Ann, going on from where a child had left off, told the story of Robinson Crusoe and Man Friday. We sang a song or two, but it had been a long day and the children were drowsy. One by one they went to find their sleeping-bags, settled down near the fire and drifted off to sleep.

Although it was the height of summer and the entire south-east Cape coast was heaving with holiday-makers, we beside the fire might have been the first family in the Garden of Eden. The adults were soon left alone to watch the rosy glow of the fire as it died down. There was an occasional crackle and sparks whirled upwards like a dance of fireflies.

Then we too found our bags and soon joined the sleepers under the stars.

Next morning we were up with the sun. One of the boys found spoor in a patch of mud beside the river.

"Maybe we'll find Man Friday's footprint," suggested Ann.

"Aw, come on Mum, you know he was just make-believe."

"Or perhaps," said the other boy, "the footprints of the fishermen's ghosts."

"Ghosts don't have footprints," announced the smallest of the girls.

But we did find spoor; during the night a bushbuck had visited us. This discovery was followed by the finding of a most unusual spoor with clearly defined footprints on either side of a roughly defined line. It was of course the trail left by a water monitor or leguaan, dragging its tail behind it, but when one of the girls suggested a crocodile, the two boys laughed her to scorn.

"Pretty small crocodile!"

"Well, it might be a baby crocodile," she conceded, "but still a crocodile."

The dispute was interrupted by Brian: "Come and have a look at this."

"Wow! A leopard! Look at this" exclaimed the boys.

The two smallest girls stood wide-eyed.

"See, no claw marks. It must be a leopard"

"A leopard right next to where we were sleeping!"

At this point Brian gave a hoot of laughter. Crinkle-eyed and grinning widely he leant down and with a few swift movements of the heel of his hand and his knuckles created another "leopard" spoor.

"Ah, Dad, you let the cat out of the bag," said the eldest boy.

"I think you mean the leopard," said Brian.

It is no longer possible to camp as we did and wear the equivalent of fig leaves in our Garden of Eden. The mouth of the river is now listed as a recommended day-hike starting at Nature's Valley. One walks the beach before scrambling along a rocky coastline to reach the estuary. It is well worth the effort. There are breath-taking seascapes to admire when pausing for unfit muscles to recover, and although you are unlikely to find any trace of the Griqua fishing community, it is more than likely that you may find the tracks of a leguaan, the hoof-prints of a bushbuck or even the spoor of a genuine leopard. Sit beside the river for a moment, where once our earliest ancestors sat, or perhaps a much later Griqua family who arrived beside the Salt River in search of their Promised Land.

* * *

When in the early 1880s Thomas Bain started work on the road through the forests to Humansdorp, postal officials began planning a new service, and with this in mind that the post office at Plettenberg Bay was, in 1886, raised to the status of Head Office in the Western Administrative District. In effect this meant that post offices to the east, Keurbooms River, Forest Hall, Covie and later Nature's Valley, would fall under the jurisdiction of Mr G C Waites, postmaster in the Bay.

Seven years later a post office was established at Covie, east of present day Nature's Valley.

In 1895 Arthur Victor was contracted to convey post once a week on this new, eastern route. Delivery was on horseback and naturally enough he was required to keep "strong and serviceable horses." He was also obliged to provide a rider equipped with a horn or bugle which was to be blown when approaching any post station. For the delivery service Victor was paid £36 per annum, but a penalty of 15 shillings was incurred for every period in excess of two hours that the post was late, unless there was *proof* that the detention was caused by swollen rivers. There was no mention of delays of any other nature, but it seems that Victor's rider was, apart from the odd flooded river, always on time.

The post left the Residency at Plettenberg Bay at 7 am every Tuesday. Thereafter arrival times were: Keurbooms River – 8:30; Forest Hall – 11:00; Covie – 2:30 p.m. On Fridays the post to Plettenberg Bay left Covie on the return journey at 11:00 a.m.

* * *

Returning from Forest Hall to Thomas Bain's now macadamised road, one comes to the former farm of Woodlands, which is now named Kurland. It was in 1941 that the Read family sold the farm to a Baron Ulrich Behr, a Russian whose family had fled the country of his birth at the time of the Revolution. In the Netherlands the young Behr found a job with the Hollandse Oos-Indiese Kompanjie and was sent to Java. From there he moved to South Africa where he met the famous discoverer of Lydenburg platinum and the Free State goldfields, Dr Hans Merensky. This may well have led to Behr's involvement with the Lichtenburg diamond fields and his awareness that to operate mines large quantities of timber were needed. From that developed his interest in the forests of the Tsitsikamma and the purchase of Woodlands.

At Saasveld Behr met a young forester, E E G Ellis, who was to become his estate manager, trusted friend and, in effect, partner in the years to come. Tens of thousands of pine saplings were planted on Kurland. As Behr acquired more land so the number rose to millions. But trees take time to mature and in the meanwhile various other crops were planted to generate income; tung nuts, soya beans, youngberries, Cape gooseberries and chicory. None came to much and a lot of money was lost.

Grootrivier

Above us, apart from a thin line of wind-blown white cloud on the eastern horizon, is a clear blue sky. Quite unexpectedly we drop down into the gorge of the Grootrivier and the surrounding foliage changes from fynbos of a coir-mattress consistency to a tangled mass of trees and creepers. By modern standards the road is narrow and winds down the side of the gorge with frequent tight bends. We soon catch up with an elderly Mercedes Benz with an equally elderly and cautious driver, together with a white-haired companion. Bain built passes with ox-wagons and Cape carts in mind, passes which today suit not only us, but also the couple in the Mercedes.

Reaching the bottom of the pass the Mercedes heads on eastwards, but we turn off into Nature's Valley and drive down St George's Lane to the café at the western end of the village for cups of coffee.

* * *

In November 1855 the American poet Henry Wadsworth Longfellow wrote an epic poem, *The Song of Hiawatha,* that is today arguably his best remembered work. Written in thumping trochaic dimeters, it tells the story of the Ojibwe stalwart Hiawatha and of his love for the Dakota maiden, Minnehaha. The opening lines introduce Hiawatha's grandmother, Nokomis, and give some idea of the repetitive rhythm of the poem:

> *By the shores of Gitche Gumie*
> *By the shining Big Sea-Water,*
> *Stood the wigwam of Nokomis,*
> *Daughter of the Moon, Nokomis.*

The poem was immensely popular. Within 12 months it sold at least 70 000 copies, an unheard of amount for a piece of poetry. It remained popular for many years and a century after it was first published, school-children were still given pieces to learn and to recite as choral verse. The correspondent of the *New York Times* wrote in the 1850s, "The madness of the hour … everybody writes trochaics, talks trochaics and thinks in trochees."

Perhaps because of the rhythm and repetition the poem lent itself to the writing of parodies, of which, over the last century and a half, there were hundreds if not thousands. That amiable clergyman and archeologist, the Rev W G Sharples of Plettenburg Bay, whom you may remember once entertained Pauline Smith and her Aunt Jean, was one of many parodists. He wrote of "the mighty hunter" of Grootrivier,

Hendrik "Barney" Barnardo, known to Afrikaans speakers as Hendrik "Grootrivier" Barnardo. Today Barnardo is remembered for his efforts to protect the green environment of Nature's Valley, and in particular the trees. However, as Sharples intimated, Barnardo had no such scruples when it came to elephants, buffalo or any lesser form of animal life. The last Tsitsikamma elephant was shot by a Barnardo, possibly Hendrik, in 1881.

After the completion of the pass in 1880 three lots were proclaimed in the valley and granted to the Anderson, Barnardo and Read families. All three families later moved up to the plateau, but in 1889, Hendrik Barnado and his first wife, Grieta, returned to the land beside the Grootrivier lagoon and added to their land by buying the Anderson and Read properties. There they built a house of yellowwood and settled down to raise a family.

Grieta died after producing six children. Her place was taken by Jacomina who added a further eight children to the family before she was killed by an ostrich. Then came Hendrik's last wife:

> *There beside the mighty water*
> *Lived the hunter, Barnardo,*
> *There he married John Tait's daughter,*
> *Married the lovely Lohanno (sic)*

(By now you should be well into the swing of things and able to continue the story in this style of epic poesy,)

Lohanna Virginia Tait, to give her full and properly spelled names, brought another seven children into the world. Not only was Hendrik Barnardo a mighty hunter, but also now the chief of his very own Barnardo tribe. Nevertheless he, together with his tribe, might have continued to live beside the Grootrivier in relative obscurity had he not, in 1918, allowed Wilhelm Mark Maximillian "Bill" von Bonde and his wife Nel to spend a holiday camping beside the lagoon. Shortly thereafter the Carel van Hasselt family also discovered this idyllic spot, as did Bobby and Marjorie van der Riet while on honeymoon. The news began to spread, and friends and friends of friends made their way on holiday to the gorge of the Groot-rivier.

It was the start too of the Barnardo legend. Every evening Barney, or Grootrivier, depending on the language of the campers, visited their sites. Ostensibly this was to ensure that they were observing his strict rules regarding the environment, but it was also to find out if there was anything they required, to deliver a bottle of milk, a water melon, sweet potatoes or a loaf of bread, and not least, to enjoy a *sopie* or two with his guests. Despite, as the years went by, the ever increasing number of campers and thus of *sopies*, there was little likelihood that these drinks might result in Barney's discomfiture, although it was not unknown for him to fall from his camp-chair during the course of the evening, much to the delight of the younger campers. "Do it again, Barney! Please do it again."

During these evening visits, Barney had plenty of stories to tell. Not all of them coincided with the known facts, but no one bothered too much about that. Whether an ancestor acquired the land in exchange for £50 and a horse with no saddle or bridle, or whether it was granted by British Governor Lord Charles Somerset, made little appreciable difference to the evening's entertainment.

By 1930 there were nine families that were regular holiday-makers beside the river and the first cottages were in use. The following year a one-roomed post office together with public phone was erected beside the Barnardos' yellowwood house. Phone operator and postmistress was a Barnardo daughter. The year of the post office happened also to be the year of the flood, when the bridge over the Keurbooms was washed away, groceries could not be delivered, campers were washed out and the Grootrivier lapped at cottage doors. Lohanna, known as "Ma Barney", spent her time drying clothes, baking bread and feeding them on spotted dog (flour, baking powder, suet and dried fruit). Barney entertained everyone with his stories. Someone played the concertina and in the evening they danced to the music of a wind-up gramophone and sang songs. For a week they were cut off from the outside world, but the week, far from being a nightmare, became the stuff of legend. The Barnardos cared for all, to the extent that six of their children shared their parents' feather bed. There were those who eyed the valley for business reasons. In the 1920s Peter van Reenen of Reenendal acquired from Barnardo an option to buy the land, but for one reason or another he never took up the option. Many others came to knock on the Barnardo door with offers to buy, but Barney was not tempted to sell. When Baron Ulrich Behr of Kurland first approached Barnardo in 1939, the answer was still "No". Despite repeated refusals, Behr persisted and was eventually successful.

There are various stories as to how the Baron accomplished the deal. Some maintain that it happened on a night when the old tribal chief looked too deeply into the bottle. Others state that Barnardo was anxious, when his time came, to be buried beside his first two wives, both of whom were interred on the Baron's property at Kurland. It was the Baron's undertaking to arrange the burial that won the old man over, together, of course with the £4 750 that would go to providing Lohanna, his surviving spouse, with an income after his passing.

The story is told of how, despite the Baron's extensive business interests, there was barely enough money left for the Behrs to pay the legal fees and develop the property. The Baron and his wife Ena, together with employees, worked side-by-side clearing the bush and making roads, and everywhere that Ena went, so did her dogs. Perhaps in part thanks to the ebullient, unconventional and forthright Baroness, there was a good working relationship between the Behrs and their employees.

At the suggestion of a friend, they decided to market the property under the name Nature's Valley. The sale of plots was at first slow, but with the tarring of the pass in 1950, soon picked up.

Hendrik Barnardo died at the age of 86 on the 24th of April, 1948. There was a flurry of activity in the valley. A suitable vehicle in which to drive the old man in his coffin was at last found. He travelled in some style to his final resting place next to Grieta and Jacomina at Kurland. A canary-yellow station-wagon was decided upon. It was driven by its owner, Brig-Gen Sir Henry Scott, KCB, DSO, MC. It would have been difficult to choose a more suitable vehicle and driver for Barney's last journey.

* * *

Many years ago I read of a wise and ancient tribe that believed that when one died one lived on in the memories of family and friends, acquaintances and others, even enemies. It was up to us while alive to ensure whether or not we would be remembered fondly or not, whether we would be in heaven, or in hell. Eventually, like a sea-mist, we would all fade into the unknown. Only the very good and very bad would be remembered for a little longer, but even they would finally be forgotten in the bright sunshine of a new day.

I know how the old tribal chief, Hendrik Barnardo, is remembered.

What remains of Bain's causeway lies to the right of the present bridge at Nature's Valley

Oakhurst, Coldstream

15.

Tsitsikamma – where the waters begin

It is not easy, some would say "not possible", to drive through the Bloukrans Pass. Actually the western side of the Pass is well maintained and other than that it is a road designed in the 19th century and meant for animal-drawn traffic, it presents no particular difficulties, excepting perhaps for rock-falls after heavy rains.

On our way down the road, travelling from the west, we met a maintenance crew at work. We stopped to talk to them in their eye-catching orange overalls: Foreman Gilbert Pietersen and his crew of Marshall Alexander, Franklin Platjies, Xolile Ntlanga, Elvis Mkanin and the sole woman, Maria Daniels. No major repair-work was being undertaken. The road, so Gilbert told us, was in good condition and the road markings still bright and clear. The gang were simply cleaning drains and brushing away leaves and the occasional stones and small branches.

"But," said Gilbert, "over the bridge there on the Eastern Cape side, man they don't know what they doing. In fact they don't do nothing." Then looking at the number-plate of the Isuzu and noting the EC plate he added, "Maybe itsa government an' they can't help it".

Maria Daniels told us how she enjoyed her work. It was so much better being outdoors. She travelled around and saw new places. She could see that what she did made a difference and was a help to other people. No two days were the same and the men were nice guys with whom to work.

Down at the old bridge the difference between Western and Eastern Cape was immediately obvious. Dense bush overhung the road on the eastern side of the bridge, and in places we could not easily walk abreast along the road, let alone drive along it. A few years ago we did drive through and in fact it is still possible: while we were standing beside the bridge a young man came through on his motorcycle. He gave us a wave before accelerating up the hill past the road crew.

Coldstream

On the eastern side of the pass one emerges on a plateau, which we reached by back-tracking and crossing the Bloukrans Bridge, the world's largest single-span concrete arch bridge. Here, for the adrenalin-junkies, is operated the 200 m Flying Fox Zip-slide, or *foefie* slide to fellow South Africans, as well as the highest, at 216 m, commercial bridge Bungee-jump in the world. You pay R1 350 for some moments of sheer terror.

Foregoing the doubtful pleasure of a bungee-jump, we crossed the bridge and found our way through to the old R102. There we found a suitable spot near the top of the pass for a picnic lunch.

At one time, when the old R102 was the National Road between Port Elizabeth and Cape Town, we made regular use of the Bloukrans Pass. In those days there was, during daylight hours, an almost constant flow of traffic on the R102. Today, while eating our sandwiches, we saw no vehicles and not a single passerby. Nor was there any sign of baboons. Back then one could with some assurance, guarantee a baboon-sighting. Caryl then remembered that we saw some baboons crossing the N2 near the Bloukrans Bridge. Have the baboons, in search of hand-outs from passing motorists, followed the vehicle traffic to the new road?

We set off eastwards along the old road and after a few kilometres, came in sight of the tall smokestacks of the Coldstream saw-mill, an industrial enterprise established by the Whitcher family within the Tsitsikamma forests in 1902.

Charles James Whitcher, founder of the Coldstream Whitchers, was an English civil-engineer. He and his wife, Mary Caroline, née Browne, together with their infant son, Edwin, arrived in Durban from the United Kingdom in 1882. By the following year the young family had moved to Knysna where Whitcher met up with Charles Wilhelm Thesen, who headed the family firm of timber merchants. Whitcher and Thesen apparently took to each other, for Whitcher was soon involved with the development of the new Thesen mill at Brackenhill.

With the saw-mill up and running, Whitcher moved, in 1887, to the Millwood Goldfields. There he found a small gold nugget, now the property of the wife of a descendant. However, together with the majority of other Millwood diggers, he did not make his fortune.

Whitcher now turned to the forest lands of the Tsitsikamma, where he purchased a large tract of forest situated between the Boukrans and Lottering Rivers. There at the turn of the century he built his own saw-mill, the first in the area. By the time it was completed in 1902, he was joined by his firstborn, Edwin and Edwin's younger brother, Alfred Charles Whitcher. In 1920 Edwin left the family firm at Coldstream and moved to Humansdorp. Alfred stayed on until his death in 1947.

Initially, using local indigenous timber, the mill concentrated on the production of furniture. Later, with the increasing availability of pine from nearby plantations, a switch was made to tool-handles. Today (2020) only pine is available from the mill.

Founder C J Whitcher did not spend all his time with his nose to the grindstone. His name appears also in connection with the yellow-striped mountain lizard – *Tropidosaura gularis* – which he found at Coldstream Cave and which would have interested the Irish-born herpetologist of the Port Elizabeth Museum, Frederick William Fitzsimons.

Fitzsimons also had an interest in archeology and is associated with the excavation of another cave in the vicinity named, not surprisingly, Whitcher's Cave, situated approximately eight kilometres north-east of Coldstream. It was Whitcher who drew the cave and its contents to the attention of Fitzsimons. The dig took place in 1926 and is regarded as the most important that Fitzsimons ever undertook. Apart from the usual stone tools, pottery and waste flakes, he unearthed more than 50 Late Stone Age burials. No doubt the Whitchers were as excited by these finds as Fitzsimons himself. Unfortunately proper records were either not kept, or no longer exist, for the information that is available regarding the excavation is regrettably scanty.

Which brings us to the change in Whitcher fortunes. In the 1920s the decision was taken to up-grade the mill. New machinery was ordered from the Mangold Brothers in Port Elizabeth at the expense of £5 750 (the equivalent today, taking inflation into account, of approximately R7.4 million). The amount was paid off over two years, but so it is said, the receipts were destroyed. Mangolds apparently came to hear of the lack of receipts. A demand for payment was submitted which led to a court action. C J Whitcher was adamant that he had paid, but being unable to produce the receipts, was ordered to pay the outstanding amount. Thus in 1929 he was forced to sell his family home, Oakhurst, together with much of his land in order to clear the "debt".

The founder of the business and of the Coldstream community never really recovered from this setback. Whether from stress and shock, increasing age or a combination of factors, the C J Whitcher era at Coldstream drew to an inevitable close. His son, Alfred took over the reins. At the gates to the mill the sign "C J Whitcher & Sons" came down and a new name went up: "A C Whitcher".

* * *

Oakhurst, the Whitcher family home, was completed in 1918. From it, prior to 1929, the family looked across sweeping lawns to the farmlands and mountains beyond. The only sign of the major source of their income was the smoke from the mill, drifting across the peaks, ridges and shaded gullies of the Tsitsikamma Mountains. We set out to find the house, leaving behind us the saw-mill and the R102 as we drove down the rutted, dusty track towards the sea.

After traversing some kilometres of dirt road, with pine plantations to the right and also off to the left, but with land in between once cleared for agriculture, a white-walled building appeared on a rise, standing out like a fairy castle in a pantomime against the dark green and black backcloth of the plantation beyond. It was only as we came nearer that it was seen to be not an icing-sugar castle beside the Rhine, but a double-storied, grey-roofed, four-square house situated within a large fenced-off area on a rise, and surrounded by a recently cut lawn and a few scattered, mature trees. The white walls and colonnaded *stoep* with an upper balcony of the Coldstream manor were now more reminiscent of an American Southern States cotton estate.

* * *

It was later in time and further in distance from Coldstream that we sat beside the sea with Raymond Ritchie who headed the Whitcher family interests in the Tsitsikamma.

The Ritchies, how do they fit in?

Peter Ritchie, my Scottish grandfather, had a farm, Blink-klippies, near Kimberley. With a name like that

341

and situated where it was you can guess the nature of the blink klippies, the "shining stones". He sold it to De Beers in order to buy a property beside the Modder River. There he built a weir to supply water to a mill and to provide irrigation. The farm was divided into a number of irrigated agricultural small-holdings which he hoped would help in the rehabilitation of ex-convicts and others in distress. In time it came to be known as the village of Ritchie.

It was perhaps no wonder then, that he became friendly with fellow Scot, George St Leger Lennox, better known as Scotty Smith, or South Africa's own Robin Hood. To the authorities Scotty Smith was a cattle-thief, smuggler and dealer in illicit diamonds, but there were many, including my grandfather, who saw him as a horse-lover and friend of the poor.

My father, James Bernardus Ritchie, went from the village of Ritchie to Saasveld to train as a forester. On completion of his training at Saasveld he was posted to Lottering Forest where he met a local teacher, May Whitcher, daughter of Alfred Charles Whitcher.

With the outbreak of War in 1939 James Ritchie enlisted and in due course was sent to North Africa. When a nearby ammunition dump was hit by enemy fire, he survived but lost his hearing and was repatriated to South Africa. In Johannesburg he was operated on and while recuperating contacted May, the teacher from Coldstream, who travelled up to Johannesburg.

In due course they decided to marry. May paid for the wedding ring and James's sister in Johannesburg baked the wedding cake. There followed the necessary visit to the Magistrates' Court where James and May were declared man and wife and they returned to the apartment for a cup of tea and a slice of cake.

After my father's military discharge, he rejoined the Forestry Department and was sent to Tokai.

At Coldstream, after the death in 1947 of Alfred Whitcher, his son Albert, or "Bertie" Whitcher took over the reins. One day the Ritchies at Tokai received a call from Bertie. Would they consider joining the family firm at Coldstream? As soon as they could the newly-weds left for the Eastern Cape.

I put in an appearance in 1956. It was the same year that the Storms River Bridge was completed. I arrived shortly before the bridge was opened to traffic. When my father, James, was notified that my arrival was imminent he set out with May for the Humansdorp Hospital. On reaching the bridge he pushed aside the barrels blocking their way, ignoring remonstrations from the assembled padwerkers. The family threesome reached Humansdorp safely and there were no later repercussions. Today, my claim to fame is that I am one of the very first to have crossed the Storms River Bridge.

* * *

From where we sat aboard *Grace*, a James Wharram designed double-hulled sailing craft – James Wharram preferred this term to the more usual catamaran – we could keep an eye on activities in Port St Francis, while Raymond told the story of *Grace*.

One afternoon Raymond and a friend, Dave Wilson, dreamt a typically Sunday afternoon dream: wouldn't it be fun to build a yacht and sail away to some exotic destination?

Unlike most such dreams this was followed by research, estimation of costs, and the choice of a site on which the work could be done, followed by the acquisition of building plans and the ordering of Israeli marine-ply.

A shed was built on a property at Witelsbos, and when the marine-ply arrived sections of a keel were cut out, glued together and laid down. There in the Tsitsikamma an ocean-going, double-hulled sailing craft began very gradually to take shape, it's three integral structures, hulls and central platform, held together, as Wharram directed, not by fiberglass, but by rope, which at sea give a shock-absorbing effect.

With meticulous craftsmanship, for after all their lives would depend upon it, the job took 12 years. Then, complete at last, *Grace* was moved to her future home of Port St Francis and launched. Imagine how Dave and Raymond felt, seeing their creation moving to the gentle surge of the harbour waters.

Raymond went on to tell of some of their subsequent adventures; of the circumnavigation of Madagascar and of anxious moments at the Bassas da India, but wherever they might be, although authorities might be less than helpful or electronics unexpectedly fail, their workmanship was sound and their confidence in *Grace's* ability to weather the storms unshaken.

So Raymond Ritchie, besides being one of the first to cross the Storms River Bridge, has other claims to fame. Wearing a T-shirt, shorts and slops, sun-bronzed and with a fine head of untamed, curly hair, greying in places and receding at the temples, he certainly fits the image of surfer, fisherman and yachtsman. Not everyone would immediately recognise him however, as a former businessman, forester and head of a family firm that is now close to being 120 years old.

Today Raymond's son, Raymond Gene Ritchie, is in charge of the timber business, the fifth generation of the family at Coldstream. Raymond senior is likely to be spending more time aboard *Grace.*

Tsitsikamma Coastal Park.

Back to the N2 and speeding traffic. During the 2017 fires we found ourselves behind a police vehicle with flashing blue lights. Every so often there were flames from patches of bush beside the road, but the fires along the N2 were largely under control. There was, however, no time to stop and assess the damage, for we had been instructed to keep up with the police car. For the first time in our lives we were a part of a blue-light brigade and travelling at 120 km/h and sometimes more. Trailing us there were half-a-dozen other cars. At the end of the line a small Toyota Tazz that was soon left behind. At one hotspot I checked the rear-view mirror, but there was no sign of the Tazz.

On this occasion we passed the entrance to the Tsitsikamma Coastal Park without giving the Park a second thought. This is not always the case. From the entrance gate to the Park not far off the N2, the road drops gradually down over a stretch of 11 km to the mouth of the Storms River. On the landward side greenery dotted in season with statuesque white arum lilies tumbles over like a green waterfall towards the sea, while below great white-topped waves crash relentlessly against the broken black rocks of the shore. We once saw a Cape clawless otter down on the rocks, silhouetted against the waves, a magical sighting that lasted but a moment before the animal disappeared over the rocks and down towards the ocean.

The amber waters of the Storms River have carved a cleft to the ocean through 200 m cliffs. Spanning the mouth of the river is a suspension bridge from which one has a fascinating view of activity in the meeting place between the waters. On one sunny morning we witnessed a school of small sharks lining up while waiting their turn to enjoy some watery tidbits brought downstream by the river.

Storms River is the start of the ever popular Otter Trail, stretching 45 km westward to Nature's Valley. So popular is it that one may only walk it by appointment, yet despite its popularity and the fact that it is seldom far from one of the busiest tourist routes in the country, there are no passersby and one is alone but for one's companions and the creatures of earth, sea and sky. From Ngubo's hut, only eight kilometres from the camp, one climbs hillsides overlooking the breakers to reach Scott's shelter beside the Geelhoutboomrivier. Then it is on to the Oakhurst shelter, just west of the Lottering River and not far removed from the Whitchers' old home of Oakhurst. Finally there is Andre's hut on the Kliprivier, before the last leg to the Grootrivier estuary at Nature's Valley.

* * *

345

South Africa's first coastal national park opened in 1966 under the watchful eye of its first conservator and marine biologist, Dr G A "Robbie" Robinson. He it was, together with Victor Cunningham who, amongst all their other tasks, laid out the Otter Trail. Robinson also, together with R M Tietz, produced the first guide to the park, *Tsitsikamma Shore - Tsitsikammakus.* Our own copy, now dog-eared and tatty, dates back to the 1970s, but it remains a treasure trove of information on the natural history of the south-eastern Cape coast.

Robinson, who died in 2017, went on to establish South Africa's first community-owned park in the Richtersveld, and in 1990 was appointed CEO of the National Parks Board.

The earliest mention of a coastal park in the Cape that I found dates back to 1928, nearly forty years prior to Robinson settling in at the mouth of the Storms River. It appeared in the now dusty pages of the *Eastern Province Herald* where it was recorded that a Mr H B Smith, while addressing a meeting of the Port Elizabeth Rotary Club, pleaded for an early start to be made on the preservation of the natural amenities of the Eastern Cape with particular reference to the Tzitzikamma – as was the accepted spelling at the time. His championship was echoed by Mr A H T Perry of Queenstown in April of the same year. The *Cape Argus,* also, on the 25th of April 1928, reported approaches by Mr Smith, which were sympathetically received, to the Cape Town Mountain Club.

With the bit between his teeth, Smith now appealed to the High Commissioner for the Union of South Africa in London. The High Commissioner, Mr Jacobus Stephanus Smit, replied appreciating the virtue of the idea not only in the context of nature and wildlife conservation, but also as a valuable tourist attraction. He promised to bring it to the attention of the Minister of Lands back home in South Africa. And there the whole matter apparently fizzled out, for I could find no further references to it.

It is interesting nevertheless to read of some of Smith's proposals. He envisaged a park with an initial area of 100 square miles (259 km^2) with the possibility of the area increasing tenfold when funds became available. The area of the present park is roughly 260 km², of which 186 km² is ocean, not taken into account in Smith's document.

The park he envisaged would incorporate hostels, shelters and camp-sites with roads and paths to the main features. He suggested that a mule-path to the top of Formosa Peak would be a definite attraction. Noting that throughout the coastal area there was evidence of its occupation by "strandlopers", he stated that every effort should be made to preserve their "cliff dwellings".

Finally there was the question of cost. Smith believed that the acquisition of the land and the establishment of basic services would cost in the region of £5 000.

In 1928, Smith, far ahead of his times, believed that if his proposed coastal park were not developed in the near future, the coast would soon be "sullied" and lost forever. How fortunate we are that his worst forebodings did not come to pass and that by the time Dr Robinson was installed in 1966 there was still a coastline to preserve.

It is interesting too, certainly in the light of recent discoveries along the south-eastern Cape coast concerning our earliest ancestors, to note his insistence that the cliff-dwellings of the original inhabitants of the area should be preserved.

The Tsitsikamma Coastal Park, apart from its importance as a tourist attraction and provider of work to the local community, is also of ecological importance and a centre for scientific research. It also serves as a memorial to those that worked to develop and maintain this important cultural asset. Foremost of these would be the late Dr Robbie Robinson, but I would also suggest Mr H B Smith of Port Elizabeth, a man of foresight whose dream at long last became a reality.

Henry Georges Fourcade: silviculturist, botanist, surveyor, inventor, businessman

At first we cannot find the way into the property. Although we have not been there for 20 years, we know that it is almost immediately opposite the entrance to the Witelsbos Forestry Station. Then the penny drops; in the last two decades trees have grown up along the R102 which completely hide the house, general dealer's shop and various other buildings we knew. We find the gap in the trees, go through and there is the former general dealer's shop. A glimpse of red roof indicates the position of the house, but there are also two large sheds, of which we only remember one.

Back then a yacht was being built in the shed, a catamaran which we were shown over by the builder. (Little did we know that some 20 years later we would come across this yacht again in Port St Francis, by which time it had acquired the name *Grace.*)

Work is going on in the sheds, for we can hear the whine of power tools. An elderly Datsun bakkie with faded paintwork drives by. The grey-haired driver eyes us quizzically, but does not stop and it is only after he has passed that we realise we met him on our last visit, when his hair was black. Hesitantly we step forward to explain our visit, but the Datsun disappears in the distance. We are at what once was the home of Henry Georges Fourcade, a remarkable man of whom very few South Africans are aware.

Little is known of Fourcade's early years. He was the son of Justin Jade Fourcade and Marie Prat. Born in Bordeaux, in 1865, he lived briefly in Japan before passing the school-leaving exams at the Lycee in Bourdeaux at the early age of 14. He went on to the Ecole Superieure de Commerce et d'Industrie where he passed the first-year examinations with ease.

Shortly thereafter, the young Fourcade, together with his mother and sister, Jeanne Marie Fourcade, left for the Cape. The reasons for the move are unclear and nothing further is known of his father.

At the Cape Fourcade completed his formal education by obtaining, in 1882, the Certificate in the Theory of Land Surveying at the South African College. Soon after this his mother and sister returned to France. Fourcade chose to remain and applied for a job with the Forestry Department in Cape Town. He was put in charge of the herbarium at the age of just 17. A fellow Frenchman, the Comte de Vasselot de Regne, who headed the Department, took the young man under his wing and guided his studies in the science of forestry.

In 1883 Fourcade was moved to Knysna, where he became an assistant forest officer under Capt Christopher Harison, who soon recognised Fourcade's ability, and in 1889 he was seconded to the government of Natal to prepare a report on the forests of that colony, and to advise on the establishment of a forestry department. The time that he spent in Natal was both happy – he was his own boss – and productive. His Report on the Natal Forests, 1889-1890, was regarded by forestry experts as outstanding and was received enthusiastically by government. It was a remarkable achievement for a 24 year-old.

On his return to the Cape, Fourcade decided to link the forest surveys with which he was busy with the Geodetic Survey of the Cape being undertaken by the astronomer Dr (later Sir) David Gill. This new task, performed during off-duty hours, involved surveying the entire coast from Mossel Bay to Humansdorp. Gill, like De Vasselot, soon recognised Fourcade's genius and willingness to work long hours. It was during this time that Fourcade designed and built the first of the white concrete trig beacons which now appear on high points throughout South Africa.

Gill was one of the pioneers of photographic astronomy, so when Fourcade began to experiment with photography as a surveying tool, he received enthusiastic encouragement. At the time there was a world-wide craze for stereoscopic photos. Fourcade believed that stereoscopic photos could be of use in topographical mapping. He gradually developed a technique that enabled him to draw contour lines from such photographs. At a meeting of the South African Philosophical

Society in Cape Town on the 2^(nd) of October 1901 he presented his historic paper, *On a Stereoscopic Method of Photographic Surveying.* Gill, president of the Society and a scientist of world renown, saw to it that Fourcade's paper was also discussed by the Royal Astronomical Society in London, and that it was published in the journal, *Nature.*

Meanwhile, in Germany at the University of Jenna, Dr C Pulfrich was working along similar lines, and in March, May and August of 1902 published a similar paper covering much the same ground in the *Zeitschrift für Instrumentkunde.* Fourcade's paper not only predated Pulfrich's, but besides establishing a theory on three dimensional measurement, also set out the design details of a camera and measuring stereoscope.

In Europe one could count on the fingers of one hand those who were aware of an obscure forestry official from the Cape, who had already published ideas similar to those of the academic from Jena, who was to be hailed as the founder of photogrammetry.

The Cape Government granted Fourcade the money needed to build a theodolite-camera and measuring stereoscope to his own design. The mechanical parts were made in England by Troughton and Simms, and the optical parts in Austria by Zeiss.

On the 26^(th) of August 1904, Fourcade went up Signal Hill, overlooking Cape Town, with his new camera and from a carefully measured base-line took photographs of Devil's Peak. Using his stereoscopic measuring apparatus he produced a contour map of all those parts of the mountain that were visible. This was the first ever topographic map produced by photogrammetry. Eighty years later the exercise was repeated by Prof L P Adams of UCT using the most precise modern equipment. The differences were negligible.

Fourcade was a perfectionist. He had a short temper and did not suffer fools gladly. He was said to have an eye for the girls, but remained a bachelor, perhaps because of an inability to establish close relationships with people. When the position of Surveyor General fell vacant, he was eager to apply, but Sir David Gill warned his protégé that his difficult temperament and lack of tact would rule him out as a candidate, although his intellectual ability was far superior to any other likely applicant. Disheartened, Fourcade, at the early age of 40, retired after more than 22 years in the Civil Service.

During the first 40 years of his life Fourcade had achieved more than most achieve in a lifetime. During the next 40 his achievements, if anything, outshone those of his early manhood and his "retirement" became the most creative period of his life.

He first moved to his farm Ratel's Bosch, now a part of the Lottering Forest, but in 1913 he bought a property at Witelsbos from Frederick Damant. Here he set up a saw-mill to produce wagon parts. He also ran a general dealer's business. By 1920 he had made sufficient money to enable him to devote the rest of his life to science.

While visiting Britain in 1925, Fourcade became convinced that European photogrammetrists were mistaken in their approach to the production of maps from aerial photographs. This led him in the following year to postulate his *Theory of Relative Orientation*, which has subsequently become the basis of almost all work in photogrammetry. This also led to his involvement with the British Directorate of Military Intelligence, in particular with MI4, the department concerned with topographical information and military maps.

Apart from his work in the sphere of stereophotogrammetry, Fourcade's greatest contribution to science during those years was his work for the Botanical Survey on the plants of the George, Knysna, Humansdorp, Langkloof, and Uniondale districts. Because of this he became as well known at Kirstenbosch and the Royal Botanic Gardens at Kew, as he was at the Trigonometrical Survey in Mowbray, Cape Town and the War Office, in Whitehall, London.

With the occasional help of Louisa Bolus at Kirstenbosch and of Dr Selmar Schonland in Grahamstown, Fourcade set out to produce a check-list of all the plants found in the southern Cape. This was eventually published in 1941 as Memoir

No 20 of the Botanical Society of South Africa under the title *Check List of the Flowering Plants of the Divisions of George, Knysna, Humansdorp and Uniondale.* It contained nearly 3000 species, including 34 species he had discovered and 16 new species named after him by other botanists.

Fourcade died at Witelsbos in 1948. His name is commemorated in the names of 27 plants. He was the author of 73 plant names and synonyms. Both the University of Cape Town and Rhodes University College (as it was then) awarded him Honorary Doctorates of Science. He left his substantial estate to the University of Cape Town and the interest on the money he bequeathed is today used for botanical research and the publication of works on botany. It was at the time the largest single bequest ever to the university. Fourcade's collection of plants, housed in cabinets he made from the wood of the Butter-spoon tree, *Cunonia capensis,* is in the Bolus Herbarium in Cape Town, His photogrammetric instruments may be seen in the Department of Surveying at the university.

The inscription on his tombstone in the Humansdorp cemetery reads:

> *Henry Georges Fourcade.*
> *Died January 19, 1948.*
> *Age 82 years.*
> *A Seeker After Truth.*

* * *

The yacht *Grace* is not the only connection between Fourcade, his property at Witelsbos, the Ritchies and Coldstream. Fourcade was a friend of the Ritchie/Whitcher families, and at Witelsbos a not too distant a neighbour.

On his occasional visits to Coldstream he was much taken by a young child, a five year-old girl. (His relationship with children was often more relaxed than that with adults.) The child died young and was interred in the family graveyard at Oakhurst, and Henry Fourcade was moved to write an elegiac poem, commemorating her life.

Christopher Harison: retired soldier, failed farmer, scientific forester

Perhaps 50 metres from the R102 at the entrance to the Witelsbos Forestry Station is a stone building with a chimney at one end – the Witelsbos can be cold and damp in winter – a steeply pitched roof, two windows and a wooden door.

The single room has a wooden ceiling and floor and the fireplace has been boarded up, which may explain why it is now used as a storeroom for dusty old files, piled high on grey-painted wooden shelves. Anyone looking for a little warmth in winter would have to move to the new offices a couple of hundred metres away. However the building still looks as though it could be put to use at a moment's notice: the quaint wooden desk is covered with a red and white check tablecloth on which there stands one of those old-fashioned black telephones to be found in any government office sixty years ago. A chair awaits the next occupant of the desk.

This was the office that Capt Christopher Harison had built for himself while serving at Witelsbos. Perhaps it was at this desk that he sat drawing up a plan to help save the indigenous forest, the task with which he was charged, and at the same time improve the lot of the woodcutters. It was this dream of his which he shared with Thomas Bain and which sent the pair of them searching for a route through the Tsitsikamma, or "Zitzikamma", the spelling upon which the tetchy Henry Fourcade from across the road would have insisted.

Harison's efforts to improve the lot of the woodcutters were not appreciated by the prospective recipients. We seldom approve of those authorities that do their best to improve our lives. Limiting the number of trees the woodcutters could fell, while at the same time providing them with an alternative source of income, and so saving trees for them to cut in the future, was as unpopular as banning smoking to save smokers' lives during a pandemic.

After serving in South Africa in the 2nd Battalion of the Black Watch, Harison resigned his commission in 1853 and married Marie Louise Moorman, the daughter of a Commander Moorman, RN, a distinguished naval officer who had served under Nelson. The young couple came to the Cape to farm near Agulhas, but the venture failed and in 1856 Harison joined the forestry service and was sent to Witelsbos. There he stayed until 1874 when he was promoted to the Knysna head-office, Witelsbos remaining under his control. Although lacking any formal forestry training, he was the first official to apply a scientific approach to the conservation and regeneration of the natural forests, which he recognised as a natural heritage. That indigenous forests still exist in this area is at least partly due to the unrelenting efforts of Christopher Harison.

In 1888 Harison was again promoted, this time to Conservator of the Western Forests, in which position he served until his retirement, aged 70, in 1895. He died two years later.

Harison has a living memorial at Witelsbos. Not far from where his old home stood in the Tsitsikamma forest is a mighty Yellowwood. A plaque has been fixed to the tree:

Captain CHRISTOPHER HARISON tree.
Named in memory of a valiant
pioneer of forest conservation
who was conservator of forests
for this region from 1856 to 1888.

Of Christopher and Marie's three children, Lancelot became a well-known magistrate in the Eastern Cape and Kate married the son of a Dr Hare of Knysna, but then moved to England. Bessie married Charles W Thesen, the merchant prince of Knysna. Her life, you may recall, is commemorated by the lych gate, of old St George's in the Main Street, Knysna.

Irma von Below: nursing sister, mother, botanical artist

It is unusual to find in the forests the homes of two such prominent members of the local community in such relative proximity to one another as those of Fourcade and Capt Harison. The entrances to these two are within a few metres of one another, and within that distance was the name board of another, "Keokamma", home for a short while to Irma von Below.

The name Keokamma was the creation of Dr Ted Kerr. He enjoyed working with bees and after acquiring the farm in about 1976 he decided to give the farm a name suggestive of bees in some form. He therefore made up the word Keokamma from the Khoe words for "honey" and "water". What more suitable a name for a farm in the Tsitsikamma?

Irma von Below, of farming stock, was born on the 13th of January 1920 in Middelburg, Cape. She was schooled in Durban and Cradock and thereafter qualified as a nursing sister at the Johannesburg General Hospital, where she met and married neuro-surgeon, Ted Kerr. She now became a housewife and a mother, but still found the time during the early 1950s to attend part-time art classes at the Technical College. She experimented with a variety of media before settling down to concentrate on watercolours.

Her love of plants took her to the Wilds, in Johannesburg, and there she became fascinated by small flowers, which she began to paint. From there it was a short step to the Ericas, and her first painting of one, *Erica pattersonia*, was soon followed by *E. jasminiflora.* On holiday visits to the Cape south coast she found herself in the Cape Floristic Region and with not only ericas, but a wealth of other small-flowered plants to admire and record.

Perhaps she was mildly apprehensive when she first drove across to Pretoria to visit the Botanical Research Institute to meet Dr R A Dyer and botanical artist Cythna Letty. If this were the case there was no need for it: both the director and

355

the artist were encouraging and urged her to continue with her paintings. Years later Cythna Letty, a renowned artist, was to state, "If only I could paint (details) like Irma." Three of Irma's paintings appeared in *Flowering Plants of South Africa.*

Irma was now put in touch with Colonel H A Baker of Cape Town. He together with E "Ted" Oliver was busy collecting ericas for the British Museum. This resulted in Irma being commissioned to paint specimens for the book. Plants were collected in the Cape and sent to Johannesburg by airmail. Many arrived in a less than a perfect state and she had to resurrect the plant, so to speak. In all she painted 65 species before the break up of her marriage resulted in her moving to the family farm, *Keokamma,* in the Tsitsikamma.

While the isolation of Witelsbos did not apparently effect either Fourcade or Harison adversely, it became a major problem for Irma von Below. The delivery of specimens became so erratic that she was unable to finish the assignment and Fay Anderson completed the plates for Baker and Oliver's *Ericas of South Africa,* published in 1967. Irma was nevertheless awarded the Grenfell Gold Medal of the Royal Horticultural Society for her contribution to the project.

After Irma's marriage to property developer John Booysen she moved to Cape St Francis and painted not only flowers but also the rock pools and fish that were a stone's throw from her doorstep. There were also exhibitions of her paintings both locally, in the hotel at St Francis Bay, and further afield: Port Elizabeth, East London, Grahamstown, Johannesburg, Pretoria, Pittsburg and London. She was also commissioned to paint the plants of the Addo Elephant National Park.

It was at Cape St Francis that she met a young student, Richard Cowling, busy with a doctoral thesis on the local flora. Together they planned a book on these plants, and despite Cowling's temporary move to Australia she began work on the plates. By December 1983 she had completed 97 of the paintings when she fell ill. She died early in the new year soon after her 64th birthday.

Irma first became aware of the fynbos at Keokamma, near Witelsbos, but at Seal Point she recorded a veld-type together with its ecological cohorts that was particularly suited to her talents. The Irma Booysen Reserve at Seal Point commemorates the all too short life of a plant-lover and artist whose intense love for the small-flowered plants resulted not only in works of art, but valuable scientific records. Keep an eye open for the small flowers when next you visit the reserve. The sandy stabilised dunes beside the ocean were Irma's happy hunting ground, and to some of us this will always be "her" veld.

* * *

A French-born land-surveyor, a former British Army officer and a Karoo-born nursing-sister all lived for a while in the vicinity of Witelsbos, and all played a part in making us aware of a natural heritage which for far too long was largely ignored by most South Africans.

Clarkson

It was in 1838 that Governor Sir George Napier approached the Moravian missionaries at Genadendal with a request to set up a station to act as a refuge for Mfengu living along the eastern border who were threatened by the Xhosa. The missionaries responded positively and a suitable farm, Koksbosch in the Tsitsikamma, was acquired. On the 14th of October of that year the Rev Johann Halter preached the first sermon at Koksbosch. A decision was made to name the new mission after benefactor Thomas Clarkson, an Englishman and friend of slavery abolitionist, William Wilberforce.

During the following year the Rev Christian Kuster arrived at Clarkson from the mission at Enon, together with five Khoekhoe families and a group of Mfengu under Headman Manqoba.

The dedication of the first small church took place in 1840 together with a school and by 1844 a mill was in operation producing flour not only for the inhabitants of the mission, but also for neighbouring farmers.

There are two roads in Clarkson, Bazia and Church Streets, running parallel to one another in a north-south direction. At the top, near the church, there is an east-west link-road. Each street is lined with what once were small, whitewashed mission houses, but during the past nearly two centuries there have been additions, alterations and even completely new houses. Very few of the original houses remain, so sadly, from a visitor's point of view, the streets are no longer as picturesque as was once the case.

The original church building is no more, but in 1871 a new church was completed, a building that in 1890 was renovated and enlarged. White walled and dark roofed, with a bell-tower beside the entrance, it stands a proud symbol of the enduring faith of the inhabitants of the little settlement. Across the road is the school, an equally important feature of the village. It was a proud moment for the entire village when, in 1864, young Edward Louis, born and schooled at Clarkson, left to train as a teacher at Genadendal.

Nearby is the parsonage where in the early days those stern but loving German Moravian missionaries lived: Kuster and Nauhaus, Schärf and Bauer and more. In the local graveyard you will see many of their memorial stones.

It was only in 1945 that the villagers stopped singing hymns in German. A new hymnal was introduced with the familiar tunes, but with Afrikaans words. The old people complained, as old people do, but eventually everyone was singing in the same language. It made little difference to the members of brass band, nor to the organist, for there was no change to the tunes. The organist played an instrument that was bought from the Dutch Reformed Church in Humansdorp in 1938 for £170, and installed just in time for the centenary celebrations of the mission.

Life in this small community, like all others, had its ups and downs. They were proud of the entry in the 1860 Report of the Humansdorp Civil Commissioner:

Some of the best servants in this district come from the Moravian missionary institute at Clarkson, where all notions of social equality are discountenanced and habits of industry, sobriety, and obedience enforced and acquired with unusual success and permanency. [Which understandably would not be entirely acceptable to present-day residents of Clarkson.] *This* [continued the Civil Commisioner] *in contrast to discharged British soldiers, men who for the most part are described by their present masters as drunken and lazy rascals.*

The Great Fire of February 1869 brought death and destruction to Clarkson, the worst hit of all communities in the Humansdorp Division. Fourteen lives were lost and 27 houses destroyed, while many who survived lost everything they had. As, during the 10th of February, the day after the fire, they began to pick up what was left and carry on with their lives, the Rev Benno Marx reminded them of the Biblical book of Job: "The Lord gave, and now has taken away. May the name of the Lord be praised."

The year 1939 marked not only the centenary of Clarkson, but the outbreak of World War II. It brought a demand for labour and many of the young men found work in the Union Defence Force. At the same time those that chose to remain were working on the building of the National Road from Cape Town to Port Elizabeth. The average workman at the time earned between 2s 3d and 2s 6d per day (say 22½ and 25 cents). It was not easy, even in those days, to feed a family on that amount. Their minister, the Rev Ernst Dietrich, was understanding, but the only consolation he could offer was that half an egg was better than an empty shell.

There were great celebrations in the community when in 1972 the library building was completed. For years both church and school had worked towards this. With its completion it was hoped that it would result in others in the community following in the footsteps of Edward Louis, teacher, and Frank Jantjies, minister, both born and bred in Clarkson, who had risen to be leaders in the community.

The 150th birthday celebrations of Clarkson in 1989 saw an influx of visitors from other Moravian congregations. The church was too small to seat everyone and they were forced to hold the main service in a marquee outside the church. The founding fathers of the village, the German missionaries, were not forgotten, but the celebrations were particularly joyful, for the Clarkson community were by now, and had been for two decades, fully fledged, no longer a mission, but in complete control of their own affairs.

* * *

In 1993 we went, together with local farmer's daughter Julie Ballantyne, to visit Daniel Jeptha, oldest resident of Clarkson. He was the grandson of another Daniel Jeptha who had arrived at Clarkson in 1841 together with his wife, Paulina. Both husband and wife were born slaves, but the emancipation of the slaves at the Cape on the 1st of January 1834 brought freedom. Their son, Andreas, married Ernestina, daughter of Christiaan and Arieta Williams at Clarkson. The Daniel Jeptha we were visiting, being the son of Andreas and Ernestina, was born at Clarkson on the 12th of September 1897.

The old man was not feeling too well that day when his daughter took us into the bedroom to meet him. He lay tucked up under the blankets in the small room, barely big enough to hold all of us. While Daniel remembered his grandparents and had often heard tales of their joy at being set free, he was perhaps more keen to let us know about his own descendants. Only two of his six children were still alive, but he had 25 grandchildren, 68 great-grandchildren and an unknown number of great-great-grandchildren. He smiled at us, "The Lord said that we should go forth and multiply."

Because of his state of health we did not stay long. When I took his hand to say goodbye I was struck by how soft it felt. Perhaps I had imagined that it would be work-hardened. Despite the lack of callouses, there was something special about it: this was a hand that once had held the hands of slaves.

On our way out of the house his daughter stopped to show us a photograph of her father standing outside a white-washed Clarkson house surrounded by a mass of spring flowers. "When he is gone", she said, "I will always remember him like this, in his garden. He loves flowers. When he was still active he was always working with plants, sowing seeds, taking cuttings and weeding. Plants are the joy of his life."

In 1996 the church, bell-tower, graveyard and former mill at Clarkson were declared National Monuments. In my mind, and perhaps that of his daughter, the late Daniel Jeptha's garden is also a National Monument.

Klasies River

Off on a warm, blue-skied day down the coast with Richard, Shirley and Ross. It is not long before we turn from the tar and follow winding farm roads flanked by tracks for dairy herds and paths that disappear over grass-topped dunes. The road drops down into a thickly wooded water course and swings sharply up again to emerge in yet another kikuyu-grassed farmland. It is only in recent years that this has become an area of dairy farms. Huge areas of indigenous plants have disappeared in the conversion to modern needs.

Nearing the ocean we enter less disturbed veld, a mixture of thicket and grassy fynbos. Suddenly we are on a crest with the ocean spread before us. There is a fishing-shack on our left and here we leave the bakkies, unsure as to whether, on the way back, they will climb the steep ascent without four-wheel drive.

Walking down the hill we have beside us the stream of the Klasies River, both hidden and sound-proofed by a tangle of coastal scrub. Before long we are in sight of the great cave that dominates the steep slope near the mouth of the river; high sandstone cliffs with calcium carbonate intrusions. So striking a feature is it that countless beachcombers clambered up from the shoreline over the years to investigate, but it was Paul Haslem and Ludwig Abel who in recent times found evidence of ancient human occupation and brought the cave to the attention of archeologists.

In 1960 Ray Innskeep and Ronald Singer made preliminary excavations and identified various artifacts dating back to the Middle Stone Age (MSA).

They were followed by John Wymer in 1967-68, whose findings were published by the University of Chicago Press in 1972.

There followed a lull in archeological activity until, in 1984, Hilary Deacon took over research work at the mouth of the river.

Hilary Deacon had a 50th birthday party at Klasies River on the 11th of January 1986, the day after his actual birthday. Given the circumstances it is difficult to imagine a more suitable spot for such a party. (It is possible that his wife and fellow archeologist, Janette Deacon, who was surely also in charge of catering for the party, did not entirely agree regarding the choice of venue. Lugging foodstuffs across the sand to the campsite could not have been easy.)

One of the guests at the party, Keith Sutton, the columnist of the *Eastern Province Herald,* drew our attention to another party that was being held that evening, a little further down the coast. There the National Party faithful were gathered to celebrate the 70th birthday of State President P W Botha.

Sitting around the camp-fire we listened to Keith: "Here, at Klasies River, beside a cave that was home to early man, we celebrate the 50th birthday of a man dedicated to teaching us more about our cave-dwelling ancestors. Meanwhile, to the west of us, at the Wilderness, are gathered together the only living – and soon to be extinct I believe - troglodytes, toadying to their leader."

Today at the bottom of the road we are met by tall, sun-bronzed archeologist Jan de Vink, with black baseball cap, T-shirt and shorts, and with just sufficient hair showing under the cap for my late father to have said, "That man needs a haircut." Jan worked here as a student under Deacon. With him is Hayley Cawthra, a Botticelli girl with an infectious grin and lovely, russet-brown hair. After matriculating she attended an art school in Sweden, before returning to study geolo-

The experts speculate at Klasies River. From left to right, botanist Ross Turner, ecologist Richard Cowling, archeologist Jan de Vink, geologist Hayley Cawthra and archeologist Sarah Wurz

gy. She now specialises in underwater geology. During past glacial periods when the sea-level dropped, a plain stretching some two kilometres from the mouth of the cave was exposed. That plain is now under water, hence Hayley's presence.

We go with them across to the cave to meet Sarah Wurz, Professor of Archeology at the Witwatersrand University, and her team of students. Sarah has an impressive list of qualifications that include, besides a doctorate in Archeology, a master's degree in Musical Science. Her blonde hair is pulled back in a scrunchy. She wears a practical, short-sleeved bush-jacket and khaki longs. It is interesting to see her interaction, soft-voiced and smiling, with the students: she is a good listener, and assists them with quiet efficiency.

She now calls her team to attention, and there in the cave, while the students perch on rocks, or stand beside a theodolite or beside excavations, there is a round of introductions. This is followed by a brief explanation of the work that is in progress.

The main cave has been associated with human habitation since about 125 000 BP. For lengthy periods, some as long perhaps as 1 000 years, the caves were unoccupied, but people came and went. The sea was never very far away, at the most two to three kilometres, unlike other caves along the coast, such as Blombos. The association with the MSA is very important, for it was then that people first started thinking and acting like modern humans.

Dating deposits in and around the cave is not easy. There has been considerable movement of material, both natural and caused by man. Outside the main cave, for example, is a large "dump" consisting of both MSA material and that moved by Wymer. At the time (1967) there was little that archeologists could glean from this material, but since then great strides regarding interpretation have been made, but dating is often a problem.

A natural displacement since last we were in the cave has been the fall at the back of the cave of a massive stalactite. This in turn has resulted in the exposure of a large midden. The midden, dating back to just 50 000 years BP is of the Late Stone Age (LSA) and apart from shells and bones, traces of bedding, burnt for hygienic reasons, have been found. It is similar to finds in middens associated with the Howison's Poort culture (roughly 66 000 BP to 60 000 BP).

Going through a 20 metre thick accumulation of deposits indicates that the people hunted small game, fish, gathered plants and roots, cooked corms, seals, penguins and antelopes on open hearths. Among this material are charred and carved human bones amongst other food remnants, which may indicate cannibalism.

We move on to an adjoining cave. What is the relationship, if any, between the two caves? Amongst the finds here is a human mandible. Is this another indication of cannibalism? Many questions still remain to be answered.

Later we walk down the beach to the old campsite situated in a hollow behind the frontal dune and beneath a canopy of verbena trees – *Clerodendrum glabrum.* Jan de Vink remembers camping here in 1990 when, as a student, he worked at Klasies under Hilary Deacon. Here it was that Keith Sutton drew our attention to the other celebration at the Wilderness.

Up the dune from here was another shelter where Johan Binneman, as a junior member of the team, unearthed a remarkable succession of LSA burials, one above the other. Excited as he was at his find, he remembered Deacon being pleased that "Binneman's graves" were now out of the way and work could start on what really mattered, the MSA material.

On the return journey Hayley Cawthra points out some discoloured stains on the rock faces; traces, she explains, of stromatolites, the first known organisms to produce free oxygen, the earliest fossil evidence of life on earth.

Regarding the habitation of the caves we were thinking in terms of tens of thousands of years, and of dates going back almost 200 000 years, now suddenly we are faced with evidence of cyanobacteria dating back to the very origins of life on earth, billions of years ago.

It has been an interesting, an inspiring day spent on a magical shoreline with pleasant and stimulating company.

Eersterivier Community

Christopher Harison's vision of small agricultural settlements spaced out through the forests of the Tsitsikamma, where former woodcutters could make a living from the land, did not work out quite as he planned. However some former woodsmen stayed on in the Tsitsikamma and others, looking for land, gradually moved into the area, one of the last in the Colony to be developed. At Eersterivier a Dutch Reformed Church was established to serve local families: Meyers, Potgieters, Du Plessis and Rademeyers, amongst others. There is still a church on the farm Heidehof, although local church members now fall under the aegis of the church at Kareedouw.

Lands were cleared and, with varying success, vegetables, mielies and wheat were grown. At first this amounted mainly to subsistence farming, but gradually more use was made of Thomas Bain's road to take produce to market. It was only after the Second World War that the first dairy farms were developed. Pioneer dairy farmers were the Elliotts of Grasslands, bordering the Storms River. Today dairy cattle are a common sight throughout the Tsitsikamma.

Sods were used to build many of the earliest homes, and it is still possible to find houses or sheds that, beneath the plaster, are constructed partly or entirely of this medium.

During the first half of the 19th century the Tsitsikamma, or Zitzikamma as it was known at the time, was in the Uitenhage District. For some years the *Veldkornet* of the Tsitsikamma was "Grootpiet" Rademeyer of the farm Driefontein. More formally he was Nicolaas Petrus Hendrik Rademeyer, born in 1812. As his nickname suggests he was a giant of a man with hands, arms and shoulders capable of working day-long with a sledge-hammer, yet gentle enough to coax tunes from a violin. He died in 1890.

Often, particularly in the 19th century, the womenfolk are overlooked, so it is pleasing to be able to report that Grootpiet Rademeyer married Martha Jacoba van Niekerk, two years his junior, in 1834 and that at least some of their descendants are still to be found living in the Kouga area. One of these descendants, great-grandson Hoffie Williams, told us about Grootpiet and the watermills.

It is not entirely clear when the events took place. Although Field-cornet posts existed, and in the early days Field-cornets were expected to be able to provide fresh mounts for postal-riders, these government officials never normally delivered post themselves. They were occasionally used as a form of *poste restante,* distributing mail quarterly at *nachtmaal,* but this was the limit of their postal delivery concerns. It must therefore have been after he relinquished his duties as Field-cornet that Grootpiet Rademeyer became involved with postal delivery.

Before the completion of Thomas Bain's road through the forests of the Tsitsikamma in 1885 the postal route from Humansdorp to Knysna and George would have been through the Langkloof. The first mention of a Humansdorp to Knysna postal route occurs in 1869. The service was operated by post-carts and it is likely that Rademeyer provided the cart, horses and drivers, but did not otherwise play an active role. Penalties were incurred for late- or non-delivery.

According to family tradition there were particularly heavy rains one year and as a result postal deliveries were erratic. Rademeyer, so the family maintain, found himself facing a debt to the Postal authorities of £1 800. This amount is unusually large, for operators were not liable to penalties if they could show that there were circumstances, such as inclement weather, that were beyond their control. Perhaps the amount included other expenses arising from the flooded rivers and damaged roads.

No matter how the debt was incurred, Rademeyer was faced with the possibility of having to sell Driefontein, the family farm, in order to pay what he owed. Instead he and the family knuckled down to raise the money by building water-mills, at least 18 of them, on farms from the Alexandria District in the east to Mossel Bay in the west. Many were situated along the route we travelled. At Grootbrak, for example, Charles Searle the teetotal community developer had one built, while nearer home there was a mill on Michiel Meyer's farm Jagersbosch in the Langkloof. On Rondebosch, the farm north of Humansdorp of former German soldier, Frederik Wagner there was a Rademeyer mill, and further on along the road to Hankey, at Ruttger Meterlekamp's farm Zuurbron, there was another. Dotted about somewhat like Robert and Sophie Gray's churches, but more numerous, they were for a while special features of the local landscape. Today, unlike the Grays' churches, they are largely forgotten and lie in ruins.

The remains of a Rademeyer mill at Eersterivier

Karretjie volk children, December 2000

16.

Memories of a journey

It is that time of year again. A sweetish, vaguely foetid smell hangs in the warm air. Visitors to the Eastern Cape coast lift their feet and surreptitiously look at the soles of their shoes. It is February and the Milkwood trees are in blossom.

Exactly a year ago our journey began in Port Elizabeth. No sooner begun than Covid-19 brought it to a standstill. It then continued on the road in fits and starts, and also virtually while sitting at the keyboard of my laptop. It was a journey like no other we have undertaken.

On Jouberts Kraal I stumbled and fell, banging a knee and flinging my camera to the ground. I lay silent as Caryl ran across. "Are you alright? I've got nothing to give you, not even sugar!"

Suddenly I am reminded of a story told by Lawrence Durrell. The British Prime Minister, William Gladstone, while on a visit to Greece, was introduced at a formal gathering to the Bishop of Paxos. In an excess of bonhomie they made to kiss one another's hands, but in so doing banged their heads together and were momentarily stunned. Fortunately a by-stander had a picnic basket from which he produced a bottle of homemade ginger-beer. This soon restored the two men and proceedings continued as planned.

I told Caryl the story. The camera was retrieved undamaged, and we went on our way laughing.

* * *

Xoliswa told of how as a child she lived with her Gogo – grand-mother – in a rural village. Gogo would sometimes send her down to the trading-store to buy some urgently needed item, a responsible task for a small girl. Clutching the money tied up in a clean handkerchief she would prepare to set out. Before she left Gogo would remind her to greet any adults she might meet on the road, "We are all 'family' in this village and it is only polite to greet one another, especially elders."

When in later years Xoliswa moved to Johannesburg she found her grandmother's teaching difficult to follow; there were just too many people. Then one day when Xoliswa was about to enter a crowded lift, she was greeted by a young white girl standing beside her mother in the lift.

"I was immediately reminded of my Gogo. I returned the greeting and asked the child if she was out shopping. By the time we reached the ground floor the mother and I had also exchanged a few words and everyone in the lift seemed more relaxed, even smiling. If only we took the trouble to greet one another when possible there might be less talk of racism in this country."

* * *

Sitting next to the taaibos, looking out to sea, I am aware of the small noises in the bush, but put them down to a four-striped mouse or other diminutive creature. My attention is held by the activity of the terns near the river-mouth.

Suddenly I realise that a pair of bright eyes is watching me from the taaibos. The face is not that big, but immensely larger than that of a four-striped mouse. The white spots on the rufous cheeks are the giveaway; it is a young bushbuck doe.

She spends some time watching me before slowly, carefully, daintily, emerging from the bush and stepping towards me. She stops not more than two metres away and we gaze solemnly at one another. How long this lasts I have no idea, but eventually she moves away and now with her back to me starts nibbling at some fresh, new grass. She obviously has summed me up, quite correctly, as harmless.

After a few minutes she loses interest in the grass and moves off, disappearing into the surrounding thicket.

Out at sea the terns have also disappeared.

* * *

On Elandsfontein I pass a small white cottage with an old woman standing outside in her minute garden. Her face is as wrinkled and as dust-coloured as the drought-stricken landscape. A few wisps of grey hair have escaped from under her brightly coloured doek.

We greet one another and I walk on towards a cattle-grid where three young men are standing abreast, blocking the road. Hands in pockets, one with a cigarette dangling from his lips, they make no move as I walk towards them. One is carrying his shirt. Is this because he is hot, or because on his bare chest there is a tattoo, "Lover boy"? Unsmiling, they look at me as I approach the cattle-grid. Visions of Burt Lancaster and Kirk Douglas in *Gunfight at the OK Corral* flash through my mind.

The eldest steps up to the grid, "Does sir need help across the grid?"

Visions of confrontations in the American Wild West fade.

"No thank you, I think I can manage. Where are you going?"

"Just to fetch Grennie", he says, pointing in the direction of the house of the old woman, "to take her to church".

We exchange mutual good wishes and continue on our separate ways.

* * *

The 2020 journey started normally enough, but at an early stage there was a change, we were locked down by Covid-19. As a result our travels became a part of the "new normal", a virtual journey based on previous experiences, a journey during a pandemic.

In 1808 the Moore family, while travelling in their Irish homeland during a plague year, was afflicted by smallpox. Poet Thomas Moore's wife, Elizabeth contracted and was badly scarred by the disease. This resulted in Thomas writing a poem, *Believe Me If All Those Endearing Young Charms*, which he set to a traditional Irish air. It is said that he sang it to Elizabeth repeatedly until her self-confidence was restored and she ventured out once again into the outside world.

Our trials were not as dire; in fact while housebound we rather enjoyed re-living our earlier wanderings in the Langkloof and along the Garden Route.

* * *

Conversation with a cyclist in very broken country while on the road to the farm Ouplaas:

"Is dit die pad na Ouplaas?" [Is this the road to Ouplaas?]

"Ja meneer, net oor die bult." [Yes sir, just over the hillock.]

"Hoe ver is dit tot Ouplaas?" [How far is it to Ouplaas?]

"Net oor die bult, meneer, en miskien nog 'n bult of twee." [Just over the hillock, sir, and perhaps another hillock or two.]

Apparently in the Balkans prior to the Second World War, it was customary to measure distance in terms of cigarettes smoked, thus the distance between Mitrovica and Vučitro might be given as five cigarettes. Presumably this took into account an interval between the smoking of one cigarette and the lighting of the next. But do not laugh at customs that may appear quaint to city-bred travellers; they make perfect sense to the locals.

* * *

On a ridge overlooking Seal Point in November is when I contemplate throwing away my notebook and pencil, donating the laptop to a needy school and taking out once again the brushes and paint-box that have lurked so long in the bottom drawer of the desk. Of course I soon realise that such a move would be as fruitless as is the search for words to describe the scene.

Close at hand are brilliant blues and softer mauves, strident reds and laundry-day whites, but taken as a whole it is the great bushes of yellow senecio and the wild pink cineraria that strike the eye. White laced blue waves fringe the point while the scavenging white gulls with black velvet-sleeves patrol the beaches. The tall, admonishing finger of the 1878 lighthouse demarcates the western end of the bay.

By the time the Gauteng holidaymakers arrive all the flowers will have faded.

* * *

Sitting supposedly alone in the forest at Witelsbos I am suddenly aware that I am not in fact alone. A slight sound causes me to turn and from the corner of my eye I notice the movement of a fern frond. A shiver runs down my spine. Only moments earlier the forest seemed a peaceful refuge from the hazards of everyday life. Now it has become a place of unseen menace. Names of young men and women flit through my mind, whatever became of them? Woodcutters' children too, missing without trace. Then there were the outsiders that met their ends in the trees, even a national sporting hero. Parts of an aircraft found in the undergrowth on a mountain; a dusty Datsun bakkie not that far from the Grootrivier Pass, but un-noticed for years.

Slowly I rise to face the possible danger. As I do, the old male baboon behind the tree barks and with a glance over his shoulder turns and disappears in amongst the seven-weeks fern. I heave a sigh of relief and walk slowly back to the forestry track.

* * *

There is much to be said for travel besides broadening the mind, but so often while going in search of something new and unusual, we cling nevertheless to that which is known and familiar. We'll get something to eat at the next Petroport, Ultra City or look out for a Wimpy. That is not travelling, that is driving.

We live in fear of being molested and robbed by passers-by; swindled by shopkeepers and overcharged by restaurateurs. Who are those people with long hair and beards? Should we rather turn down here and avoid them? Let's try a shop in Main Street; there are more people there. Is it safe to drink the water? Perhaps we should take the tarred road in case we have a puncture.

That too is not travelling.

One must get out of the car and walk down the street or in the veld. There is not a snake waiting to attack behind every bush. In fact you'll be lucky to see one. There is a most wonderful world out there, but you'll never experience it without leaving the car and walking, which is also good for your health!

This being the case it is strange that many people choose to go overseas rather than see what their own country has to offer. While I do not have anything against going off to see the world, and in fact encourage it, there seems little point in it if you are going to take South Africa, with its corruption, racism, violence and other dangers with you. Surely you have left your own country to find something different? You'll have to take some chances if you really want to start travelling. Why not start by first practising at home?

I have long since forgotten the facts related by the guide at the Tower of London regarding the Crown Jewels, but I do remember meeting there a Beefeater, Captain of the Tower of London Cricket Team as it turned out, who was delighted to discover that I knew Protea cricketer Mark Rushmere. That the Beefeater, a Scot, became a cricketer, is a story in itself, but must wait for another day. Useless but memorable information acquired because we decided to talk to a Beefeater and found the life of a Scotsman living in London of more interest than the Crown Jewels.

While it would seem better for the timid to start at home, even here there is so much to fear if one is that way inclined. One simply has to disregard unreasonable fears. Go out and investigate the back roads and talk to those you meet along the way. We stopped one day while on the road to Beaufort West to talk to some itinerant karretjie volk, direct descendants of the San. It was a memorable meeting with the gypsies of the Great Karoo: an experience which is unlikely to happen again, for the karretjie volk have finally, or so it seems, settled down, many on the outskirts of Colesberg.

One never knows what serendipitous encounters one might have, but you'll have to forget your fears and face whatever may be behind the bush, and talk to those you meet on the road. You'll never know what wonders are out there unless you look for them.

As South African travel-writer Dana Snyman has noted, every person one meets has a story, although he does add that some have more interesting stories than others!

When everything else is forgotten, the stories, the adventures remain.

Co-ordinates

Co-ordinates are given in the form 335506/251325, which indicate 33° 55' 06" south, 25° 13' 25" east.

Assegaaibosch Hotel – 335643/241844.
Avontuur – 334338/231009.
Backhouse Hoek – 334913/245114.
Bakkieshoek – see Backhouse Hoek
Ballotts Bay – 340047/223234.
Barrington – 334940/222118.
Bartlesfontein – 340927/215942.
Belvidere – 340240/225947.
Bergplaas -335251/224000.
Bitou River Bridge – 340029/232334.
Blanco – 335646/222429.
Bloukrans Brug – 335800/233845.
Bo-Langvlei – 335916/224052.
Bonniedale farm – 332227/215630.
Braamrivier – 334422/232038.
Brandhoek – 334459/235402.
Cadles Hotel - 335506/251325.
Camfer Station – 335000/222605.
Cape St Blaize – 341109/220935.
Cape St Blaize Light – 341109/220923.
Cape St Francis – 341148/245214.
Cape St Francis village – 341222/244948.
Churchill Dam – 340001/242938.
Clarkson – 340050/242029.
Coldstream – 335752/234257.
De Seven Fonteine – 340921/220614.
De Vlugt – 334846/231030.
Diepriviermond – 340224/243431.
Diepwalle Forest Station – 335655/230927.
Eenzaamheid – 334621/224711.
Eersterivierstrand – 340355/241256.
Elandsfontein – 335125/235753.
Essenbos Station – 335753/242539.

Essenbosch – 335726/242444.
Fancourt – 335719/222451.
Forest Hall – 335923/232938.
Fourcade's house – 335942/240700.
Gamkaberg Reserve – 334436/215646.
Gamtoos Ferry – 335455/250139.
Gamtoos Rail Bridge – 335449/245715.
Gamtoos Road Bridge – 335519/250138.
George – 335912/222710.
Goedgeloof – 344840/244813.
Goose Valley – 340131/232302.
Goukamma Mouth – 340435/225655.
Gouna – 335658/230200.
Groot Brak Rivier – 340256/221413.
Groot Rivier Brug – 335619/233325.
Haarlem – 334402/232019.
Hankey – 334959/245258.
Harkerville – 340158/231356.
Hartenbos – 340718/220554.
Heights – 335059/235800.
Heights Station – 335122/235829.
Hendrikskraal – 335231/240157.
Herbertsdale – 340049/214542.
Herold – 335027/223155.
Herolds Bay – 340300/222353.
Hoeree – 334256/235033.
Holgate Siding – 334853/222136.
Honeyville – 335608/244535.
Hoogekraal – 340100/222657.
Humansdorp – 340128/294607.
Jagersbosch – 335447/241149.
Jeffreys Bay – 340200/245458.
Joubertina – 334938/235123.
Jouberts Kraal – 334628/240947.

Jubilee Creek – 335321/225755.
Kaaimans Mouth – 335952/223325.
Kandelaarsrivier – 334110/220936.
Karatara – 335449/225033.
Kareedouw – 335707/241723.
Kareedouw Pass – 335756/241546.
Keokamma – 340247/241104.
Kerkplaats – 335942/244013.
Keurbooms River Bridge –
340009/232401.
Klein Brak Rivier – 340514/220850.
Kleinrivier – 334301/235035.
Knysna – 340222/230302.
Koksbosch – see Clarkson.
Kompagnjiesdrif – 335250/240407.
Krakeelrivier – 333840/234350.
Kranshoek – 340525/231745.
Kromme Dam – see Churchill Dam.
Kromme Mouth – 340838/245033.
Krommerivierhoogte – see Heights.
Kruisfontein – 340011/244348.
Kruisvallei – 335313/230937.
Kurland – 335644/232940.
Leeuwenbosch – 340109/243746.
Louterwater – 334722/233732.
Market Square - 335744/253725.
Melkhoutkraal – 340217/230416.
Misgund farm (J-Bay) –
335627/245123.
Misgund settlement –
334520/232946.
Molenrivier – 334654/224938.
Montagu Pass Toll – 335507/222458.
Mooihoek – see Backhouse Hoek.
Mossel Bay – 341121/220810.
Natures Valley – 335848/233322.
Nocton Farm – 335456/250418
Oakhurst – 335912/234318.
Ongelegen – 334418/232510.
Onzer – see Joubertina.
Opkoms – 334103/240001.
Opkomst – 334415/235759.
Osbosch – 340820/244854.
Pacaltsdorp – see Hoogekraal.
Pampoenskraal - 335703/223155.
Pellsrus – 340334/245523.
Pinnacle Point – 341229/220525.

Plettenberg Bay – 340257/232201.
Port Elizabeth City Hall – see Market
Square.
Port St Francis – 341104/245106.
Portland – 335151/230000.
Redclyffe Hotel – 334428/232612.
Rheboksfontein – 340127/244700.
Rheenendal – 335643/225556.
Robberg Peninsula –
340616/232342.
Rondebosch farm – 335829/244616.
Rondevlei – 335938/224242.
Rondevlei Siding – 335902/224149.
Ruigtevlei Siding – 340122/225117.
Saasveld – see Pampoenskraal.
Safraanrivier – 335240/220155.
Schoonberg – 334857/223211.
Seal Point – 341252/245008.
Sedgefield – 340119/224810.
Simola – 340017/230139.
St Francis Links – 340947/244844.
Storms River Bridge –
335805/235553.
Storms River Village –
335813/235257.
Swartvlei – 335951/224519.
Tenax Reserve – 335723/241652.
Thesens Island – 340254/230313.
Thornhill - 335338/250819.
Tistsikamma Coastal Park –
340123/235348.
Trifolia – 340159/243620.
Twee Riviere – 334959/235359.
Uitvlugt – 334215/240003.
Uniondale – 333923/230725.
Van Stadens Pass – 335440/251343.
Victoria Bay – 340009/223253.
Voorbaai – see De SevenFonteine.
Vuyisili Mini – see Market Square.
Wilderness – 335934/223426.
Witels Forestry Station –
335933/240703.
Wittedrif – 340027/232018.
Wolwedans farm – 335240/221936.
Woodridge – see Cadles Hotel.
Zuurbron – 335400/244938.
Zwartenbosch – 335933/244454.

Further Reading

Ferreira, OJO. 2003. Onder-Kouga: Bakkermat van Gerbers en Ferreiras. Adamastor, J-Bay.

Franklin, M. 1975. The Story of Great Brak River. Struikhof, Cape Town.

Fransen, H & Cook, MA. 1980. The Old Buildings of the Cape. Balkema, Cape Town.

Frescura, F. 2002. The Post Offices of the Cape of Good Hope. Archetype, Pretoria.

Logie, B. 1999. Governor's Travels. Bluecliff, Port Elizabeth.

Logie, B. 2003. Two for the Road. Blue Cliff, Port Elizabeth.

Mackay, M. 1983. The Knysna Elephants and their forest home. Wildlife Society, Knysna.

Martin, D. 2005. The Bishop's Churches. Struik, Cape Town.

Matthee, D. 1985. Circles in a Forest. Penguin, Harmondsworth.

Matthee, D. 1987. Fiela's Child. Penguin Harmondsworth.

Matthee, D. 1987. Moerbeibos. Tafelberg, Kaapstad.

Matthee, D. 2003. Toorbos. Tafelberg, Kaapstad.

Moir, SM. 1963. Twenty-Four Inches Apart. Oakwood, Lingfield.

Mountain, A. 2003. The First People of the Cape. David Philip, Cape Town.

Nimmo, A. 1976. The Knysna Story. Juta, Cape Town.

Parkes, M & Williams, VM. 1988. Knysna the Forgotten Port. Dando, Knysna.

Parkes, M & Williams, VM. n.d. Exploring Knysna's Historical Countryside. Knysna Museum.

Parkes, M & Williams, VM. n.d. Wandering through historical Knysna. Knysna Museum.

Paterson-Jones, C. 1992. Garden Route Walks. Struik, Cape Town.

Price, CH. 1973. George Rex, King or Esquire? Timmins, Cape Town.

Ross, G. 2002. The Romance of Cape Mountain Passes. David Philip, Cape Town.

Skead, CJ. 2000. Observations on Khoekhoe Placenames. Blue Cliff, Port Elizabeth.

Skead, CJ. 2002. From Oldenland to Schonland. Privately published. Port Elizabeth.

Smith, P. 1981 (1935). Platkops Children. Balkema, Cape Town.

Storrar, P. 1982. Portrait of Plettenberg Bay. Centaur, Cape Town.

Storrar, P. 1984. A Colossus of Roads. Murray & Roberts/Concor, Cape Town.

Storrar, P. 1990. The Four Faces of. Fourcade. Maskew Miller/Longmans, Cape Town.

Tapson, W. 1961. Timber and Tides. Juta, Cape Town.

Thesen, H. 1974. Country Days. David Philip, Cape Town.

Turner, M. 1988. Shipwrecks & Salvage in South Africa. Struik, Cape Town.

Uithaler, WC. 1994. Honderd en Vyftig Jaar Op Pad. Universiteit van Port Elizabeth., C.

Van Waart, S. 2008. Briewe uit die Tuin van Eden. Lapa, Pretoria.

Magazines, journals and newspapers.

Adkins, B. 24 Apr 1981. Thornhill elephant lost a tooth. Eastern Province Herald.

Burman, J. 21 Mei 1965. Vlammsee Skend SA se Aansig. Huisgenoot.

Clarke, MJ. 1967. Who was Jane Hartley Boys? Looking Back, Vol. VII, p 119.

Ferreira, OJO. Julie 1983. Onder Kouga. Kontrei, No 14.

Fraenkel, W. 12 Jan 1985. Georgian Home for Museum. Weekend Post.

Hallack, C. June 1965. East to West, a Bicycle Journey from PE to CT. Looking Back, Vol V p 13.

Harradine, M. 2014. A Bulldog Named Rex. Looking Back, Vol LIII

Jongbloed, B. 9 Feb 1983. Bid to replace historic church. Eastern Province Herald.

Langham-Carter, RR. 1976. William Tyssen of Gamtoos River. Looking Back. Vol. XVI, p 123.

Langham-Carter, RR. 1980. Boys and Tyssen. Looking Back, Vol. XX, p 61.

Logie, B. 1 July 1996. Striking not a recent innovation in E. Cape. The Herald.

RH. Sept.1965. Nocton Farm. Looking Back, Vol. V No.3 p 9.

Roberts, D. Nov/Dec 2020. Farm Cottage Restoration. South African Architecture.

Smith, J. 15 Feb 1995. Finding treasure in the past. La Femme (The Herald).

Smith, NB. 1978. Redclyffe Hotel, Misgund. Looking Back, Vol. XVIII, p 88.

Sutton, K. 13 Jan 1982. The Philby Spider. Eastern Province Herald.

Sutton, K. 13 May 1981. Link with Conrad. Eastern Province Herald.

Sutton, K. 13 Sept 1975. Mount Stewart. Eastern Province Herald.

Sutton, K. 14 Mar 1980. Good party in wreck. Eastern Province Herald.

Sutton, K. 16 July 1980. First SA chapel in Mossel Bay. Eastern Province Herald.

Sutton, K. 28 Jan 1980. Speedwell of Good Hope. Eastern Province Herald.

Sutton, K. 4 Aug 1981. Story of the old passes. Eastern Province Herald.

Sutton, K. 8 Sept. 1978. Last of the wool clippers. Eastern Province Herald.

Van Niekerk, P. 25 Aug 1979. Millwood: all that is left of golden dreams. Weekend Argus.

Woolford, J. 11 Dec 1982. A Victorian author in 'Fort' Elizabeth. Weekend Post, 11 Dec 1982.

ooOoo

Cape Times, 24 Sept 1963. National Bird is Now 'A Menace'.

Cape Times. 20 Mar 2009. George Bernard Shaw's crash course on South Africa.

Eastern Province Herald, 12 Feb 1869. [Great Fire].

Eastern Province Herald. 16 Feb 1985. Elephant skeleton found in Knysna forest.

Looking Back. Sept 1998. In Memoriam Alfred Porter 1910-1988. Vol XXXVII.

Personal Communication.

A number of people, some now deceased, have over the years provided verbal information, which appears in this book, regarding the Langkloof and/or Garden Route. They are listed here in the alphabetical order of their first, or nick-names, for that is how I know (or knew) them:

Adriana Barrett

Anton Boonzaier

Bert Behrens

Bruce Snaddon

Chip Snaddon

Dougie Diedericks

Erik Roux

Francois van Niekerk

George Ferreira

Gladys Snaddon

Graham Ross

Hayley Cawthra

Helen Mudge

Jack Skead

Jan de Vink

Jan Vlok

Jean Groombridge

Jiggs Snaddon Wood

Jimmy Zondagh

Johan Binneman

Kate Snaddon

Keith Sutton

Kevern Burger

Linda Baldie

Mollie Moolman

Nico Hesterman

Raymond Ritchie

Richard Cowling

Ross Turner

Sarah Wurz

Saskia Boonzaier

Sue van Waart

Maps

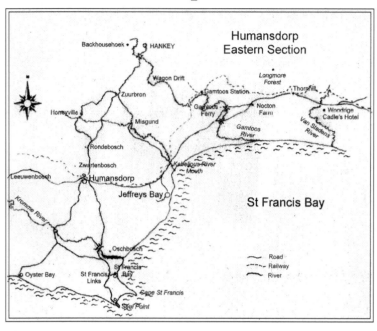

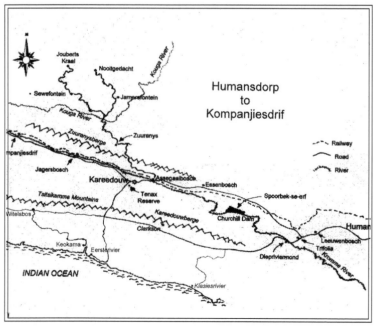

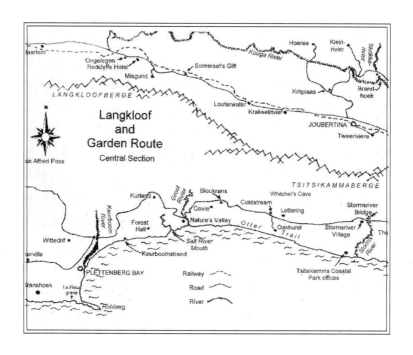

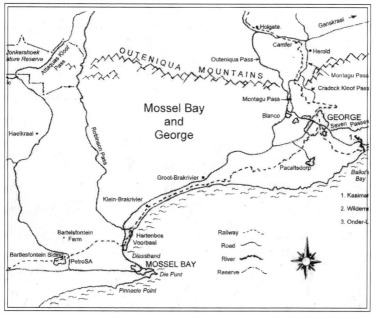

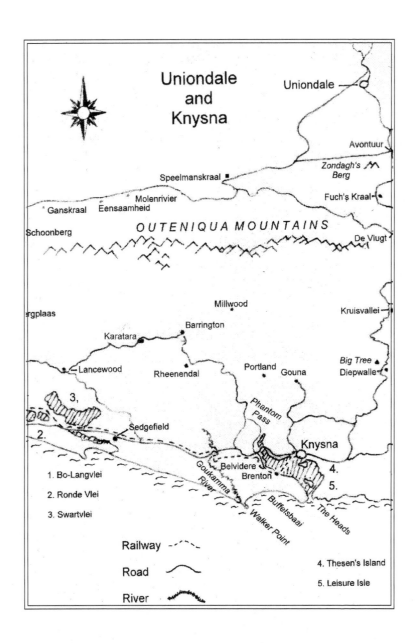

Uniondale
and
Knysna

Uniondale

Avontuur

Zondagh's
Berg

Speelmanskraal

Fuch's Kraal

Molenrivier

Ganskraal   Eensaamheid

Schoonberg

OUTENIQUA MOUNTAINS

De Vlugt

rgplaas

Millwood

Kruisvallei

Barrington

Karatara

Big Tree

Lancewood   Rheenendal

Portland   Gouna

Diepwalle

3,

Phantom Pass

Sedgefield

2.

Knysna

1. Bo-Langvlei

Belvidere
Brenton

4.

Goukamma River

5.

2. Ronde Vlei

Buffelsbaai

3. Swartvlei

Walker Point

The Heads

Railway

Road

River

4. Thesen's Island

5. Leisure Isle

Photo Credits

Page 69.:Assegaaibosch Hotel

Page 220: Chip Snaddon (SAR No 3669).

Page 313: Garden Route Tourism (Keurbooms ferry).

Page 241: George Herald: (Jan Vlok).

Page 256: Knysna Museum: (Locomotive and crew).

Page 199: Mossel Bay Tourism: (Beach a century ago).

Pages 2, 89: Port Elizabeth Historical Society: (Alf Porter and Margaret Harradine & Dassonvilles and Gladiator).

Pages 193, 194: Sean Grant: (Lynx & Robin & Bokmakirrie).

Page 194: Sjirk Geerts: (Sunbird).

Page 34: South African Railways: (Gamtoos Railway Bridge).

Page 364: Unknown: (Rademeyer mill).

Page 256: Veld and Flora: (Von Below).

Wikipedia: pages 7 (Vuyisele Mini); 71 (Norwegian mill); 209 (St Mark's Cathedral); 236 (Millwood); 256 (Fairmile); 257 (Le Fleur and Cullinan Diamond}.

Woodridge Preparatory School: pages 14 (Hannah Cadle); 18 (Woodridge Prep); 97. (Chatty Knight and Joy Hofmeyr).

About The Author

Bartle "Bart" Logie is a retired teacher and former headmaster of Woodridge Preparatory School (an independent school near Thornhill, between Jeffrey's Bay and Port Elizabeth), and now lives in St Francis Bay. He was born in Johannesburg, but has strong Eastern Cape connections, having spent the greater part of his life in the province.

As a result of his particular interest in the history of his favourite province, he has written magazine articles on various aspects of the region. A study of old farm buildings in the former Humansdorp Division of the old Cape Colony led to the compilation in 2010 of an historical gazetteer for the area, and in 2014 he completed, in association with Margaret Harradine, a similar volume for the Uitenhage and Port Elizabeth Divisions on behalf of the Historical Society of Port Elizabeth.

He has contributed towards reports on localities such as the Baviaanskloof Mega Reserve and the village of Hankey for various central government and local authorities. His research and writings have also appeared on a number of tourism websites.

Together with his wife, Caryl, a keen botanist, he has been involved – when not writing or travelling – in a variety of projects connected with the preservation of biodiversity in the Eastern Cape.

Bart's books – 20/20 is his tenth – are a unique combination of travelogue, local history documentary, and fireside story, all told in a free-flowing, easy-to-read and relaxed style. His approach combines meticulous research with hands-on, personal experience of the places and people he describes. Bart and Caryl have probably logged more kilometres, both on foot and by car, since he retired, than most people do in a lifetime!

Printed in Great Britain
by Amazon

27993522R00223